AMBUSH ALLEY

AMBUSH ALLEY

THE MOST EXTRAORDINARY
BATTLE OF THE IRAQ WAR

TIM PRITCHARD

BALLANTINE BOOKS

NEW YORK

Published in the United States by Presidio Press,
an imprint of The Random House Publishing Group,
a division of Random House, Inc., New York.

Presidio Press and colophon are trademarks of
Random House, Inc.

Library of Congress Cataloging-in-Publication Data
Pritchard, Tim, journalist.
Ambush alley : the most extraordinary battle of the Iraq war / Tim Pritchard.
p. : ill., maps ; cm.
Includes index.
ISBN 0-89141-880-6
1. Iraq War, 2003—Campaigns. 2. Iraq War, 2003—Personal narratives, American.
3. Pritchard, Tim, journalist. I. Title.
DS79.76.P755 2005
956.7044'342—dc22   2005043033

Printed in the United States of America

www.presidiopress.com

2 4 6 8 9 7 5 3 1

First Edition

Book design by Jo Anne Metsch

For my father,
who continues to be an inspiration

A NOTE ON SOURCES

The individual marines experienced the events of March 23, 2003, as a series of chaotic moments, which bear no relation to any normal understanding of time and place. Time seemed to stand still or speed up. Marines had little idea what was going on with the other marines at their sides, let alone with another company a couple of kilometers away.

Through interviews with some fifty marines, I have tried to piece it together to produce a detailed account of what turned out to be the most terrifying battle of the war in Iraq. My aim has been to re-create combat as the marines experienced it. The dialogue and feelings expressed by individual marines are their best recollection of what happened that day.

While this is predominantly about the thoughts and deeds of a group of U.S. marines, there is another side to the battle that can only be imagined. Because of the deteriorating security situation, few Iraqis felt able to talk openly about the events of March 23. However, I hope that my account will give some idea of the confused feelings of relief, rage, anguish, and suffering experienced by combatant and noncombatant Iraqis on the streets of Nasiriyah that day.

During the battle, many enlisted marines and some officers commonly referred to the Iraqi fighters as "hajjis." In the Arabic world, a "hajji" is a Muslim who has made the pilgrimage to Mecca. It is both a mark of respect and a common surname. The vast majority of marines would not have been aware of the religious connotations of the name. One marine believed that the name came from a character in a TV sitcom.

My interviews with marines have been supplemented by official documents, diaries, and photographs. Many of the facts relating to the attack on the 507th Maintenance Company are taken from the U.S. Army report on the Private Jessica Lynch incident. The facts relating to the A-10 friendly fire attack are taken from the Department of Defense inquiry into the case. Newspaper articles that have helped my research include Mark Franchetti's dispatch from Nasiriyah for *The Times* of London on March 30, 2003, and Rich Connell and Robert J. Lopez's report of September 5, 2003, in the *Los Angeles Times*.

I'd like to thank all those marines at Camp Lejeune and elsewhere who gave me so much of their valuable time, especially Chief Warrant Officer David Dunfee, Captain Scott Dyer, Captain Teresa Ovalle, and First Lieutenant James Reid. Special thanks to David Coward, David Mack, everyone at Darlow Smithson, Jean Reynaud for his helpful comments, and my family and friends for their love and support.

CONTENTS

IRAQ MAP

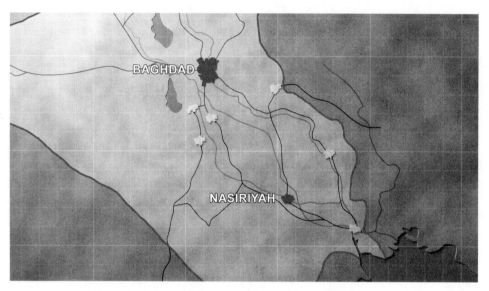

Major routes to Nasiriyah and Baghdad

NASIRIYAH MAP

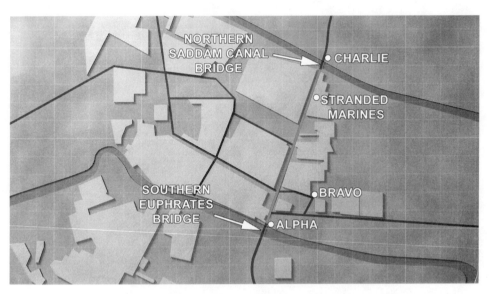

Company positions at the height of the battle. "Ambush Alley" between
the Northern Saddam Canal and Southern Euphrates bridges

LIST OF CHARACTERS

TASK FORCE TARAWA—BUILT AROUND 2nd MARINE REGIMENT
Brigadier General Rich Natonski, Commander

2nd MARINE REGIMENT
Colonel Ronald Bailey, Regimental Commander

1st BATTALION, 2nd MARINES
Lieutenant Colonel Rick Grabowski, Battalion Commander
Major David Sosa, Operations Officer

CHARLIE COMPANY, 1st BATTALION, 2nd MARINES
Captain Dan Wittnam, Company Commander
First Lieutenant James "Ben" Reid, Weapons Platoon Commander
Corporal Jake Worthington, Javelin Gunner
Lance Corporal Thomas Quirk, Rifleman
Private First Class Casey Robinson, Squad Automatic Weapon (SAW) Gunner

First Lieutenant Conor Tracy, AAV Platoon Commander
Sergeant William Schaefer, AAV Platoon Section Leader
Lance Corporal Edward Castleberry, AAV Driver

ALPHA COMPANY, 1st BATTALION, 2nd MARINES
Captain Mike Brooks, Company Commander

BRAVO COMPANY, 1st BATTALION, 2nd MARINES
Corporal Neville Welch, Riflemen Team Leader

ALPHA COMPANY, 8th TANK BATTALION
Major Bill Peeples, Company Commander
Captain Scott Dyer, Executive Officer

MARINE AIRCRAFT GROUP 29
Captain Eric Garcia, CH-46 Medevac Pilot
HM3 (Hospital Man 3rd Class) Moses Gloria, Navy Corpsman

PROLOGUE

On September 17, 2003, I was traveling with U.S. forces in a convoy of Humvees through the western outskirts of Baghdad, to report on the success of the military operation that had toppled Saddam Hussein. Yet talk among U.S. soldiers and marines that day was not of their achievements, but of the local population's growing mood of resentment after the euphoria of the U.S. forces' initial sweep into Baghdad. It was an airless, sunny afternoon as we traveled along a dirt road to our base in a former Iraqi army compound. It was eerily quiet. Suddenly, an ear-shattering explosion cracked through our vehicle and a rush of hot air and debris swept past my face. The heavily armored door of the Humvee warped inward into my legs and the vehicle lifted off the ground. There were cries of "Get down, get down." As I dived to the floor, I looked up to see a shattered windshield and clouds of dust, reflected against the sunlight, falling slowly toward the ground. The acrid smell of explosives filled my nostrils and stuck in my throat. We had been ambushed. Hidden members of the Iraqi resistance had detonated an improvised bomb made from an old shell casing filled with stones and debris underneath the wheel of our vehicle. Soldiers were screaming in terror and anger, clutching bloody arms and backs. They were rushed to field hospitals with broken arms and shrapnel wounds. Within twenty-four hours I had been evacuated to Germany with ear damage.

The sheer terror of that moment gave me a new understanding of the realities of war—the sights, smells, sounds, taste, and touch of combat. That gave me a starting point for this book. But what drove me to write it was meeting the marines of 1st Battalion, 2nd Marines, a couple of months after I got out of Iraq, at their home base of Camp Lejeune, North Carolina. These marines had been at the heart of the U.S. forces' push to Baghdad and they had an amazing story to tell—a story of boundless camaraderie and bravery amid the anguish, suffering, brutality, and stupidity of war.

Like the rest of the coalition forces who went to Iraq, the majority of the men of 1st Battalion, 2nd Marines had never tasted combat. They arrived in Kuwait as unremarkable, brash young men hyped up by the prospect of testing themselves, of firing their weapons for real, of killing people. They also arrived as part of the world's most technologically advanced fighting machine, bristling with awesome weaponry and backed by top-class military training.

Yet nothing prepared the marines of 1/2 for what happened next. It was March 23, 2003, the third day of the war. Their commanders had tasked them with an important but relatively straightforward mission in Nasiriyah, a city in one of the least hostile parts of Iraq. As they attacked into Nasiriyah, the marines of 1/2 were brimming with the confidence of a military force that knew what it was doing and why it was doing it. As the day went on, they were caught up in the chaos and uncertainty of combat, what has been called "the fog of war," fighting for their lives against an enemy that they hadn't anticipated and didn't recognize. This is the story of what happened to that group of ordinary young men on the battlefield that day. It was a day that changed them forever. And a day that revealed some of the reasons for the confusion and chaos that still reigns in Iraq.

I

THE
ROAD
TO
NASIRIYAH

MARCH 23, 2003

0600–1230 Hours

1

Private First Class Casey Robinson readjusted his lanky body, trying to squeeze his wide, swimmer's shoulders into any gap that he could find. He was lying on the deck of vehicle C201, one of Charlie Company's twelve AAVs, trying to get some sleep. As soon as he dozed off he'd get a cheesy whiff from the feet of his fellow marines and he'd wake with a start. There were twenty of them squashed into each AAV. Some sat on metal benches; some were perched on ammunition boxes; some, like Robinson, lay on the metal floor, squeezed between interlocking legs, M16 rifles, machine guns, Javelin antitank missiles, and enough cans of ammo to do serious damage to a small town.

It had been like this for two days now. The AAVs, short for amphibious assault vehicles, were not much more than tub-shaped, watertight, metal boxes that on land ran on tank treads rather than wheels and in water deployed small but powerful propellers. They had been designed in the 1970s to transport marines, in short stretches, from ship to beach landings, but now, two days into the combat phase of Operation Iraqi Freedom, many of the marines' AAVs, including C201, had clocked more than 150 kilometers of southern Iraq's moonlike landscape. The plan was to drive them even farther, all the way to the gates of Baghdad. The marines called them amtracks, or just tracks. While 201's treads allowed it to go over rough terrain, the marines inside were taking a pounding. Robinson was not happy. *This is like riding in a sardine can.* There were no windows, just tiny slits of reinforced glass that passed as spy holes. With no sense of space or direction, Robinson was tossed from side to side, at the mercy of the AAV's rubber and metal tracks meeting hard-packed rocks, dirt, and pitted Iraqi earth.

Robinson fought back a wave of tiredness and boredom. *What am I doing here?* Except for a few short breaks for vehicle maintenance and to relieve the pressure on the bladder, they had hardly stopped. The previous night he'd spent a few hours pulling security in a fighting hole by the side of Highway 8, a few kilometers east of the air base at Jalibah. His job was to stop the Iraqis from interfering with the long military convoys that the Army was moving up to supply its combat troops just ahead of the Marines, along the MSR, the main supply route. Robinson and the rest of the Marines from Charlie Company were in a blocking position with their tracks pulled up by the side of the road. Luckily, they were on 50 percent security watch. He got an hour's sleep while another marine took watch, and then they switched. He made sure he stayed awake on his watch. He'd heard that the previous night, a marine sleeping outside his AAV had been crushed in the dark by a passing tank.

Robinson yawned and got a blast of his own foul-smelling breath. He'd not washed for two days, and oral hygiene was no more than an occasional scour with a sand-and-grit infested toothbrush. The sun was coming up over the horizon. He didn't really know where he was. He knew they were heading northward toward a city but he couldn't remember its name. The previous night they'd been told that they were going to stop short of the city and set up a blocking position on its southern approach. Then they might have to go into the city and seize some bridges to secure a route so the rest of the Marine Corps units could pass through. He was hazy on the details. Humble grunts like him were only handed out information on a need-to-know basis. But what he did know was that it was going to be an easy mission. His commanders had warned them against complacency, but they had all been told that the city's population was Shiite Muslims and that they hated Saddam. *They are going to greet us with open arms and give us the keys to the city.*

Robinson had been a marine for two years, and even during the preparations to ship out to Iraq he was convinced that he would never see combat. The only gunshots he'd heard so far were some dumb-assed POGUES who had accidentally fired off their weapons. That's what the infantry marines called anyone who wasn't a hard-core, frontline rifleman—people other than grunts. Now that they were in Iraq, the prospects of getting involved in a fight were not good. There was a rumor going around that his unit, 1st Battalion, 2nd Marines out of Camp Lejeune in North Carolina, was merely a supporting force for the Hollywood Marines. That was the semidisparaging, semienvious nickname that East Coast marines like Robinson gave to the marines out of Camp Pendleton, California. *They are too soft. But it would be nice to have those Californian girls and beaches so close.*

Another wave of frustration swept over him. For two years at Camp Lejeune and on maneuvers in the Californian desert at the Twentynine

Palms Marine Corps base, he'd learned the art of mechanized infantry warfare. He'd learned about geometry of fire, how to form a defensive perimeter, how to employ machine guns, how to strip and reassemble an M16 in seconds, how to kill the enemy with his bare hands. He was supposed to be one of "the Few, the Proud." Now, instead of fighting the enemy, he was being jolted around in a metal box, fending off the diesel fumes and the taste of vomit slowly making its way up his throat. He took a gulp from a bottle of tepid water and had the uncomfortable feeling that his two years in the Marine Corps had mostly trained him in tedium and loneliness. Private First Class Robinson had had enough. His parched mouth was sucked dry of any moisture by the fine sand that coated everything and the warm, fetid heat that clung to the AAV's deck. He was fed up, weary, and very hungry. For the first time he felt envious of the POGUES and the REMFs, the *rear-echelon motherfuckers,* who were probably sitting on their clean, fat asses in an air-conditioned dining hall well away from the front line, getting ready to bite into a hot breakfast of ham and eggs, washed down with coffee.

He kicked the shin closest to him.

"I'll trade you a chicken teriyaki for the Mexican burrito."

The track erupted in a frenzy of bartering.

"Oh man, I got the jambalaya again. Who'll swap it for the vegetable tortellini? How about you, Worthington?"

"Peanut butter for a chocolate milk shake?"

"Fuck you, Wentzel. You can keep your cinnamon cake."

Swapping food from their MREs, meals ready to eat, was the one activity that kept the marines entertained during the endless wait for battle. Robinson had it down to an art. He thought of himself as a real chef. He would take the spaghetti from its plastic bag, mix it with the ravioli, get some jalapeño cheese, take the salsa from the Mexican burrito, cut the brown plastic MRE sleeve, and mix it all up under a flame so it was real hot. For dessert he'd take the wheat bread, cover it with peanut butter, shake some cocoa powder on it, and decorate it with M&M's. He would wash it down with water mixed with a drink powder from the MRE packet. Marines called the garishly colored liquid "bug juice." It looked vile, but it made a change from bottled water. If he could get all the elements to make a meal like that it was a good day. It would be an even better one if he could get rid of a jambalaya or the nasty-tasting beef hot dogs he'd nicknamed the four fingers of death. Fortunately, there were some weirdos out there who liked the nasty ones. That was how Robinson and his fellow Marines passed the time. They were young men, at the peak of physical fitness, who had spent months and years training hard in the art of warfare. But for the past two days as they rolled around inside their track, all they had done was trade food, play cards, tell dirty jokes, eat, and fart. And those MREs really did make you fart.

The 176 marines of Charlie Company had formed a tight bond during their time together. Some had been with the company for several years. Others had joined straight from Boot Camp only a few months before. They reveled in their nickname of "Crazy" Company, convinced that they always came out on top during training exercises with Alpha and Bravo, the other companies in their battalion. But what really set them apart was that they were a wild and determined bunch. Marines took pride in their reputation as untamed warriors, but somehow Charlie seemed to have more than its fair share of troublemakers.

Private First Class Robinson was one of the wildest. He didn't mean to get into trouble. Trouble somehow always found him. It probably started sometime when he was a kid and his dad went off the rails and ended up in prison. But how can you really know? He didn't really like talking about it. As a six-year-old kid, Casey Robinson lived with his mom and stepdad in Santa Cruz, California. He admired his stepdad for looking after his mom and working hard in his construction business, but the two of them just didn't get along. The freedom of growing up in a beach community probably didn't help. By day he would work at the Chicken in a Basket stall on the Santa Cruz Beach Boardwalk; by night he would drink and hook up with girls or get in a fight with the Eastside surfers.

He had no idea how the rivalry between the Westside and Eastside surfers began. Ever since he'd surfed the waves at Steamers Lane as a kid it had been like that. The waves there were short and tricky and exhilarating, not like east of the San Lorenzo River, where the waves were longer and more consistent. But sometimes the Eastside surfers would ditch their longboards for shortboards, cross to the Westside, and start surfing on the waves there. And if you took someone else's wave you'd better have a lot of friends, because otherwise they would whip your ass. That's how the fighting would begin. What started with a young Casey Robinson getting into trouble from his mom for staying out late, ended with a police record for drunkenness and assault after he smashed a rival surfer within half an inch of his life during a beach brawl. A police record, beach life, and sex real young had made Casey Robinson grow up pretty quick.

The assault charge almost cost him his place in the Marines. He was a fine swimmer and a junior lifeguard. At first he wanted to be a Navy SEAL. A lifeguard he'd looked up to, a guy who he saw as a sort of mentor, had told him stories about life in the Special Forces. But when he'd gone to the Navy recruiting office, the officer there told him that the SEALs was too tough.

"Sign up for the Navy and you might get a chance at it later."

Casey Robinson saw through the ruse. He'd heard stories about people being sucked into a contract and then given shitty Navy jobs. Instead, he went next door to the Marine Corps. There the recruiter was real straight with him and sold him on Force Recon, the Marines' elite, fast-reaction reconnaissance force.

"Join the infantry first and then you'll get your shot at Force Recon."

Right then and there, soon after his nineteenth birthday, Casey Robinson had signed up to be a grunt. But somehow, as usual, things just didn't work out. He'd done really well during his three months at Boot Camp and was the only one to come out as a private first class. But when he went to the School of Infantry at Camp Pendleton in California, a routine inspection uncovered steroids in a locker. A couple of marines snitched on him. They weren't his steroids. Yes, he was going to buy them, but they weren't his. His urine and fingerprint tests came up negative, but they still investigated. When he joined the Fleet Marine Force he was sent to 1st Battalion, 2nd Marines out of Camp Lejeune. No one there knew about the steroid allegations, and he was promoted to lance corporal and given his own fire team to lead. Then somehow they found out and his platoon sergeant started talking about NJPing him. That meant giving him a nonjudicial punishment, slapping him on the wrist, and busting him back to private first class. Robinson wanted to have a full court-martial hearing so he could fight his case, but by the time it came up they were on ship on their way to Iraq, and he was told he couldn't refuse NJP and didn't have the right to a lawyer. A few days after they'd weighed anchor he was summoned to an onboard hearing and was given an NJP. He was lucky, he guessed. He thought the 1/2 battalion commander, Lieutenant Colonel Rick Grabowski, might throw the book at him, bang him up, and put him on bread and water for the rest of the sea journey. His company commander, Captain Dan Wittnam, had stood up for him and had told the board he was a good guy and was responsible. That was a surprise. He thought Captain Wittnam would have been really tough on him. Wittnam kept Charlie Company on a tight leash. He worked them hard during physical training and didn't let any of them step out of line. He was a classic Marine, the guy Robinson wanted to be like. He got a kick out of running faster, harder, and for longer than any of his marines. That's why they'd nicknamed him Captain Insano.

Robinson regretted the episode with the steroids, but somehow he couldn't help himself. He was already tall and powerful, but it wasn't enough. *No matter how fast I go, I want to go faster. No matter how much I lift, I want to lift more.* He knew it was kind of messed up, but the world was against him and he had to get stronger and bigger to fight his way through it. Maybe he was trying to prove something to his father who was never there. Or maybe he was proving something to himself. Whatever it was, twenty-two-year-old Casey Robinson, recently demoted from lance corporal to private first class, was currently somewhere in the middle of Iraq, trying to fend off the stench of diesel, the body odor of twenty unwashed grunts, and deep, dark thoughts that sometimes made his two years service in the Marine Corps feel like a prison sentence.

His steely blue eyes darted around at the faces in his track. They were mostly, like him, from Charlie Company's 1st Platoon. Opposite him, attached from Weapons Company, were the Javelin gunner, Corporal Jake Worthington, and his "A" gunner, Lance Corporal Brian Wenberg. On his left, in the commander's hatch, was his platoon commander, Second Lieutenant Scott Swantner, and on his right were Lance Corporal Douglas Milter and his squad leader, Corporal John Wentzel. He didn't know whether it was resentment, but he had a tough time with Wentzel. Wentzel had been promoted to squad leader just as Robinson had lost his job as team leader. He liked the guy but thought he was too soft, a bit of a pussy. When he went into combat he wanted to know that he could rely on the guys to the left and right of him. Somehow he didn't think Wentzel would make the grade. Driving the AAV was the lanky tracker, Lance Corporal Edward Castleberry. In the AAV commander's hatch was another tracker, Sergeant William Schaefer. The trackers, from the 2nd Assault Amphibian Battalion headquartered at Courthouse Bay, Camp Lejeune, were a breed apart. Their job was to drive and maintain the AAVs and to work the tracks' up guns, the 40 mm Mark 19 grenade launcher and the .50-caliber heavy machine gun. There was some rivalry between the two groups. The infantrymen thought of themselves as the heart and soul of the Marine Corps and considered the trackers as a mere appendage. The trackers thought the grunts were arrogant and cocky. At Camp Lejeune, the two groups never mixed much, but in Kuwait, Robinson had gotten to know Castleberry and liked the guy.

None of them had even been near a combat zone before. Some were only seventeen years old, barely out of high school. Robinson had gone through Boot Camp with a couple of them. Others he'd met on ship. But now after weeks together living side by side he knew everything about them, even down to the sex games they played with their girlfriends and wives. He'd watched them laugh hysterically at a dumb-ass prank on a drill instructor or sob at bad news from home. The faces he knew so well were obscured behind the hard, metallic face of war. They were all equipped with Kevlar helmets, with night-vision goggles attached, taut body armor with bulky ceramic plates in the front pocket, gas masks and weapons hanging clumsily by their side. They were used to most of the equipment, but what really made them uncomfortably hot and sticky were the charcoal-lined MOPP (mission-oriented protective posture) suits they had to wear over their desert cammies in case of a nuclear, biological, or chemical attack. Over the past few weeks they had practiced putting them on and taking them off again as part of their NBC drills, but they'd never really grown comfortable with them.

"My turn at air security."

Robinson stood up, grabbed hold of the ridge of the hatch above him, and pulled himself up to take over posting security. Precariously balancing himself on an ammo box with his torso half out of one of the AAV's two rectangular hatches, he pulled up his M249 squad automatic weapon, or SAW, after him. There were four marines up there already, scanning the horizon from each corner of the amtrack's hatches, their M16 rifles at the ready. As a SAW gunner, Robinson had specialist training. His M249 fired the same 5.56 mm round as the M16 but, at a rate of up to one thousand rounds per minute, it packed a much bigger punch. He mounted it on the top of the AAV and, using the sandbags around the hatch as support, looked down the sight. There was very little out there. The sun was slowly rising over a flat, scrubby, burned-orange landscape dotted with small mounds of dirt and the odd mud brick house. Every so often an Iraqi tending goats would give the marine convoy a desultory wave. *The hajjis don't look too hostile.* In front and behind him stretched a long line of military vehicles. He knew that somewhere at the front of the column were the tanks assigned to their battalion, followed by the AAVs of the three infantry companies, Alpha, Bravo, and his own company, Charlie.

Robinson felt better with his head out of the track. It was hot and dusty, but the air was fresh and the wind on his face felt good. The past few weeks of life in a hot, featureless desert had been mind-numbingly boring. But maybe today would be a better day.

2

"Viking 6, this is Timberwolf 6. Sitrep. Over."

Using his call sign, *Timberwolf*, Lieutenant Colonel Rick Grabowski, the commander of 1st Battalion, 2nd Marines, stood by his Humvee and called back to Viking, the regimental command post, with a situation report. With his husky voice, which some of his marines made fun of behind his back, he told the regiment that he had reached the 22 northing, a position about twenty kilometers south of Nasiriyah. The night before, his boss, Colonel Ron Bailey, the commander of the 2nd Marine Regiment, had given him the 20 northing grid reference as his holding point. He was told to be there by 7:00 a.m. local time. Grabowski had made it with time to spare. Now Grabowski had been asked to move north for a few kilometers to the 22 northing to give room for 1st Battalion, 10th Marines to set up their batteries. They were going to provide artillery support for the upcoming mission. He was feeling confident. There was a chill in the air, but the sun was coming up on the horizon and he felt good about the day ahead. The two days since they had left Kuwait had been uneventful. But today they might get their first proper mission accomplished.

For months, Grabowski and his company commanders had pored over maps and satellite photos of Nasiriyah. It was a featureless, medium-size Iraqi city with a population of five hundred thousand living in the densely packed center and surrounding areas. It was unremarkable except for two bridges of strategic importance. On the southeastern edge of the city was a bridge over the Euphrates River. The Euphrates was one of the main obstacles facing the U.S. military in its push toward Baghdad. A road from the Euphrates Bridge led to another bridge, about 4.5 kilometers to the north, over a narrower waterway, the Saddam Canal. That bridge led directly to a highway that took a northeastern route all the way to Baghdad.

Grabowski and 1st Battalion, 2nd Marines had been given the mission of capturing the two bridges. That would open up a route for the Marines to enter Baghdad, some three hundred kilometers to the north.

The mission was straightforward. But there was one major difficulty: how to get from the southern bridge to the northern bridge. The road in between the two bridges went right through the heart of Nasiriyah. Grabowski knew that Operation Iraqi Freedom was built around speed. The aim was to get to Baghdad as quickly as possible without being slowed down by urban fighting. Moreover, no one wanted public opinion to turn against them because of civilian casualties from a big firefight in an Iraqi city. On February 6, on ship, Grabowski was at a planning meeting when Colonel Ron Johnson, operations officer for the 2nd Marine Expeditionary Brigade, had pulled out an aerial map of the city and pointed to the road running between the Euphrates Bridge and the Saddam Canal Bridge.

"Army planners call this stretch of road Ambush Alley. But we're not going to call it Ambush Alley. This is not Mogadishu."

Johnson was referring to the chaotic urban fight that Army Rangers and Special Forces had been sucked into in the Somalian capital in 1993. Most of the marines knew it as the terrifying but exhilarating battle portrayed in the Hollywood movie *Black Hawk Down*. No one wanted a repeat of that debacle. That was why, when tasked with the mission of taking the bridges, Grabowski, with Johnson's agreement, decided to find a route around to the east of Nasiriyah so they wouldn't have to push along what was officially called Route Moe. But somehow the comparison with Mogadishu had slipped out. Inevitably, some of Grabowski's marines were already referring to that stretch of Route Moe as Ambush Alley.

To accomplish his mission, Grabowski had a battalion of nearly a thousand men under his command. First Battalion, 2nd Marines was composed of his command element, three infantry line companies—Alpha, Bravo, and Charlie—a weapons company, a headquarters and service company, and a tank company of Marine Reservists who had been attached to his unit for Operation Iraqi Freedom.

During the weeks on ship and in Kuwait, Grabowski and the staff of 1/2 worked on a plan for approval by the 2nd Marine Regiment. It was based on the Marine concept of maneuver warfare. His three line companies, the tanks and weapons company would work in support of each other to seize the bridges through a series of rapid, violent, and unexpected maneuvers. Alpha Company, supported by M1A1 Abrams tanks, would roll onto the first objective, the Euphrates Bridge. Bravo Company, accompanied by tanks, would then roll across the Euphrates Bridge, pass through Alpha's lines, turn to the east, and circle around the outskirts of the town. Bringing up the rear would be Charlie Company. It would move through Alpha's position on the Euphrates Bridge, follow Bravo Company to the east, and pass through its lines to take the second objective, the northern Saddam Canal Bridge. Then Bravo would pass through Charlie's lines to take a third objective—a T intersection a couple of kilometers north of the Saddam Canal Bridge. It was a maneuver designed to surprise any Iraqis defending the city by avoiding Ambush Alley, the more direct, but potentially hazardous, four-lane highway connecting the bridges.

The seizure of the bridges was a "be prepared to" mission. Grabowski still didn't know whether they were going to carry it out that day. It might never happen. What he did know was that they were going to advance toward the city and take up a defensive blocking position around the southern Euphrates Bridge and await further instructions.

Veterans of Desert Storm had talked with disappointment about turning up for battle during the last Gulf war, finding the Iraqis had all fled, and then having to wait in the desert for buses to take them back to their camps in Saudi Arabia. Grabowski hoped this war wasn't going to be like that. He was a gruff man who wore a trademark blue scarf around his neck to keep the sand out. He'd been commander of 1st Battalion, 2nd Marines for two years. He'd enlisted in the Marine Corps while still in high school and spent four years with the infantry. After college, inspired by the stories his father had told him of life as a pilot in Vietnam, he tried out for flight school. His hearing wasn't good enough, though, and he failed his physical. He went back to Camp Lejeune and worked his way through the ranks. For over twenty-five years his life had been with the Marines. He'd humped hundred-pound packs up and down hills, ridden through steaming jungles, floated on hot, sweaty ships in the Pacific and the Caribbean, and fired millions of rounds from M16 rifles and M60 machine guns. Although he'd been sent to Haiti in 1994, during the unpredictable weeks before the chaos that took Jean-Bertrand Aristide back to power, he had never really tasted combat. Now it was dawn on Sunday March 23, 2003, and Rick Grabowski, commander of 1st Battalion, 2nd Marines, part of the six-thousand-strong Marine Task Force Tarawa, was finally at war. They were on their way to kick Saddam Hussein's ass.

The intel 1/2 Marines had received from CENTCOM, U.S. Central Command, was reassuring. In 1991, after Desert Storm, the Shia population in Nasiriyah had launched a rebellion against Saddam's ruling Baath Party. The Americans had failed to support that rebellion and it was brutally squashed by Saddam's henchmen. This time, though, the higher-ups believed that the Shia population would again rebel against Saddam once the Americans entered the city. Grabowski was confident. *They are going to be happy to see us.*

For several weeks he had tried to find out how the enemy was positioned around the city. In particular, he had wanted to know more about several large complexes on its northern edge. He knew that Nasiriyah was a military town, but Intel had only managed to tell him that they were "military compounds." But they did have intelligence that Iraqi soldiers from the 11th Infantry Division, based around Nasiriyah, were carrying civilian clothes and that once they saw the Americans, they would just slip out of their uniforms and disappear into the local population. Any Iraqi units guarding Nasiriyah would then crumble and surrender. It was one of the reasons why it had been decided not to "prep" the area beforehand with air and ground fire. Grabowski and his staff had carried on long discussions into the night about the enemy. Although they had little information on paramilitary fighters in the town, they were pretty sure that no one would put up much resistance. He hoped it wasn't misguided optimism, but there was a serious amount of talk about the number of EPWs, enemy prisoners of war, they would take. That very morning there had been reports that around Basra, the 51st Iraqi mechanized brigade had already given up.

Grabowski looked back at the snaking column of military hardware stretching back several miles as far as the eye could see. He was toward the front of the column, traveling in his HMMWV, or high-mobility multipurpose wheeled vehicle, known to the military and civilians alike as a Humvee. He hated traveling in the C7, the command-and-control track that contained most of the battalion staff and comms equipment. It didn't have windows and he could never see what was happening on the ground. He'd divided the battalion command post into two groups. He had decided that he would take some of his senior staff with him as a forward command post that would control the battalion's movement from a position just behind the tanks and frontline troops. That way he could see exactly how the mission was unfolding and could react to it. The main command post, led by the executive officer, Major Jeff Tuggle, would be at the rear of the column. Tuggle would take over if he got hit or couldn't communicate.

Grabowski reached for the radio handset of the PRC-119, the Marines' basic tactical radio.

"Panzer 6, this is Timberwolf 6. Sitrep over."

He wanted a situation report from the tank company up ahead. Grabowski monitored two nets. He used the battalion tactical network 1 to communicate with his company commanders. To speak to the regimental commander and staff, he used regimental tac net 1. There was also a battalion tac 2, which was for nonurgent logistics and administrative purposes, but he hardly ever used it. The sun was up, the chatter on the radio was calm. Lieutenant Colonel Rick Grabowski was excited and happy.

Driving in a Humvee alongside Grabowski was Major David Sosa. Sosa was the battalion's operations officer, or number three. While Grabowski oversaw the whole mission, Sosa's job was to oversee the practicalities. Sosa was a wiry, energetic, and intense marine, with dark, soft eyes. There was something deliberate, almost machinelike, in the way he walked and carried himself. He had been born in Brooklyn, New York, to Puerto Rican parents. Straight out of high school he had enlisted in the Army's 82nd Airborne. But after two years as an infantry paratrooper with the Army he went back to college. He found it tough and dropped out because his grades were bad. But then suddenly some sort of switch was hit. He went back to college and his GPA began to improve. He decided to try out as an officer in the Marine Corps and had been there ever since. Nine months before coming to Iraq, he had been appointed operations officer for 1/2 Marines. It was a bit like a homecoming. He had started his career as a weapons platoon commander in Alpha Company 1/2.

Sosa could call on overwhelming firepower to support the battalion. Most Marine and Army units supporting Operation Iraqi Freedom received much of their equipment from huge prepositioned cargo ships floating permanently in the Indian Ocean. It gave U.S. forces the ability to attack into trouble spots anywhere in the world with speed and ease. The equipment was brand new and state of the art. Task Force Tarawa, though, was unique. It had brought most of its equipment with it from Stateside on seven ships provided by the U.S. Navy. Two of the ships were big enough to carry the task force's eighty-one helos and jets from the Marine Corps Air Station at New River, North Carolina. The others carried the task force's tanks, amtracks, support vehicles, and weapon systems supplied out of Camp Lejeune.

Sosa felt the thrill of being part of such an overwhelming force. They had M1A1 Abrams battle tanks with 120 mm guns that could hit a target over three kilometers away with deadly accuracy. Mounted alongside the main gun was the coaxial machine gun. The tank's stabilization system made it the most accurate machine gun in the world. The regiment's artillery could lock in on incoming fire, track where it was coming from, and take it out in seconds. The Marine Air Wing Huey and Cobra attack helicopters could light up an Iraqi T-72 tank five miles away with Hellfire missiles and rockets. The battalion could call for close air support from CAS Harrier jump jets and F/A-18s carrying precision bombs to take out targets with pinpoint accuracy. That was one of the differences between the Army and the Marines. The Marine Corps was a much smaller force than the Army, but it was the only truly integrated air-ground combat team in the world. It was designed to be a self-sufficient total force that could operate by itself. Sosa almost felt pity for any Iraqi that dared take them on.

Sosa remembered what the S-2, the battalion's intelligence officer, had told them of the Iraqi military's capability. Theoretically, there was no contest. The Iraqi air force had been virtually destroyed in Desert Storm, while the Iraqi army's tanks and artillery pieces were antiquated and its troops demoralized. Intelligence was unequivocal. The Iraqi military did not stand a chance.

Sosa looked around. The infantry companies were lined up along the side of the road, their amtracks pulled into a staggered column. Way ahead of him were the tanks and the CAATs, or combined anti-armor teams, Humvees bristling with heavy machine guns, and antitank missiles. The marines around him were pulling security, lying in the prone position in a perimeter around their amtracks, just as they'd been trained. Everything was going to plan. It was just as it should be.

It was 0715. All of a sudden Sosa heard a rumble in the distance. Then, seconds later, there was another rumble. He turned to Lieutenant Colonel Grabowski.

"I think that's artillery."

"No, I think that's thunder."

Sosa wasn't sure. There was another rumble. Sosa knew it couldn't be friendly forces because there were no units in front of them. First Battalion, 2nd Marines was the lead element.

"No, I think someone is shooting at us."

Then, about fifty meters to the east of where he was standing, a plume of dirt splashed up from the ground, followed by another loud clap.

He saw a flash about five kilometers off toward the northeast and another splash off to the side of the road. Over the radio he heard the voice of one of the CAAT marines.

"We've got small-arms fire coming in at us from both sides of the road."

Sosa couldn't believe it. *They're actually shooting at us.* Like the others, he'd been briefed that there would be little resistance but he thought he'd been pretty careful about not allowing himself to fall into a false sense of security. He'd warned his marines to prepare for the worst, that the Iraqis were going to fight. Now he realized that he'd bought into the capitulation theory. He was angry with himself for making assumptions about enemy action. *If you don't validate those assumptions, you might be in a world of hurt.*

3

"Panzer 5, this is Panzer 6. Have we got air on its way? Where is the helo overwatch?"

At the head of the 1st Battalion, 2nd Marines column a company of M1A1 Abrams tanks from the 8th Tank Battalion out of Fort Knox, Kentucky, was pushing forward toward Nasiriyah. The tank crews were reservists, part-time marines who left their civilian lives for one weekend a month and two weeks every summer to train as marines. They had been activated on Friday, January 10, 2003, assigned to 1/2 Marines, and within seventy-two hours they had packed, left Kentucky, arrived at Camp Lejeune, embarked on ship, and were on their way to Iraq.

The company was commanded by Major Bill Peeples, a thirty-five-year-old city planning officer from Jackson County, Indiana, a suburban area south of Indianapolis. For four years in his early twenties Peeples had been an active duty Marine Corps maintenance officer but then had left to do other things. Two years later he faced a choice. Unless he rejoined the Marine Corps, he would be taken off the reserve officer list. He decided to rejoin as a reservist, and after five years working in a tank company he was appointed commander of Alpha Company, 8th Tank Battalion. That was a year ago. Now he was leading his men into battle from his M1A1 tank, which his crew had named "Wild Bill" in his honor. He'd named the machine gun "Maximus" after his newborn son.

He had organized his tanks in a wedge formation with one up front and two tanks behind like an arrowhead. It gave the lead tanks maximum sectors of fire. The lead took the twelve o'clock sector, or front. The tanks behind protected the flanks to three o'clock on the right and nine o'clock on the left. The tanks at the back had their turrets to the six o'clock position to protect the rear. With his torso half out of the tank commander's, or TC's, hatch he could see the sun rising on the right side of the road, illuminating a flat, scrubby, and endless wasteland stretching off into the distance. The early morning light glinted off the swirls of dust, kicked up as the convoy passed. Much earlier that morning, Peeples had seen, off to the west, ribbons of light belonging to a never-ending convoy of Army support vehicles making their way north toward Baghdad along Route 1. It was eerie. It looked like a California freeway. Now, though, there was no one on the horizon. They were on their own.

For two days his twelve tanks had led the battalion through the desert. It had been uneventful apart from one tank breaking down; it was currently under tow at the rear of the column. Now they were on a road speeding toward the city of Nasiriyah. His tank company possessed enormous firepower. *We are the tip of a very hard spear.* In consultation with the battalion command, he'd configured his eleven remaining tanks into Team Mech and Team Tank. Team Tank consisted of seven tanks plus a platoon of infantry from Bravo Company. In return, Peeples gave a platoon of four tanks to Bravo Company to create Team Mech. At one stage, during heated discussions about how to best organize the battalion, Lieutenant Colonel Grabowski and his operations officer, Major Sosa, had wanted to give each of the three infantry companies a platoon of tanks. Peeples had persuaded them that he could offer more support as a separate Team Tank maneuver unit. His crews had trained as a company and knew how each other thought and worked. He didn't think they were so effective when they were put under rifle company commanders who had little experience of working with tanks.

It was not the first time Major Peeples had crossed swords with the battalion staff. His war had not started well. When his company arrived at Camp Lejeune from Kentucky, less than twenty-four hours after being activated, he had discovered that they didn't have time to inspect or fix the original fourteen tanks assigned to them from Camp Lejeune's 2nd Tank Battalion.

"You can fix them on the way over."

Peeples didn't like the answer. The battalion staff was already on ship when they arrived so there was no welcoming party, or any chance to discuss what the battalion expected from them. To make matters worse, his company of 125 marines was split into three groups and embarked on different ships; the USS *Ashland*, the USS *Portland*, and the USS *Gunston Hall*. Communication between the ships was virtually impossible so they could not coordinate with each other or talk to the battalion's logistics officer to tell him what they needed. When at last they did manage to inspect the tanks, they found that they were in terrible condition—to the point where ten of them were deadlined and totally unsuitable for combat.

When they finally got together in Kuwait, it was no better. He felt as though he was treated as a second-class citizen. Even though, as a major, he was the third most senior marine in the battalion, he suspected that he was excluded from a lot of the battalion-level planning. No one really said anything about it, but he put it down to a feeling among the active-duty marines that they were somehow better than the reserve community. *Of course, they mouth the usual platitudes about how the Marine Corps is a total force and that the reservists and those on active duty are the same. But that's all it is. Talk.* What made it worse was that there was an undercurrent in the Marine Corps that the infantryman was its heart and soul and that any other specialty was somehow not the real thing. It was true that the Marine Corps was built around the infantry, and he understood that armor and airpower were there to support the infantry companies. However, since he'd joined the battalion, he'd never really felt that the command staff had a proper appreciation of the support and firepower tanks could bring to a fight. The M1A1 Abrams was a $4.3 million killing machine. It could light up vehicles and buildings three kilometers away with its accurate 120 mm laser main gun that had a 360-degree firing capability. Its 7.62 mm coaxially mounted gun and .50-caliber machine gun could rip human beings in half. Its twelve-hundred-horsepower engine could move it along at speeds of up to forty-two miles per hour. It had a range of over 450 kilometers and a stabilization system that meant it could fire its main gun accurately when moving. There was no faster or more accurate tank in the world, and he loved being in command of it.

Peeples picked up the radio. He wanted a CAS update from Captain Scott Dyer, his executive officer. He had requested and been promised a flight of helicopters, but as yet there was no sign of them. *It's all quiet at the moment, but it would be good to have some air support as we move forward.*

"Panzer 5, this is Panzer 6. Any news on air support?"

Captain Scott Dyer, call sign Panzer 5, was riding in his tank just behind Major Peeples in the center of the wedge formation. His huge six foot eight inch frame, ridiculously tall for a tanker, was clad in a green Nomex tanker's jumpsuit, and jutted out of the TC's hatch. On his head he wore a bullet-resistant CVC, or combat vehicle crew helmet. His tank was named *Dark Side*. It was a reference to the fact that as an enlisted marine he had once been one of the guys. Now that he was an officer, they teased him for crossing to the Dark Side. He'd marked his turret with a huge red hand-print like the Native Americans marked their ponies. He and his crew liked to call it the red hand of death. His driver, Lance Corporal Michael Shirley, and his gunner, Corporal Charles Bell, had painted a large Playboy Bunny on the left side of the tank's skirt. It was a ruse to get *Dark Side* in the magazines. It hadn't yet worked.

It was Dyer who had borne the brunt of the battalion's hostility toward the reservists. He had responsibility for getting the tanks back up and running in Kuwait. They were lacking so many pieces of vital equipment that he had put in a parts request that exceeded the budget for the entire battalion. He'd watched a succession of generals and experts come down to inspect their tanks. He could tell what the battalion and regimental staff were thinking. *Those nasty reservists don't know what the hell they are talking about.* Part of him understood why they were so freaked. Peeples and Dyer had one-tenth of all the tanks available to the Marine Corps in Iraq. *If 80 percent are deadlined, that's cause for pause.*

It took several weeks before he convinced the battalion staff that he did know what he was talking about. Only then did they pull together to help him get the tanks up and running. Navy engineers had managed to machine some of the parts on ship, like firing pins and bustle rack extensions, to carry even more gear. He, his maintenance chief, Staff Sergeant Charlie Cooke, and the tank crews had begged, borrowed, cannibalized, and even stolen parts from other units waiting in Kuwait. On March 19, after days working around the clock, they had managed to get fourteen working M1A1s up to FAA Hawkins, the force assembly area, for the push into Iraq. While they were there, waiting for the order to cross the line of departure, one of the tanks broke down. Another was driven into a hole and couldn't be recovered. In spite of their achievements in getting twelve tanks ready for combat, it was a bad start, and Dyer realized that it had left a nasty feeling between them and the battalion staff. He knew that Major Peeples had felt it, too. There was bad blood from which they might never recover.

It was doubly frustrating for Scott Dyer because he had started his career as an infantryman with 2nd Marines and was looking forward to working with them again. He had enlisted when he was seventeen. It was looking for a fight that had got him interested. He'd been on his way to enlist in the Army when, because of his height, he'd banged his head on a sign hanging outside the Marine Corps recruiting office. He started cussing. The recruiting officer had yelled at him.

"What the hell are you doing to my sign?"

"Well, if your sign wasn't so friggin' low I wouldn't have bashed my head."

"You've got an attitude, kid."

Dyer had followed the marine into the office, ready to continue the fight, when he saw a sign on the marine's desk: IF YOU ARE HERE TO BE ONE OF THE BOYS YOU ARE IN THE WRONG OFFICE.

On the walls were posters and action photographs of tanks speeding through the desert and helicopters swooping over blue seas. They started talking. The recruiter didn't tell him about college money or job training. He talked about challenges and teamwork. He made no promises other than that the Marine Corps would train him harder than he'd ever worked in his life.

"Not everyone is tough enough to be a marine. We are the Few and the Proud for a reason."

When he'd told his mom that he was joining the Marines, it was the first time he'd ever heard her swear.

"The fuck you are."

She had refused to sign the papers. Even though she worked for a civilian contractor that made spare parts for the defense industry, she had a bad view of the Marine Corps. She said that marines beat up on their women, drank too much, and behaved badly. For a whole month they argued, but eventually he wore her down. Sure enough, as soon as he got out of Boot Camp, she put a photo of him in his dress blues on the mantelpiece. Each time people she respected and admired made a fuss over her for having a son in the Marine Corps, she glowed with pride.

He'd spent seventeen years as an active duty and reserve marine. The higher he rose, the more he disliked the careerism. The grunts would help each other out, but the officers wouldn't hesitate to stab each other in the back. Once he'd become an officer, all he could see was a succession of desk jobs. *There's no way I am going to become a staff weenie.* He'd left the Marine Corps to study law but hadn't wanted to cut his ties completely. He knew, though, he wasn't going to return to Camp Lejeune. His wife was an attorney, and he couldn't see her processing divorces in North Carolina or working in the Marine Corps store. He rejoined as a reservist for a second time. He'd chosen to be a tanker. *If the Marines go to war one day, they won't leave their tanks behind.*

"Palehorse 6, this is Timberwolf. Can you give us your current position?"

"Roger, Timberwolf. We are pushing through the 22 northing."

"Timberwolf, this is Mustang 6. Marines dismounting to pull security."

As they pressed ahead, Dyer listened to the radio chatter on the battalion net. It was routine stuff, delivered with calm authority. Company commanders were giving situation reports and updates on their positions. Up ahead saw the first real signs of human activity since leaving Kuwait. There were a few groups of brick houses on both sides of the road. Farther south, they'd only seen mud huts. Women and children were being hustled into white pickups and driven away. He didn't think it was suspicious. He thought that they had just taken fright at the sight of the might of the U.S. military on the move. It was quiet. *We are still several klicks south of the city. We are well south of anywhere we might make contact.*

Dyer knew they were going into a fight, and he lived by the motto "Plan for the worst, hope for the best, and accept whatever happens." He tried to drum it into his marines. Nevertheless, he wasn't convinced that they would see any action that day. They had spent weeks discussing a plan to seize the bridges at Nasiriyah, but a few days ago that plan had lost priority. The order he had been given was to get to the interchange of Routes 7 and 8, well south of Nasiriyah, and occupy blocking positions to isolate the city. He remembered what he had been told. *The enemy hasn't left their barracks. They have prepared no defensive fortifications. There is no indication that the enemy is prepared to fight. They may well capitulate.* Anyway, there were all sorts of rumors, fueled by radio reports on the BBC, that the Army had already taken the city.

Traveling alongside the tanks, five hundred meters in front of the rest of the battalion, were the CAAT vehicles, the Humvees of the combined antiarmor team. They were equipped with state-of-the-art TOW antitank missiles, .50-caliber machine guns, and MK19 grenade launchers. They were lighter and quieter than the tanks and were useful in scouting out the terrain and enemy situation ahead of them. With the thirteen-power sight on their TOW systems, they could see almost five kilometers. They had a lot of firepower, but Dyer knew their punch was limited. The CAAT marines felt better when the tanks were around. *If you get in contact, you want to bring out the heavy right hand of the boxer. You want to bring out your bruisers.*

He read off his position from his satellite-navigated GPS, or Global Positioning System. They had crossed the 22 northing, still over ten kilometers south of Nasiriyah. There was no hurry.

Whoosh.

Out of nowhere, there was a whistle and the thud of a mortar landing nearby.

Captain Scott Dyer looked around, momentarily confused. He recognized the sound of the incoming shells as 120 mm mortar rounds. At the same moment he heard rounds pinging off the tank's two-inch-thick steel ballistic skirts. His first reaction was surprise rather than fear. *So this is what it feels like to be shot at.*

In his tank up front, Major Peeples watched as a shell landed off to his right, followed by the thud of another one, then another. *That can't be Izzies shooting at us.* While most marines referred to Iraqis as *hajjis,* Peeples insisted on calling them *Izzies,* from IZ, the two-letter military symbol for Iraq. The intel had predicted that the Iraqis would be surrendering. They were not supposed to be shooting at them. And tactically it was madness. *If the Izzies are shooting, why are they engaging a company of tanks with mortars?*

"Timberwolf. This is Panzer 6. We are receiving mortar and small-arms fire."

Peeples reported back to the battalion command post what he was seeing. Rounds were skipping off the small dirt mounds and berms in front of him. To his left and then his right the thud of mortar shells threw up a fountain of dirt. From his TC's hatch he first looked at one side and then the other. *Where are those rounds coming from?* The sensation of being shot at was odd. They weren't being overwhelmed. But he felt harassed. *I hope the fuel bladders don't get hit.* Attached to each of his tanks was a great big rubber balloon that contained fifty-five gallons of aviation fuel, so that they didn't have to go back to the rear so frequently to refuel. He'd never trained with them, and there was some debate with his marines about what would happen if they took a round. No one had come up with a satisfactory answer for his concerns. He wanted to cut them loose, but for the moment decided against it.

Captain Dyer had tried to stay buttoned up by fighting with the hatches closed, but now he threw them open. He was struggling to see his other tanks and the enemy. Even with his torso out of the turret he was having difficulties pointing out targets to his gunner. The rules of engagement they had been given said that they were supposed to identify legitimate targets before shooting. He'd been shocked that they felt it necessary to tell him this. He knew they were not there to fight the Iraqi people or demolish their buildings. *We are here to liberate them.* Yet now, the rules of engagement seemed rather hazy. The rounds were coming from groups of houses on both sides of the road. The Abrams' main gun would have demolished the buildings, but there were Iraqi civilians milling around. *We can't just shoot anyone up.*

Darting between the tanks, Dyer saw the CAAT Humvees unleashing rounds from their .50-cal machine guns and the Mark 19 grenade launcher. This was not how he imagined they would be fighting. He was expecting to be confronted by men in army uniforms. All he could see were black-robed Iraqis running from one building into another. A fresh burst of machine-gun rounds smacked into the sides of the CAAT vehicles from the direction of the building that the black-robed men had run into. One of the CAAT marines aimed a TOW missile directly at the front door and fired. It was guided by a thin wire that spooled from the missile as it was fired. As long as he kept the crosshairs on the target it would impact. There was an explosion and the building crumbled. They sent two more TOW missiles, flying at two hundred meters a second, into the other building. Half that building came down, too. Through the sighting system, marines could see black-robed men stumbling away from the rubble. Women, too, were now escaping from the battered houses. One of them was dragging a child away. Half the boy's arm was missing.

Immediately, the amount of incoming fire diminished substantially. Captain Dyer scanned the horizon for more targets. Up ahead he saw a truck heading toward them. His gunner called out the range requesting permission to shoot. *There's something odd about that truck.* Dyer looked again and saw that it had the markings of a U.S. Army truck. In one of their intel briefings, Dyer had been warned that irregular forces were likely to gather American equipment and uniforms either to commit atrocities against the local population and blame it on the Americans or to use it as a ruse to get close to them. Dyer took stock and radioed Major Peeples. *If there's a chance that it's packed with explosives, I'm going to take it out.*

"Panzer 6, this is Panzer 5. There is a truck coming down the road. Looks to be an American vehicle. Doesn't seem to be a threat at this time. Continuing to observe."

Peeples also saw the truck coming toward them. Then it seemed to take fright, turn round, and head back up the road.

"Panzer 6, this is Panzer 5. The truck is turning round. I'm going to let it go."

Dyer tried to report the sighting back to Lieutenant Colonel Grabowski at the battalion forward command post a couple of kilometers to his south.

"Timberwolf, this is Panzer 5. We have observed what appears to be an American truck to our north."

He keyed out of the radio transmission so that enemy forces couldn't track the call. He keyed back in again.

"Do you know of any friendly forces between us and Nasiriyah? Panzer 5 out."

Battalion did not reply. He repeated the message. Again there was no reply. Suddenly Dyer became aware that there was so much chatter going on over the battalion net that he could not get his message through. The CAAT vehicles were reporting every action of their firefight. The infantry companies were reporting the explosions they could see to the north. He wished they would get off the radio and give him a chance to find out what was going on.

He was puzzled. First Battalion, 2nd Marines was the lead element. And he was at the very front of the column. As far as he knew, there should be no friendly forces in front of him. And certainly not the U.S. Army.

Then, through the dust and smoke ahead, he saw three more vehicles, two of them large trucks, accelerating toward him. This time there was no mistaking. As they got closer, he saw that they were shot up and leaving a trail of smoke behind them. He watched as one of them, a U.S. Army Humvee with bullet holes in its windshield, screeched to a halt just behind Major Peeples's tank. *Who the hell are these guys?*

Major Peeples was just as confused as Captain Dyer. *What is going on?* He jumped out of his tank and ran toward a U.S. soldier who was now crouching behind his Humvee, pistol drawn. The soldier was breathless and agitated. He could hardly get the words out quickly enough.

"We've got people north of here. Soldiers. U.S. soldiers. They are pinned down and they're getting shot at."

It didn't make sense. There was nothing in front of them. His tanks were the lead element. He didn't understand. The soldier tried to explain that he was the commanding officer of an army maintenance convoy that had got lost in the night. They had mistakenly driven into Nasiriyah. Just as they realized their mistake, they had been ambushed and chased through the city. Several of his soldiers were wounded, and there were more of them caught in a firefight a few miles up the road.

"You've got to help us. Please help us."

Peeples tried to get the battalion command post on the net, but there was just a cacophony of noise as everyone tried to talk on the radio at the same time.

"Timberwolf, this is Panzer 6. I'm with a U.S. army soldier who says we've got people in a firefight to the north. Am going to investigate."

Peeples tried again. When there was no response for a second time, he called Captain Dyer on the company net.

"I'm going to head north and try and rescue these soldiers. Call Timberwolf and let them know what we are doing."

"Roger that."

As Major Peeples took off, Dyer got on the battalion net. As the XO, or executive officer, it was normal for him to act as a backup for his company commander and talk up the chain of command, communicating directly with the battalion commander. But there were so many voices on the net that he couldn't break through to either Grabowski, call sign Timberwolf 6, or Major Sosa, the operations officer, call sign Timberwolf 3. Instead, he heard individual marines talking on battalion tac 1 communicating pointless bits of information. He knew they should be on the administrative network. *Get off the net, you idiots. You should be using battalion tac 2.* He heard lance corporals doing radio checks with each other. *That's good practice in training, but not in the middle of a firefight.* He yelled at the radio in frustration.

"What the hell are you doing? Get off this net."

His job was to let battalion staff know what he was doing. It was also his duty to paint the battle for those in the rear. Now, he found he just couldn't break in. He feared this might happen. *The battalion staff has such a steel grip on operations that marines are monitoring battalion tac 1. They are afraid of doing something that the operations officer, Major Sosa, hasn't authorized.* In over seventeen years as a marine, Dyer had not seen anyone exert such control. It got to the point where he saw Major Sosa ordering individual marines how to park their vehicles. It was good for commanders to show they were in charge, but Dyer felt that Sosa and some of the others exhibited a level of retentiveness that caused confusion.

He tried the radio again. Nothing. He put out his message but got no answer. He couldn't wait any longer. Followed by tanks from the 1st and 3rd Platoons, he chased north after Major Peeples. Looking back over his shoulder, he saw that no one had come with him. The platoon of infantry that Bravo had given them to make up their Team Tank configuration had stayed behind. He cursed them silently. *Useless idiots.*

Major Peeples headed north along the dusty highway. Either side of him were fields of mud, crisscrossed with irrigation ditches and dotted with groups of mud brick houses set back from the road. A few kilometers on, he came across a bizarre scene. Ahead of him was what looked like the city dump, and in the middle of it, pulled off to the side of the road, was a column of battered and shot-up Army trucks. Thick black smoke was pouring from the engines and the trailers. Many of the Army vehicles were in flames. Through the thick smoke, sweeping across the road, he saw muzzle flashes lighting up the area. There was some sort of fighting going on. As he got closer he saw, spread out over a few hundred meters, several U.S. soldiers lying by the side of the road, firing at buildings to the east and west. Peeples drove his tank in front of them to provide cover from the incoming fire. He jumped off his tank and ran over to them. He now saw that there were six or seven anxious and scared-looking U.S. soldiers, some of them wounded. They were in a bad way. There was no room on his tanks to medevac them, and the platoon of infantry attached from Bravo were nowhere to be seen. *What do I do next?* Looking south, he saw the rest of his tanks coming up the road, including 2nd Platoon, the tanks that were attached to Bravo company. He was relieved. He now had all his tanks with him and could maneuver as a single tank company. There was machine-gun and AK fire coming at them from a building complex to the northeast and from buildings near a railroad track just ahead of them. Machine-gun fire erupted from behind some large oil storage tanks to their north, the rounds skipping off the tanks' thick armor. His tanks rumbled into position. Second and 3rd Platoons traversed their main guns to point to the east of the road. First Platoon took the west side.

Peeples radioed his platoon commanders.

"Use the coax."

He was thinking about which gun to fire. The rules of engagement that he'd received meant that he was supposed to return small-arms fire either with the loader's M240, or with the coaxial machine gun that was mounted next to the tank's main gun. His marines let off rapid bursts, kicking up dirt around the positions where most of the fire was coming from.

Whoosh.

A deadly rocket-propelled grenade, or RPG, careered between two of his tanks. That changed things. The rounds in the main gun of Peeples's tank were "battle carried." It meant that there was already a round in the chamber.

"Gunner. MPAT. Target that building."

Peeples's gunner, sitting in front and below him in the well of the turret, traversed the cannon, put the red crosshairs on the small building where most of the fire seemed to be coming from and squeezed the trigger on the power-control handles. The twelve-inch recoil on the thirty-two-foot main cannon rocked the tank. With a deafening *boom,* and an orange fireball from the muzzle, the round, traveling at Mach 5, smashed into one of the buildings. The MPAT or multipurpose antitank round was designed to penetrate a target before exploding. Peeples watched the building disintegrate.

Below him, the loader pulled a lever to access another round, loaded it with both hands into the gun, and closed the breech.

"Driver, hard right, hard right. Stop. Forward. Stop. Lower gun tube. Traverse right. Traverse right."

His tanks maneuvered around each other, making intricate adjustments by pivot steering—locking one track in order to pivot on it.

As Peeples traversed his turret, it caught in the fuel bladder and brought the main gun to an abrupt halt. Peeples was momentarily panicked. *I was afraid this might happen.* He got a knife out and cut the bladder away, splashing JP8 fuel over the road. He saw the rest of his company doing the same. It was a relief finally to get rid of the bladders. None of the tankers were happy with a hundred gallons of fuel strapped to their tanks while the rounds were flying.

Peeples could now see five army vehicles. Three of them were large tractor-trailers, which looked as though they carried maintenance equipment. One was a Humvee and the other was a fuel truck. They looked battered and beaten. He looked back at his tanks. For the past two days they had stayed, clumped together on the hard road, unable to spread apart because of the numerous irrigation canals. It was not ideal. Normally, his company tried to spread itself over an area of one thousand meters to give the tanks more maneuvering room and to present a more difficult target. Now he saw one of his tanks attempting to do that by moving off the road onto the shoulder. Moments later he received a panicked radio transmission.

"Panzer 6. We're stuck in the mud."

Peeples turned to see a tank, commanded by Captain Romeo Cubas of 3rd Platoon, sinking into some of the worst mud he'd ever seen. What looked like hard-packed dirt near one of the irrigation ditches was a pool of thick, oozing mud.

Peeples grabbed the radio handset and called Staff Sergeant Aaron Harrell, one of 2nd Platoon's tank commanders, and tasked him with the recovery. The tanks were still receiving small-arms and machine-gun fire. *Thank God it's not that accurate.* With one eye on the unfolding fight and the other eye on the stricken tank, he switched between manning his guns and giving orders on the radio. He saw Harrell's loader crouched on the front slope of the tank, unhooking the tow cables as rounds passed overhead and mortars landed in the fields off to the side. Harrell hooked up the cables to Cubas's tank and ordered his driver to push his own tank forward. Slowly Cubas's tank was pulled out.

At the same time, Captain Jim Thompson, a marathon runner and triathlete, had jumped off his tank and was running toward one of the wounded soldiers. He expected to be able to carry him to safety, but as he tried to heave him up in a fireman's carry, the weight of the soldier just crushed him. Thompson was so exhausted from the fight that he could hardly lift him. Two other marines ran over and helped the soldier limp to safety behind one of the tanks.

Captain Dyer rolled to the conduct of fire net. As the leader of the campaign's designated FiST, or fire support team, his job was to communicate with battalion staff to get more fire power. Frustratingly, he still didn't know whether he was getting through. He shouted instructions into the radio. No one acknowledged him. The amount of incoming fire had now increased. Mortar and artillery shells were throwing up mud and dirt around the dump.

"I need counterbattery support. I need to know where those mortars are coming from. We need to run some air missions."

The fire support net was silent. He tried again on battalion tac 1, not sure whether anyone could hear him.

With him was Major Donald Hawkins, the forward air controller, who supervised air support from the ground. With no reply from battalion, Hawkins called up close air support using the UHF "guard" frequency. Several Cobra attack helicopters and fixed-wing planes had come on station and were circling overhead, surveying the unfolding firefight from the air. Speaking directly to Hawkins, they told him that they could see hundreds of Iraqis beginning to encircle them. They started to take antiaircraft fire. Then one of the pilots spotted a T-55 tank moving toward them.

Dyer and Hawkins both looked. They couldn't see it because it was hidden behind a railroad bridge. The Cobra pilot had a good view of it and took aim with a Hellfire missile. Dyer saw it leave the rail and then go "stupid," losing its direction and missing the target. Hawkins called on the Cobra to laser designate the target and then contacted a Hornet circling overhead to drop a laser-guided bomb. The Cobra pulled to the right, painted the target, and the Hornet came in to attack. Just then, the voice of the battalion fire support coordinator, who was based at the forward command post, and whose job was to oversee what each FiST was doing, came over the radio.

"Abort! Abort! Abort!"

The Hornet pulled away, just before dropping the bomb. The tank, now alerted to the danger, sped off into the tree line.

Dyer and Hawkins couldn't believe it. Dyer got on the radio to the battalion command.

"What the hell are you doing?"

"We've got counterbattery fires in the area."

Dyer was furious.

"Guys, these are not tire stacks out there. This is not a training exercise. These assholes are shooting at us. I'm on the ground. I can see what is going on. I've done the deconfliction. This is perfectly legit."

Dyer was boiling with frustration. The fire support coordinator had a perfect right to call off the mission. But the FSC was sitting miles away, buttoned up in an AAV. Dyer and Hawkins had their eyes on the target and were well aware of what was going on. *When I need battalion they aren't there. But when I'm working well, they throw a wrench into a perfectly good run.*

He thought it was just another example of battalion trying to micromanage everything that was going on. They'd already made it clear that they wouldn't take Peeples's or Dyer's advice on how best to deploy the tanks. In fact, every time they suggested something, Major Sosa seemed to do the exact opposite. Dyer's resentment was growing. The relationship with battalion was not getting any better. *This is my second firefight and I'm in the game and I'm clicking. They are yet to do a goddamn thing.*

Another shell landed twenty-five meters to the east of his tank. *That's the third bracketing shot. That was damned close. And they will get closer.*

Dyer yelled at 1st Lieutenant James Carter, his artillery forward ob-server. They needed to get their own artillery, call sign Nightmare, to start tracking where those shells were coming from.

"Why haven't you got up with Timberwolf and got this artillery shut down?"

"I'm trying, but I can't reach them."

"Well, why don't you get onto regiment? Call Viking. If you can't get them, call Nightmare direct."

"What do you think I'm doing? You keep interrupting me."

The wounded soldiers of the Army maintenance company were now sheltered behind Peeples's tank. Dyer counted ten soldiers. Five of them looked to be seriously wounded. Dyer knew there were no corpsmen to give them medical attention. *How the hell are we going to get them out of here?*

Just then a track from Alpha Company came up the road. Marines jumped out and got ready to medevac the wounded.

The tanks and CAAT vehicles had destroyed most of the close-in resis-tance. Helicopters still buzzed overhead taking out mortar positions and machine-gun bunkers. The counterbattery fire from the "cannon cockers," the artillerymen of 1/10 Marines at the rear of the column by the 20 north-ing, had now begun to destroy enemy artillery positions. Captain Dyer was able to take a moment to relax. He had an extreme case of cotton mouth. He'd hardly drunk anything since the early morning. He reached over to grab his canteen. A thick black layer parted and rose off the side of his tank as a cloud of flies flew back to what he now realized was a foul stinking trash tip.

4

It was around 0900 when Captain Dan Wittnam, the thirty-three-year-old commander of Charlie Company, heard the radio reports of fighting up ahead. His twelve AAVs and three Humvees were well toward the rear of the column, but he heard the sound of gunfire and saw smoke and flashes in the distance. Overhead he heard the clattering of helicopters. It was the first time Wittnam had seen helos flying like that since they'd crossed into

Iraq. Usually they flew over the marines on the ground almost disdainfully, as though they were on some highly important mission. Now they were hovering with intent just ahead of them. His company's AAVs were herringboned, parked at an angle just off to the side of the road, waiting for the order to push ahead. Some marines were outside their tracks, pulling security; others were inside, catching up on some sleep. He knew they were weary. It had been stop and start all morning, and his marines would only have been able to snatch some unsatisfactory shut-eye.

Charlie 1/2 was the first company Wittnam had commanded, and it had been a trial. Wittnam drove his marines with an intensity that belied his soft eyes and calm, kind, and patient demeanor. They weren't elite soldiers—they didn't have the commitment of Special Forces, the fitness of the SEALs, or the expertise of the D boys from Delta Force. Most of them would be too scared to jump out of a helo, some couldn't shoot for fuck, and a few were on the chubby side. But for the year or so that he'd had them, he'd watched the Marine Corps transform them from ordinary guys who would otherwise have been propping up the local bar, wasting their lives at the bowling alley, or beating their wives, into young men with heart, capable of extraordinary things. It was frustrating, though. Some of them could be doing even better. Private First Class Casey Robinson was one of the most difficult. He was excellent in the field but was always getting into trouble. He'd had problems with steroids and with fighting. Just before leaving for Iraq, he'd hit a police officer down in Wilmington while on liberty. And then he'd had a fight with a noncommissioned officer on board ship. He'd been charged with assault and disobeying a direct order. Wittnam had tried every motivational technique in the book but none of them had worked. It was a waste. Robinson should be a corporal by now, not a private. He had the potential to be a good marine. If only he could sort his head out. He knew what the problem was. The marines who settled in quickly were the ones who managed to forget who they were before they signed on. It seemed that Robinson refused to let go of who he used to be.

Wittnam put his binoculars to his eyes to see if he could follow what was happening up ahead. He hoped that his young marines would be able to cope with the challenges that lay in front of them.

It was the roar of the M1A1 Abrams tanks setting off in front of him that woke Private First Class Robinson from his lethargy. The chat on the radio was calm, professional, but he could tell there was an undercurrent of excitement. From his position at the hatch he heard isolated booms and saw puffs of smoke on the horizon. *At last something is happening. At last I know that a war is going on.* He wanted to be in combat, but at the same time he was glad he was not up there getting hit by whatever was flying through the air. He saw marines ahead running around and vehicles going backward and forward. There was a lot of activity, but he had no idea what was going on. He guessed at some point his company would be told to do something. He was discovering that even actual combat was mostly a question of waiting around for something to happen.

Robinson, along with the rest of Charlie Company, had been looking forward to getting out of Camp Lejeune. He longed for the adventure that awaited him in Iraq. His two years of Marine Corps life had consisted of long hours doing pointless drills, humping hundreds of miles on marches, carrying ammo to a distant rifle range, scrubbing floors, walls, and shitters, sweeping the path outside the barracks, waiting to embark and disembark boats, get in and out of vehicles. Sometimes he even had to wait in line to get his pay packet of $800 paid on the first and fifteenth of each month. That was usually because the assholes from DPAC, the accountants and bureaucrats who handed out his money, had messed with his pay. He thought they did it on purpose just to have a go at the grunts for being cocky. It was on those days that the radio commercials in Jacksonville, Camp Lejeune's hometown, would go into overdrive, and tempting signs about low-cost loans would appear outside car dealerships along the town's main drag. They would spend their money at titty bars like Driftwood and at bars and clubs like Coconuts that offered free entry to women on Thursday nights. Some marines managed to spend all their pay within days of getting it. That's why they were looking forward to getting out of North Carolina. Life at Camp Lejeune could be mind-numbingly boring with brief moments of action.

The boredom had continued on ship. He had been packed beneath the decks with the rest of the enlisted marines, condemned to spend hours waiting in line to brush his teeth or get to the chow hall. When he finally sat down, he was forced to scoff his food quickly to give up his seat for someone else. They had to clean their crowded berthing area every morning, and they weren't allowed back in until the ship's XO had inspected it.

In Kuwait they were billeted in a dust bowl of a tented compound called Camp Shoup. For six weeks they had to survive the monotony of life in a featureless desert by looking at porno magazines, jacking off, and writing love letters to wives and girlfriends. They weren't allowed alcohol, but some enlisted marines managed to get their family and friends to send them miniature whiskey bottles in their care packages from home. It was never enough to get drunk on, though. He was pretty sure that the officers managed to smuggle in quantities of alcohol, too, although they would never admit it. Otherwise, life there consisted of drinking European mineral water, pissing, waiting for the hot chow that made Robinson so ill that he gave up on it, trading prepackaged MREs, drinking more water, pissing, visiting the foul smelling Porta Pottis for a shit, more water, more pissing. The only excitement was when the cry of *"Lightning, lightning,"* or *"Gas, gas,"* the code words for a SCUD launch, went up. But they had all very quickly tired of the mad scramble to put on gas masks and MOPP suits and the endless sweaty minutes that ticked by as they waited for the all-clear signal.

The one aspect of training that had energized him was the desert patrols. He loved learning about the desert and getting acclimatized to the heat and the unfamiliar terrain. It was so much more interesting than all the crap he'd learned in the classroom. They'd practiced identifying targets and threats with their night-vision goggles. Arabic speakers came over and taught them how to take down Iraqis with nonlethal stuff. They taught them how to yell out instructions in Arabic. *Stop where you are. Drop your weapons. Down on your belly.* Robinson doubted whether he would be close enough to use it. Weapons training on the range was limited so they did a lot of hand-to-hand combat. Robinson's favorite was Bull in the Ring. Two marines would kneel back to back and then fight it out in the sand. They had to wrestle, without punching, and get the other guy to surrender. Armlocks, ankle locks, or finding pressure points by the neck usually did the job. Captain Wittnam even had them doing platoon-on-platoon Bull in the Ring and they would all go at it. It reminded Robinson of his first few months in the Marine Corps when the senior marines subjected the juniors to Bull in the Ring as a form of hazing, a rite of passage. Some of the junior marines were terrorized by the experience. Robinson saw it as toughening them up. *I don't want no pussies with me when I go to war.*

What kept Robinson and the rest of Charlie Company going during the misery of Camp Shoup was the prospect of using their weapons in anger, of combat adventure with their buddies. *We are going to kill some motherfucking Iraqis.* The thought of finally going to war had sent a thrill through the marines of 1st Battalion, 2nd Marines.

The order to cross the LD, attack into Iraq across the Line of Departure, had come unexpectedly. For a while, Robinson had thought they would never go to war. They could see from the TV that people were demonstrating against it. *The whole thing is going to be shut off.* One day they were told to get ready, the next day they had to stand down. Then, on March 19, they were told they were going. It was a day earlier than the original plan called for. Rumors in the Marine Corps spread like syphilis, and this was no exception. One was that Saddam Hussein had already given up and that they were going to head straight for Baghdad. Someone else said that a "target of opportunity" strike had been made on Saddam and that the war had started earlier than planned. It didn't matter. This was it. H hour had come and gone. They were going to war.

At dawn, on March 20, the adrenaline rush took Private First Class Robinson by surprise. He'd always thought of himself as a cool dude, not easily fazed. Now, as he watched the sky light up with artillery fire and air strikes and listened to the booms and crackles of shells raining down on Iraqi positions, he was overawed by the spectacle of supreme power. The target was Safwan Hill, an Iraqi observation post on a prominent mound in the desert. The commander of the 1st Marine Division, Major General James Mattis, told his artillerymen to pound it so that after the bombardment "it would be a foot shorter." Robinson looked at the sky above and watched the Patriot missiles dueling with the SCUDs.

"Yeah. All right. Up yours, Saddam."

Marines around him cheered and yelled. Robinson whistled to himself. It was like being off his head on the Fourth of July.

In front of Robinson, inside the belly of the track, Lance Corporal Edward Castleberry, the driver of track 201, jiggled his legs in anticipation. Castleberry's position was just in front of the bank of radios so he could listen in to what was happening on the battalion tactical net. He heard explosions and people getting real excited on the radio. Unlike Robinson, he could tell from the radio transmissions why the tanks had set off at such speed.

"We need to evac. We've got several wounded soldiers. Some of them are real bad."

He was confused. The Army was not supposed to be there. *The Army beat us here? Are you fucking insane? No fucking way.*

He didn't say anything out loud, but in his head he made fun of the Army. *They must have fucked up badly. They can't fight anyway. They are screwed. It's lucky we showed up.*

In the back, some marines were trying to sleep, but others were desperate to know what was going on. They could hear nothing but the screaming motor and the odd sound of gunfire. He tried to keep them informed.

"Army is up in front and they're all shot up. Alpha is helping them out right now."

Some of the marines joined in the jokes about the Army. He felt their excitement mounting.

"Come on, let's go and join in the fight."

Castleberry would have liked to oblige, but he was a lowly lance corporal.

"Sorry, guys. It's not my call."

Just behind track 201, sitting in the troop commander's hatch of track 208, was First Lieutenant James "Ben" Reid. He was tall, with earnest, adult eyes that chimed wrongly with his lanky, almost adolescent way of carrying himself. He was in charge of Charlie's weapons platoon and was Charlie's FiST leader. It was a crucial job, and he took it seriously. Charlie was a long way to the rear of the column so he sat, huddled over the radio, listening to the battalion net. The information was coming through clearly and simply. The net wasn't clogged up, and he had time to put red and blue dots on his map board, propped up on the edge of the hatch, to mark the positions of friendly and enemy forces.

In his weapons platoon he had heavy machine guns, shoulder-launched multipurpose assault weapons known by the acronym of SMAWs, and 60 mm mortars. He had divided his mortar squad into two parts. He put two mortars in the company commander's track with enough ammo to do a quick hip shoot if necessary. He had his FiST and a third of the mortar squad and ammo with him in 208. What he had done was unorthodox, but he figured that it was safer to split up the mortar squads just in case one of the tracks got hit.

He'd picked up the news about the Army over the radio. *What the hell is going on? I thought we were supposed to be out in front here.* He stayed plugged into the battalion and company net and he switched back and forth between the two to maintain his situational awareness. He heard Lieutenant Colonel Grabowski come over the net and talk to the commander of the tanks.

"Hey, Panzer 6, you need to stay in the tanks so that I can talk to you."

Reid thought the order was a good one. His battalion commander spoke up when he needed to and yes, the tank commander did need to stay in his tank.

But then came a radio transmission that worried him. Over the battalion net he heard Staff Sergeant Troy Schielein, one of the CAAT marines fighting up ahead alongside the tanks, say he was going to launch a TOW. There was a loud explosion, and then his voice came back on the radio.

"I just took out a machine-gun position with a TOW."

He then heard Lieutenant Colonel Grabowksi reprimand him.

"Hey, I didn't authorize you to shoot that TOW."

Reid couldn't compute what he was hearing. *Hey, wait a minute. Schielein's up there on the scene and he knows what's going on. The battalion commander can't control every detail of the battle.* It worried him that the battalion commander seemed to want to influence every course of action. He kept this thought to himself.

It was followed by more radio transmissions with information that there were some soldiers still stuck in the city and that they'd been ambushed by Iraqis faking surrender. Then Major Tuggle, the battalion XO, had come back on the net and said that the Iraqis had not been faking surrender. Reid tried to work out what it all meant from the bits and pieces he could hear. *Why did we get one report and then have it squashed?* Maybe Tuggle was worried that the marines would get trigger-happy and shoot up Iraqis who were surrendering for real.

With his head out of the TC's hatch, Reid saw helos and F-18s flying over the city. As the helos passed by, they were carrying rockets and missiles. They flew back carrying nothing. *Well, they're shooting at something.* He heard the boom of the artillery shooting some counterbattery. There was more talking on the net. The radio communications were starting to build and becoming more intense. From the messages, he could tell that Alpha Company was now dismounted and the marines were clearing some buildings on the eastern side of the MSR.

Ben Reid had never wanted to be anything other than a marine infantry officer. His father had been one, and as a family they'd moved around every few years, on new Marine Corps assignments, between Virginia, Hawaii, Kansas, North Carolina, and Texas. All his friends had fathers who were marines, and he'd grown up admiring everything about the Marine Corps.

Reid was conscious that he'd come out of school just over two years ago and yet was in charge of marines who'd been in the Corps for many years. He was grateful that on the ship to Kuwait he'd shared quarters with Second Lieutenant Michael Seely. Seely was one of the few guys who had been in Desert Storm, so they talked about what to expect. He let the older and more experienced Seely do the talking because he didn't want to look like a jackass and ask stupid questions. He'd learned from him and from books passed out on ship that the Iraqis used British military doctrine but had failed to adapt it adequately to work with Soviet equipment. He didn't know whether the information would be useful, but it gave him something to look out for. He worked hard to develop teamwork with Second Lieutenant Fred Pokorney, his artillery forward observer. Fred was a big, lanky guy whose uniform never seemed to fit properly. He'd had several years in the Marine Corps and was due for promotion to first lieutenant. They would talk late into the night about FiST tactics, as well as tell each other personal stuff about wives and family.

Once, on ship, he'd sat down to eat at the same table as Lieutenant Colonel Grabowski, the battalion commander. Even though his nametag was clearly showing, Grabowski still got his name wrong.

"How's it going, Martin?"

"I'm Lieutenant Reid, sir."

That's how the conversation began and that's how it ended. Reid understood that Grabowski was probably not very good with names and had other things to worry about, but it did concern him. *The Marine Corps is a people business. If you know the names of your marines, their girlfriends' names, the brand of beer they like to drink, the chances are that you will also know about fire support, about weapons systems, about tactics.* Maybe he was being unfair, but he just feared that Grabowski sometimes gave the impression that he cared about other things more than his marines. That's when there is a danger that you will lose credibility. He had no doubt that Grabowski really did care, but somehow he didn't say the right things. It was the same when he gave the sending-off speech the morning before leaving Camp Shoup for the attack into Iraq. They were expecting a rousing speech about a "Band of Brothers" and "Fighting together for Victory." Instead, he'd said something in his husky voice about getting to Baghdad as soon as possible so they could enjoy the luxuries of the PX, the military stores where marines could buy their Cokes and favorite candy bars. It was awkward. No one laughed.

The battalion commander's apparent obsession with gear uniformity also concerned him. He wanted all the machine-gun ammo men to look the same, all the grenadiers to look the same even down to the exact location of a magazine pouch. Reid understood the point he was making. He guessed it was a good thing to know where to find ammo on a marine if necessary. But he did think it was over the top. *It's a lot of bullshit so that the battalion commander can feel important.* He didn't see how that would help him fight his battle. In Reid's view there were other concerns that deserved more time and energy. He did accept, though, that maybe Grabowski was right. Maps, compasses, and first-aid kits needed to be carried in a standard location. *I guess that's why I am a lieutenant and not a lieutenant colonel.*

Reid stuck his head out of his TC's hatch. They were moving up on the left of Bravo Company. Up ahead he could see the first sign of activity. A few cars were driving back and forth real slow and the occupants stopping to talk to people. *This looks suspicious. They look as though they are getting ready to do something.* An old man leading a mule was carrying a bundle of what looked like white sheets. As they moved up, marines in Reid's track pointed their M16s at him and shouted at him.

"Drop what you are carrying."

"Fucking drop it."

"Drop your fucking laundry."

They weren't really nervous. They were just doing what they thought they should be doing. Anyway, the harmless old man didn't understand and just walked on.

Farther to the rear of the column of Charlie vehicles, in the back of track 211, Lance Corporal Thomas Quirk of 3rd Platoon was having a hard time of it. The exhaust was coming back into the track, and the dust and dirt and smell of diesel were getting to him. He was hacking up wads of yellow pus caused from the dust infecting the lung's membranes. His vocal cords felt stretched and raw from the coughing. He no longer knew how long they'd been moving, but for hours now he'd been cramped up in his track, dozing off in the most uncomfortable of positions: a head in someone's lap, a foot on someone's stomach, a hand in someone's ear. It occurred to him that if someone had opened up the track, it would have looked like something from a nature documentary on the Discovery Channel. They were like little animals all curled up together in a dark hole.

The radio squawked into action and the marines dozing in the rear forced themselves awake. In the distance was the sound of gunfire. Quirk's squad leader, Corporal Randy Glass, who had been monitoring the radio, spoke up.

"Hey, listen up. What we heard is that the Army is pinned down in the city to the north of us and we're going to reinforce them. And we gotta watch out because the hajjis were making out like they were giving up and then pulling out AK-47s on them. They killed a couple of Army guys."

In his head, Quirk slagged off the Army. *These fucking idiots got themselves in trouble. These pussies are in the wrong fucking spot. They need to be building churches and handing out food, not fucking getting in firefights.*

Then another message came through the radio. No, the Iraqis had not pretended to surrender. *The briefs are changing all the time. What is going on?*

Quirk was glad for the minor excitement. It was something else to talk about. During the two months since leaving Camp Lejeune, they had exhausted most subjects. They talked about the stupid stuff they'd done in high school, the things they wished they could do, the things they might do in the next few days, and the things they were going to do when they got home. For the last few hours they'd laughed about the time when Quirk's buddy, Lance Corporal John Mathews, had made fun of their staff sergeant. They were digging a "SCUD pit" and Staff Sergeant Anthony Pompos had told Mathews to dig deeper.

"Hey, Staff Sergeant, do you like duck meat?"

"Yeah, I love hunting ducks and I love duck meat."

The lance corporal nodded and pointed to his dick.

"Well, why don't you duck down here and get some of this meat."

It was the funniest thing they'd heard in a long time. It was made even funnier when Staff Sergeant Pompos yelled back at him.

"Well, Mathews, you duck down in the hole and keep digging until I tell you to stop."

Quirk had grown up in Ossining, New York, a nice, suburban neighborhood of small but smart houses with three-foot-square front lawns, about an hour's journey from Grand Central Station in Manhattan. His parents were TV parents—caring, middle class, and so sweet. They were the best. His mother was a teacher and his father worked in computers. He respected his dad. He'd been in the Marine Corps and served in Vietnam. But Quirk could never bring himself to tell him just how much he admired him. Quirk, too, had wanted to join the Marines straight after high school, but he and his girlfriend had got into trouble for vandalizing a police car. They only meant to throw eggs at it but ended up jumping on it and breaking some windows. He was put on probation for three years. Then September 11 happened. He went home and saw the second tower falling on TV. His dad looked at him.

"Well, what are you going to do now?"

"I am going to join the Marine Corps."

"Hats off to you son."

He went to the Marine recruiting station in Middletown, New York, and told the recruiter about his neighbor and the local firemen who had died on September 11. Quirk laid it straight down the line to the recruiter because he knew they were conniving bastards. They tried to suck you in with stories of combat, of cheap blow jobs in Guam and Manila, of the thrill of killing and how every chick wants to hook up with a marine.

"Don't pump my ass. Don't try and trick me with your bullshit. I want to be a rifleman. I want to be a grunt. Just tell me what I have to do to make this happen."

The recruiter said he could work with his criminal record. It took him several months but finally he managed to get the waivers, and on January 21, 2002, he went to Boot Camp at Parris Island, South Carolina. A year later he was on his way to Iraq. Not that he cared about Iraq or Afghanistan. He didn't give a shit about those places, about liberating this guy or that guy. It was pure and simple. *If Americans are going to get killed, I want to be right next to them because for whatever fucking naïve, childish fucking reason, I fucking goddamn love my country.*

Quirk still showed traces of how young he was. He was short in stature, but his shoulders were broadening. He still had a baby face, but his jawline was getting stronger. Before joining the Marine Corps his biggest fear was taking a shit in front of other guys. He really didn't want to wipe his ass in front of anyone else. But now he was getting used to life in the field and for the past few days, whenever he needed a shit, he'd take a buddy and the two of them would go over a hill and chat away as they were taking a dump.

Quirk stood up and poked his head out of the AAV's hatch. He offered to swap places with Lance Corporal David Fribley. Fribley, a twenty-six-year-old marine from Lee, Florida, had been posting air security all day and he was tired. Quirk was glad to do the guy a favor. He was about the nicest guy you could ever meet, but he was an odd one. If you ever needed any money he would give you his last five dollars. He was a different kind of marine. He didn't have the let's-kill-everybody mentality that the rest of them had. In fact, he was so nice, so self-sacrificing that he got on Quirk's nerves. But it was useful when he wanted a pack of Combos—the pretzels with cheese filling that were Quirk's favorite snack out of all the shit in the MREs. Fribley would never refuse a swap. *Fribley walked into the wrong office. He should have gone to the Air Force instead.*

It reminded him of a joke he liked. He told it to the rest of the guys in the track.

"Three high school friends meet up for a camping holiday a few months after they have joined up. The one who was in the Air Force says:

"Boot Camp was horrible. They ran out of Diet Coke in the soda fountain.

"The one from the Army says:

"That's nothing. They made me sleep outside and it rained on me.

"The one who joined the Marine Corps says nothing. He carries on lighting the fire with nothing but his dick."

With his head out of the hatch he saw, for the first time, Cobra attack helicopters flying overhead toward the city. They were shooting stuff up, firing off missile after missile and exploding targets ahead in fountains of flames, smoke, and billowing dust. Quirk was in a state of euphoria. This was the first time he'd seen American marines shooting at real things. He was through the roof with excitement. He turned to his buddy, posting air security next to him.

"They are shooting the fuck out of things. This is the coolest thing I've ever seen. Hey, this is the best day of my life."

The clattering of the helos, the booms of their missiles, the smoke rising on the horizon sent Quirk into overdrive. He didn't think the Iraqis would fight back. He didn't even think he would have to fire his weapon. He certainly didn't think that within the next hour he would be shooting at and killing human beings or that they would be shooting back and killing his buddies. *This is cool. They're blowing all this shit up and I'm so glad I'm seeing it.*

That's what he liked about the Marines. All his life, growing up in a safe suburb of New York, he'd dreamed of another, more vigorous, more exciting life. And now he was in the thick of it. He was at war. The thrill was intoxicating. He had to pray to stop himself from feeling crazy. He did it a lot when he was a kid to stop himself from getting agitated. It was not an organized prayer, just something to calm him down when things got overwhelming.

"Dear God, give me a clear mind and a calm heart. Give me strength to get through this day."

He looked up again to enjoy the sight, sound, and smell of the American military war machine in action.

5

Looking down from his Huey, Brigadier General Rich Natonski saw the efforts of his planning. A long column of hundreds of AAVs, tanks, and supporting vehicles of Task Force Tarawa were strung out along Highway 8, ready for the move into Nasiriyah. Natonski had wanted to be a marine ever since he was a little kid growing up in a small house in Connecticut, but he had no idea that he would come this far. Very few marines actually got to war and yet here he was, in the thick of one, with some six thousand men and hundreds of tanks, AAVs, helicopters, and jet fighters under his command.

At over six-foot-three, he was a large and, at first glance, an intimidating bear of a man. He'd had a long and distinguished military career, and to the younger men he exuded the romance of the Marine Corps life: of jungle patrolling the Ho Chi Minh Trail, of assaults into Hue, of nights out in Saigon. In 1975, he'd commanded a platoon that evacuated American and foreign nationals from Phnom Penh just as the Khmer Rouge were moving into the city. Weeks later he was flown into Saigon in a CH-53 helicopter, where he evacuated civilians from the U.S. Military Assistance Command compound hours before the North Vietnamese Army overran it.

He'd stayed in the Marine Corps during the traumatic years of the 1970s and 1980s when General Louis H. Wilson Jr. cleaned house, tackling the drug abuse and racial problems that had plagued the Marine Corps by kicking out the bums and the slackers. He'd gotten married and had three children. Now, at fifty-one, he had risen to brigadier general and had commanded marines in Somalia, Bosnia, and the Middle East as part of the modern, professional, all-volunteer Marine Corps. The Marines chose Natonski. The other branches of the military just weren't the same: the dull professionalism of the Army doggies, the showy but boring technology of the Air Force flyboys, the impenetrable, elitist culture of the Navy. To be a marine you had to be physically and mentally tough. You had to excel at the raw and dirty art of combat. It wasn't a job; it was a calling.

He had nearly missed the latest adventure. When CENTCOM, the ground forces command base in Florida, was first planning for Operation Iraqi Freedom, it seemed as though there might not be a place for Natonski or his marines from the 2nd Marine Expeditionary Brigade, based out of Camp Lejeune.

The Allied commander, Tommy Franks, wanted to take Baghdad as rapidly as possible. Unlike the first gulf war, where General Norman Schwarzkopf had called for a forty-day air war before sending in ground troops, Franks wanted to use the Army, led by the thirty thousand soldiers of the 3rd Infantry Division, to make a lightning strike on Baghdad from the southwest across the desert. He wanted the Marines to take the roads and attack Baghdad from the southeast as the supporting effort. He gave the mission to the 1st Marine Division, out of Camp Pendleton.

That hurt. The East Coast marines thought the Hollywood marines were too soft and pampered. Those on the West Coast thought of the East Coast marines as a poorer cousin. It was friendly rivalry. But it was a real rivalry.

Then, nearly a year ago, the 1st Marine Division's commander, General Mattis, had asked Natonski to form a self-sufficient MAGTF, a Marine air-ground task force, from East Coast marines to support the 1st Marine Division. They were originally called Task Force South, and their mission was to follow the 1st Marine Division into Iraq and then block toward Basra. But two days after leaving for Kuwait, the British offered up their 1st Armored Division to the Coalition. The Brits got the Basra mission instead. On ship, they had to plan for a sudden change in task: to open up and secure an eastern route through the city of Nasiriyah so that the 1st Marine Division could pass along two routes to Baghdad. The plan had always been for the 1st Marine Division to bypass Nasiriyah to the west and then take Route 1 to Baghdad. Opening up a second, eastern route through Nasiriyah would allow Marine convoys to transport equipment north on Route 7, a less crowded and less targetable route. It would also confuse Saddam's forces if the Army and the Marines attacked Baghdad along several axes. The Medina Division of Saddam's Republican Guard up in Al Kut would have to make a decision whether they were going to block Route 1, or whether they would block Route 7. It would split their forces.

The new road they were to open up was christened Route Moe, and once Task Force Tarawa had secured it, they were tasked with guarding the 1st Marine Division's thrust toward the Iraqi capital. It would allow the 1st Marine Division to conserve its ammo for the attack on Baghdad. Natonski was disappointed. It meant that his marines wouldn't get the glory of marching into Baghdad. That would go to the West Coast marines. He tried not to let it bother him, but each time Natonski traveled from Camp Lejeune to Camp Pendleton in California for planning operations he felt as though he was treated like an outsider. Natonski consoled himself with another thought. *We're going to kick down the door to Baghdad.*

He'd formed his Task Force around Camp Lejeune's 2nd Marine Regiment. It was the 2nd Marines who had lost over two hundred men in a suicide bomb attack on their compound while on a mission in Beirut in 1983. Now they were back in the Middle East, and he was determined that this time they would come out on top. He'd brought with him the helicopters and fixed-wing planes of Marine Aircraft Group 29 from the 2nd Marine Aircraft Wing and logistics and support vehicles from Combat Service Support Battalion 22. It's what made the Marines different from the Army. He could pick and choose units to create a self-sufficient and flexible force that had everything it needed to fight in the air and on the ground. It was fortunate that many of his units had recently trained together during combined arms exercise, known as CAX, at the Marines desert base at Twenty-nine Palms in California.

It was Natonski who had come up with the name of Task Force Tarawa. He'd asked the historical branch to come up with some names. They'd suggested Plughole. During World War II, it was the U.S. Navy's code name for Iraq. But Natonski thought Task Force Plughole didn't have the right ring. Walking back into his HQ one day he'd seen a portrait of Lieutenant General Julian Smith leading the 2nd Marine Regiment in its attack on the Japanese-occupied island of Tarawa. He knew there and then what his task force's name should be. They became Task Force Tarawa to reflect that they were an East Coast unit fighting in a West Coast force.

His Huey began its descent toward his frontline troops on the outskirts of Nasiriyah. He saw the approach to the city, dominated by the three huge circular oil tanks, which he'd so often imagined from his maps. It had only taken him a few minutes to fly in from his combat operations base at the Jalibah air base. Now, as he approached the regimental command post, he was working out his next move.

He'd been watching the progress of his lead element, 1st Battalion, 2nd Marines, on his Blue Force Tracker. Through onboard GPS, each command vehicle relayed its changing location to a satellite transmission system that transferred the information to digital maps dotted with blue icons to show where his forces were positioned. First Battalion, 2nd Marines was making slower progress than he had expected, and he had come forward to see what was holding them up. *I've got to get them moving.* The regimental commander, Colonel Ronald Bailey, had reported to him that 1/2 Marines was receiving sniper fire. Natonski didn't want that to stop them. *We're a mechanized force. We can't have snipers holding us back.* He knew that the 1st Marine Division was already refueled and waiting to move through Nasiriyah on its way to Baghdad. His strategy had been built around the military concept of tempo. If he could get his units operating faster and more aggressively than the enemy, his forces would always retain the initiative and knock the enemy off balance. They would not be able to react in time. It had worked well during Desert Storm when the 1st and 2nd Marine Divisions had attacked violently and unexpectedly through Iraqi defenses to seize the outskirts of Kuwait City. He had to get that route through Nasiriyah open, and fast.

Natonski ducked as he jumped out of the Huey and hurried, bent over double, through the heat and dust whipped up by the helo's rotors. The first thing he saw were four U.S. servicemen lying on litters with bloody bandages around their arms and legs. From their equipment and the patterns on their desert cammies he realized they were U.S. Army soldiers. Alarm bells started ringing. *What's going on? What are soldiers doing here?*

He ran over to them, beads of sweat already forming on the back of his neck.

"Who the heck are you?"

The soldiers were wide-eyed and pale. They were in a state of shock. One of them tried to explain how they were part of the Army's 507th Maintenance Company. They were supposed to be following an Army convoy but somehow they had taken a wrong turn in the dark. Instead of bypassing Nasiriyah according to plan, they had mistakenly gone right into the heart of the city and been ambushed by Iraqi forces.

Natonski tried to look as calm as possible, but inside he was raging. *What the hell is going on? This shouldn't be happening.* U.S. Army units shouldn't have been there in the first place. And what Iraqi forces had they come up against? The intel he had received was that the entire Iraqi 11th Infantry Division inside Nasiriyah would capitulate rather than fight.

"Well, I'm glad you are okay. We'll get you out of here as soon as possible."

Natonski found Colonel Bailey, the regimental commander, and went forward to look for the battalion commander, Rick Grabowski. On the flanks, young marines were busy clearing buildings. Some of them were knee-deep in mud, their spongy, charcoal-lined MoPP suits dripping with water soaked up from the small irrigation ditches lining the highway. They looked so miserable as they waded through the muddy ground that Natonski felt a pang of pity for them. Many years ago he'd been in their position. When he reached Grabowski's Humvee, he was stunned to find six more U.S. soldiers gathered around an Army vehicle. *This is getting confusing. What the hell is going on?* They were soldiers from the same 507th Maintenance Company. Natonski pieced the story together. They had just made the most unbelievable wrong turn. At the junction of Routes 7 and 8, south of Nasiriyah, instead of turning sharp left to head around Nasiriyah to the west, the convoy had gone straight into the heart of the city. Iraqi soldiers waved them through several checkpoints until they emerged on the other side of the city. It was then that they realized they had made a mistake. The sun was rising, and they had just turned around to retrace their steps when they were attacked. Under fire from Iraqi fighters, the convoy's eighteen vehicles had sped back through the city, trying to avoid debris and blockades erected in their path. A few vehicles had gotten through. Most had been hit and were disabled somewhere in the city.

Natonski's eyes grew wider as he heard the full absurdity of the story.

"Is that all of you?"

"No, there are some still missing."

An Army captain, almost sobbing, explained that some twenty soldiers and thirteen vehicles were still unaccounted for. Among the missing were Private First Class Howard Johnson, Specialist Shoshana Johnson, Sergeant George Buggs, Specialist Edgar Hernandez, Private First Class Jessica Lynch . . .

As Brigadier General Natonski talked to the soldiers, Lieutenant Colonel Grabowski and Major Sosa tried to figure out how the army convoy had got in front of them. When the tanks had called back with news of U.S. soldiers, Sosa's first thought was that it might be an Army scout unit that had originally planned to link up with them. That plan had been scrapped some days ago, but maybe the message hadn't got through to them. The news that it was an Army maintenance convoy came out of the blue.

They cast their minds back. Grabowski remembered that in the very early hours of the morning, as they had been trying to cross a cloverleaf junction some sixty kilometers south of Nasiriyah, he had been aware of an Army convoy passing them along the highway. He didn't think anything of it. He assumed they were just heading toward the western side of Nasiriyah and wouldn't interfere with his mission on the eastern side of the city. The only thing Grabowski was concerned about then was not getting his vehicles mixed in with the Army convoy.

Now he realized that the Army convoy had jeopardized his mission. *How am I going to respond?*

When he'd first heard the reports of wounded U.S. soldiers up ahead and that Major Peeples from the tank company had gone off to locate them, his main concern was that Peeples didn't get stuck up there without support. They were the only tanks he had in the task force.

He had been frustrated when he had difficulty reaching Major Peeples on the radio. He knew Peeples was probably switching to his company net to talk to his marines, but he wanted a clear picture of what was going on.

"Bill, I need you to stay in your tank. You need to stay on the radio."

He was even more frustrated when he heard the tank company XO, Captain Dyer, get on the radio with another request.

"Timberwolf, this is Panzer 5. My tanks are less than half full. We need to refuel before the decision is made on whether we are going to do a blocking position."

The tanks had gone through gallons of fuel in their rush to locate the U.S. soldiers.

"Roger that. We are setting up an RP for you now."

The Abrams was fast and quiet. Its advanced suspension made it a comfortable ride. Tankers said it was like riding in a Cadillac. But its fifteen-hundred-horsepower gas turbine engine drank up fuel, and it could only go three hundred miles on a full tank. At full speed it went through fifty-six gallons an hour. Even when it was idling, it drank ten gallons of fuel an hour. It couldn't stray too far from an RP, or refueling point.

Major Sosa also had a bad feeling about sending the tanks back to refuel. It wasn't just a few tanks that would be out of action. *They all have to go back.* It had to be done, though. They didn't want the tanks stuck without fuel on the northern side of the city after the mission was completed. They would be a long way from any of the fuel trucks. Nevertheless, a wave of anger came over him. *That's what the fuel bladders were for.* He was silently fuming that Major Peeples had cut them loose. *They carried fifty-five gallons. That was an extra quarter of a tank for each M1A1.* He and Peeples had already got into a fight over the issue back in Kuwait. Peeples had said it was SOP, standard operating procedure, to drop the bladders once they got engaged. Sosa hadn't thought it was a good idea. Rather tetchily he had suggested that they review their SOP. He was also unhappy with the way Peeples passed his information. In Sosa's view, he was out of his tank too much or talking to his marines on the company net rather than keeping battalion informed. The summer before at the CAX in Twenty-nine Palms, they had trained with another tank company commander. Sosa remembered being very impressed by how effectively that tank commander had passed information across the net.

Now he could only watch with dismay as all eleven tanks rumbled back past the infantry companies lined up along the side of the road, toward the refueling point several miles to the rear of the column.

Brigadier General Natonski was still trying to digest the news that the whole of Nasiriyah would now be well aware that U.S. forces were in and around the city. This was bad. Operation Iraqi Freedom had been planned around speed and stealth. If the Army and Marines could get to Baghdad quickly, they would seize the initiative and surprise Saddam's forces before they had time to react. Speed and stealth also guided Natonski in his plans for taking Nasiriyah. He wanted to keep the Iraqi defenders guessing as to whether they were going to march into the city or bypass it. When the time was right, he would make a lightning strike into the heart of Nasiriyah and seize the crucial bridges across the Euphrates and the Saddam Canal. Now the 507th had endangered that plan. The Iraqis, alerted to their arrival, might blow the bridges before his marines could get to them. *Goddamnit.* Silently, he cursed the Army. He couldn't help thinking that the 507th got lost because the Army didn't train their support services as well as the Marine Corps. There had always been rivalry between the services, but the rivalry was greatest with the Army. Natonski believed the Marine Corps gave the American taxpayers more bang for their buck. The Army was far bigger and better equipped than the Marines. It got the latest technology, while the Marine Corps made do with patched-up helicopters from the Vietnam era. But the Marines preferred it like that. They prided themselves on doing more with less. *The Army might win the war, but it was the Marine Corps that won the battles.*

As some tanks rolled past, he looked up.

"What's that?"

Grabowski told him that the tanks were heading back to refuel.

Natonski had to make a decision. He'd had enough combat experience from Vietnam, Somalia, and Bosnia to know that the best-laid plans always fall apart at first contact. They were OBE, overtaken by events. He wished it hadn't happened so early in the campaign. Twenty thousand marines and eight thousand vehicles from the 1st Marine Division were backed up waiting for him to clear Nasiriyah so they could get their convoys on the road to Baghdad along Route Moe. He could no longer take the bridges by surprise—the 507th's wrong turn had put paid to that and there was clearly some sort of resistance along the route. But if he moved quickly he might be able to get to those bridges before they were blown. Otherwise it might take days to find another crossing site. He'd grown up with the Marine Corps doctrine of maneuver warfare as stated in its Warfighting Skills Program: "It is a state of mind born of a bold will, intellect, initiative, and ruthless opportunism. It is a state of mind bent on shattering the enemy morally and physically by paralyzing and confounding him, by avoiding his strength, by quickly and aggressively exploiting his vulnerabilities, and by striking him in a way that will hurt him the most."

He turned to Rick Grabowski. He wanted those bridges as soon as possible.

"We've got to accelerate the attack. We've got to find those missing soldiers and get to those bridges before they're blown."

As Natonski turned to go he looked back again at the battalion commander.

"Rickey. Those soldiers are still in the city. Try and find them if you can. The Army would do it for us and we need to do it for them."

"Roger, sir, I'm already working on that."

6

Private First Class Robinson's stomach fluttered with excitement as the news filtered down that Charlie Company was to move out. They were still toward the rear of the column, but now they were going to move up toward Alpha and Bravo marines who had started to see some action. As they moved forward, Robinson, from the hatch of track 201, saw four M1A1 Abrams tanks heading toward them, driving away from the city, on the other side of the road. Corporal Wentzel shouted over to him.

"Hey. Aren't those our tanks?"

The marines in the rear of the other AAVs also saw the tanks driving back the way they'd come. They were surprised. They'd all been briefed that the tanks were supposed to be leading their attack.

"They're scared. They're running away."

A few of the marines in the rear laughed. The infantrymen had never really practiced that much with the tankers or the trackers, and they didn't think of them as marines. The feeling among them was that the real marines were the riflemen who wrought havoc on an enemy with nothing more than an M16 rifle. It was all very well sitting inside a highly engineered, well-armored military equivalent of a Cadillac, but if you wanted to prove yourself in battle you relied on only three things: your training, your weapon, and the buddies on either side of you. All the same, the marines felt uncomfortable seeing those tanks disappearing to the rear with their massive firepower. Robinson couldn't really explain it. He just felt better when the tanks were around.

The chat down below turned to girls. Some of the guys talked about which girl they were going to fuck when they got home or how they were going to cheat on their girlfriends. That was all allowed. What wasn't allowed was to suggest to a marine that his girl might be cheating on him. Robinson understood the rule. *It's better to say that you want to fuck his mother than to tell him that his girl is cheating on him.* He remembered one guy on ship acting real weird after a telephone call. Later he found out the guy's wife had just told him that she was leaving him to move back to California with an Air Force pilot. He tried not to think about it too much. They were a long way away, and there was nothing they could do. He'd been ditched like that before. But once he got over the shock, he remembered that his buddies had forced him to joke about it. That's what helped him get through it.

From the hatch of 201, Robinson looked at the palm-lined streets and the two-story cinder-block houses in front of him, on either side of the highway. It looked quiet enough. *Look at those hajjis running across the road. They're probably scared.* A few locals dressed in rags stood by the side of the road and watched as the American war machine rumbled through the outskirts of their town. Robinson couldn't quite figure out what they must be thinking. None of them smiled. He briefly remembered that they were supposed to be pro-American in this town. *Clearly no one has told them that we are here to liberate them.*

Driving track 201, Lance Corporal Edward Castleberry could hear and see a flurry of activity ahead of him. He was ordered to move off the road and press north through some cane fields on a parallel axis to Bravo Company. Overhead he heard and saw Cobras fly by and shoot stuff up farther ahead of him. *This is awesome.* They had the tracks arranged in a wedge formation to give the gunners in the tracks a clear view ahead and to provide maximum firepower to the front and sides. Every one hundred meters or so, Castleberry would be ordered to stop and drop the ramp. The infantry dismounted and provided security by taking cover around the track in a 180-degree arc, looking for signs of the enemy. They didn't need to cover the right-hand side because the .50-caliber machine gun and Mark 19 could take care of anything that came from the east.

Farther back, in track 208, Lieutenant Reid had also seen the tanks drive by on their way to being refueled. *Wow, those guys have been shot at.* Reid still hadn't seen any enemy. He couldn't tell whether it was light enemy fire or something heavier that they were getting into. As they drew alongside Alpha Company, he saw that Alpha's marines were coming out of the ditches covered in mud. They were not happy. It was almost funny to see the pissed look on their faces. *I wonder how the water will affect the MOPP suits if we get gassed?*

Off to the side of him the cannon cockers of 1/10 Marines were firing "Red Rain" counterbattery into the city. They were picking up where the incoming artillery and mortars were being fired from and targeting the positions with their own artillery.

Gathered around their Humvees, Lieutenant Colonel Grabowski and Major Sosa tried to formulate a plan. Natonski had now made it clear to them that he wanted them to push for the bridges. They were not going to stop and block the road to the south of the city. They were going to attack into Nasiriyah. Sosa knew that they had rehearsed the plan on ship and in Kuwait. They had even driven out into the desert with key personnel and gone through the mission with engineering tape simulating the bridges. But that was a couple of weeks ago. *The last plan we briefed before leaving Kuwait was the defensive plan to hold south of the city.* He'd also remembered a briefing in which the regimental commander, Colonel Bailey, had stressed they would not seize the bridges if they were under fire. Now they seemed to be going against all that.

The speed at which the decision had been made had taken them by surprise. Neither Grabowski nor Sosa had realized the pressure Natonski was under from the 1st Marine Division to get Route Moe open.

Grabowski was still confident. He had gone over the mission again and again with his company commanders on ship and in Kuwait. It was a clear and simple one. They knew they didn't have to clear the route. The follow-on unit, 2nd Battalion, 8th Marines, was supposedly the experts at clearing urban areas and would deal with that. He also knew from intel briefings that there was nothing in the city that could stop his mechanized force with the heavy armor of the tanks. All they had to do was seize the two bridges.

I've got to get the tanks back from refueling as soon as possible. Their thick armor meant that they were more or less invincible to anything that the Iraqis might throw at them. He didn't really want to send the AAVs into the city without tank support. The Marine Corps AAV was only made of re-inforced aluminum. The vehicle's skin might stop an AK-47 round but an RPG, a rocket-propelled grenade, flying through the air at three hundred meters per second would cut right through it. On impact, the firing pin would shoot a jet of molten metal to pierce the skin, allowing the grenade to explode inside the track. Unfortunately, Grabowski knew that none of Task Force Tarawa's AAVs were equipped with EAAKs, or Enhanced Ap-pliqué Armor Kits, the thick antiballistic plates, developed by the Marine Corps, that could be attached to the outside of an AAV.

He consulted with Sosa.

"Let's start to send the infantry companies forward and hope that the tanks won't take too long to refuel."

He got on the radio to his XO, Major Jeff Tuggle, who was at the rear, closest to the refueling point.

"We need those tanks back here as soon as possible."

Sosa and Grabowski knew that they would have to change their original plan. That called for Team Tank to establish a support-by-fire position on the southern bank of the Euphrates, allowing Alpha to go through first and seize the Euphrates Bridge. Then Bravo, with its tanks, would cross the Euphrates Bridge onto Route Moe, known as Ambush Alley, turn immedi-ately to the east, and work its way to the northern canal bridge around the eastern outskirts of the town. The forward command post and Charlie Company would follow in trace, and Charlie would move through their lines and take the northern bridge.

The urgency of Natonski's request had changed that plan. Grabowski could see that Bravo Company was at the head of the column while Alpha Company marines were still out in the fields clearing buildings. It would take too long to get Alpha Company to leapfrog Bravo. *We'll just have to get Bravo Company to lead the attack and Alpha can follow in trace.*

The pace of their mission had just picked up. It was now up to Major Sosa to make it happen. He didn't panic, but he now realized that there were several questions about the terrain that they were going into that had never been answered by the intelligence people at regimental level. He'd wanted to know about the current, depth, and silt level of the waterway by the northern canal bridge. He had also asked about the terrain and street layout to the east of Nasiriyah. No one seemed to know what it would be like. There were maps and photos, but they had very little human intelligence. There was no one on the ground who could tell them what state the streets were in, how the Iraqis would greet them, and what sort of resistance they should expect. *It would have been nice to have answers to those questions, but maybe regiment has other priorities.*

Grabowski got on the radio to the company commanders. Natonski had given him a timeline he'd been unaware of. Natonski wanted those bridges by 1500. That was less than four hours away. And Grabowski and his men had the added complication of looking out for U.S. soldiers stranded in the city. He didn't want his marines firing on them, thinking they were bad guys.

"This is Timberwolf 6. We need to get moving. Keep your eyes open for American forces on the ground. Don't engage the enemy unless they clearly demonstrate hostile intent toward you. We've got to get those bridges."

7

"Timberwolf, this is Tomahawk 6."

Captain Mike Brooks, commander of Alpha Company, stood up in the TC's hatch of his track to get a better view of the scene ahead. On the horizon, plumes of black smoke billowed from the jagged outline of the city. Hueys and Cobras hovered overhead. The *boom* of an artillery shell echoed in the distance.

He reached for the radio and glanced down at his military-issue GPS, checked his position, and gave Lieutenant Colonel Grabowski at the forward command post a quick situation report.

His column of twelve AAVs and three Humvees was in front of Charlie Company but still several kilometers behind the tanks, the CAAT vehicles, and Bravo Company.

He'd heard on the radio that up ahead, the tanks were under fire and that they had rescued some U.S. soldiers who had been ambushed in the city. As his company had moved forward, it, too, had started receiving small-arms fire. He'd got some of his marines to dismount and to clear on foot some suspicious buildings a hundred meters or so to the east of the road. It was muddy out there, and he could see that they were not happy struggling knee-deep through the water and the dirt. *This is frustrating. The opposition isn't determined, but they are harassing us and it's slowing us down.* He hadn't been expecting to fight like this. There was no tactical formation of Iraqi soldiers, just faceless figures dressed in black, shooting at them from behind buildings and irrigation ditches. To be honest, he wasn't even sure exactly who he was fighting. He knew there might be some opposition from Baathists and fedayeen troops loyal to Saddam, but these fighters were shooting from what looked like normal, humble homes.

"Timberwolf. Tanks are going back to refuel."

Brooks had felt a chill when he learned on the radio that the tanks were going to the rear. He always felt more secure when the tanks were around. For two days the movement through southern Iraq had gone smoothly and to plan. There was no sense of urgency; they were controlled and method-ical. Even the reports of the tanks getting into contact ahead of them hadn't fazed him. But as he saw them speed past on the way to the refuel-ing point he had a strange sensation that something was beginning to un-ravel. They looked dirty and shot up, and his sense of discomfort got worse. The feeling of invincibility that the tanks gave when they were up front had gone. He checked his thoughts. *Nothing is wrong. They'll prob-ably get refueled quickly so it will be okay.*

Brooks was thirty-four, with a mild, thoughtful manner and boyish bright eyes that flashed with determination. He was married with three young sons. He'd been brought up on a farm in a small town in rural Penn-sylvania. As a kid, he hadn't done very well at high school. He hated books and exams and always seemed to get into mischief. It was nothing serious, but he did once get a disorderly conduct fine for throwing eggs at some-one's house. He did whatever it took to have a laugh and some fun. To this day, he didn't really know why he changed. He just got tired of being a smart-ass. He wanted something more focused, more solid. A friend had signed up for the Marine Corps a year before, and he had seen what that had done for him. He left high school and rather than become an officer, he enlisted at nineteen. He wanted to do it the hard way, to learn some humility, and self-respect. He worked his way through Boot Camp and then went to field artillery. That's when he decided he wanted the challenge of leading marines. He wanted to be an officer. Four years after leaving the Naval Academy at Annapolis he was made a marine captain. He was disappointed when he was given command of a headquarters company. He wanted to be in the front line, training for war. But he persevered, and a year before the invasion of Iraq he was made commander of his very own rifle company—Alpha Company, 1st Battalion, 2nd Marines.

Most of his marines had already been with Alpha for several months, even years when he took over command. But some of them had also joined at the same time, and others were straight out of Boot Camp and the School of Infantry. He made a point of getting to know everything about them. He had spent a lot of time with them in training and got to know their strengths and weaknesses and their different characters. He would push them during training, asking them to do things that he knew were hard for them. Sometimes he'd wondered whether he pushed them too hard, but when he saw them do it and do it well, he felt proud.

"Tomahawk 6, this is Timberwolf. Hey, you need to wrap up your activities there. We need to get going. We need to push."

It was Grabowski, the battalion commander, and there was a new sense of urgency in his voice. Brooks was momentarily taken aback. He had no idea why the movement forward had suddenly become more immediate.

"Bravo, you're in front, you take the lead. You will cross the bridge first."

Brooks knew that's not how they'd planned to take the bridge. He was supposed to lead Alpha Company onto the Euphrates Bridge. Bravo and Charlie would follow in trace, go around to the east, and head toward the northern bridge. He would then follow once 2nd Battalion, 8th Marines had relieved him on the southern span, the Euphrates Bridge. Since early January, when the battalion commander, Lieutenant Colonel Rick Grabowksi, had entrusted them with the possible task of taking the bridges at Nasiriyah, they'd revised and changed the plan many times. On ship with his fellow company commanders, Captain Tim Newland and Captain Dan Wittnam, he had pored over maps and satellite images to check that they could make it happen. They had war-gamed the scenario with other officers in a packed wardroom, to make sure that they hadn't missed anything. Following classic Marine doctrine, they had visualized the operation, determined the critical events, and developed a scheme of maneuver that they were convinced would overwhelm anyone defending the city. The intelligence officers provided a lot of images and information on the terrain and on the disposition of Iraqi military units built up over the last twelve years from U.S. Air Force sorties monitoring the no-fly zone for Operation Southern Watch. It was supposed to be like any other combined arms drill executed over and over again at CAX the previous summer. They had perfected their scheme of maneuver and now, suddenly, the battalion commander had changed their attack formation. *What's going on?*

He saw it made sense to go with Bravo across the bridge first. He still had marines out in the fields, and it would take some time to get his company to leapfrog Bravo. Nevertheless, he felt that something was not quite right. He wanted to be fluid, to adapt to change, but the urgency with which it was unfolding didn't give him a good feeling. *Where would that leave Charlie?* In the original plan, Charlie was going to follow Bravo. But they were even farther away, in fields to the west of the road. It would take them even more time to mount up and get into position between Bravo and Alpha.

He heard Captain Wittnam, company commander of Charlie, on the radio.

"Sir, Alpha is already behind Bravo. I recommend we follow in trace of Alpha."

That at least made some sense and was closer to the original scheme of maneuver. He felt a bit more comfortable. If only the tanks were up there he would feel better. He was glad he knew Dan Wittnam so well. Implicit understanding between commanders enabled them to work better as a team. It was something they had focused on at CAX.

He got back to the work ahead. *What can I do now? What do I need to do?* He called his men back and tried to make it clear that Bravo was now going to take the lead. He got messages out by radio to his platoon commanders that he wanted everybody back to the tracks as quickly as possible.

8

Corporal Neville Welch was in the hatch of AAV B203, the third track from the front of the column of Bravo Company vehicles. He was scanning the fields and houses on either side of him when he heard his platoon commander say that they were moving out. Now that the tanks had gone to the rear to refuel, Bravo was at the very front of the battalion, with Alpha and Charlie following in trace.

Like many of the other marines, he had heard that Army units were in trouble up ahead and that tanks had gone to help, but that didn't strike him as odd. He didn't know that there should have been no units in front of them. He was an ordinary grunt, at the bottom of the chain of command. It was not surprising that some information just never got to Corporal Neville Welch, or that when it got there, like an elaborate game of Chinese whispers, it sometimes wasn't exactly the same as what was sent out. *Maybe the Army is there to escort us into the city.* He trusted the higher-ups to know what was going on with the big picture. Most grunts drank up the slightest piece of news because they got so little information. Not Welch. He tried to ignore the rumors. He just kept his focus on his job.

At that moment, his job was to watch out for hostile targets. There had been some firing up ahead, and he was told to look out for any suspicious activity. The sun, no more than a dull glow of light, was peeping through a mixture of clouds and thick dust that seemed to clog the air. To the east, set back a hundred meters from the road, were some tumbling mud brick buildings. They looked as though they were abandoned, but flying from the roof was a black flag. It looked threatening, but he'd been told that it was no more than a sign that Shia Muslims lived there. Helos flew overhead, scaring the goats and dogs standing by the side of the road. A loud thud rocked the horizon and black smoke billowed out from a target ahead. A whoop of joy went up among the marines around him.

Corporal Welch did not join in. For him, this was a serious business. He'd enlisted in the Marine Corps days after September 11, 2001, outraged by the terrorist attack on innocent people. He'd felt victimized and vulnerable and saw it as a call to war. He felt the attack had penetrated the soul of America. It was his generation's Pearl Harbor. He didn't want to sit on the sidelines. He had decided then and there that he was going to give something back to the country that had put him on the path of self-actualization.

He'd been born in Guyana into a traditional and poor family. He'd gone to school and technical college there, but at the age of twenty-one he realized that Guyana was no place for an ambitious young man desperate for education. He was given federal grants to study at Kingsborough Community College in Brooklyn, New York, where he improved his reading and writing. Then he got a place at Howard University in Washington, D.C., where he studied health systems management and immersed himself in African American literature. Every day he'd spend hours at the Moorland-Spingarn Research Center reading an eclectic mix of writing: August Wilson, Paulo Freire, Kenneth Clark, Frantz Fanon, Kwame Nkrumah, even Sir Walter Raleigh. He wanted to understand the consciousness of black America. The more he read, the more he felt that African American activists were missing something, that their focus was too narrow and local. He realized that even the civil rights movement was a parochial struggle. What he wanted was for African Americans to think bigger, in a more universal way, to understand that what was happening in America was just a small part of a larger struggle being played out in the Caribbean and Africa. That's how he met his wife, Bashen, an African American from Birmingham, Alabama.

Welch was tall and educated, and had a severity about him that could be intimidating. He spoke with a lilting Caribbean British accent. Straight out of college, Welch had set up a janitorial business that had been quite successful. Then September 11 happened, and Welch closed the business down. It was no surprise that when he walked into the Marine Corps recruiting station on Flatbush Avenue in New York, the recruiter was taken aback. He tried to persuade him to work in the public affairs office or pick some other specialty in which he could use his bachelor's degree. But Welch had seen the videos. He wanted to be in harm's way, out in front. He wanted to be an infantryman, a grunt. He signed on right away for four years. Bashen was upset. Her father had done several tours of duty in Vietnam and had come back a changed and wrecked man. She didn't see him anymore because he drank too much. Neville Welch did what he could to comfort her, but he had made up his mind. Within days he was on his way to Boot Camp.

"Dismount. Dismount."

The rear ramp of Welch's AAV dropped and marines poured out into the road and started setting up a security perimeter around his track. In front of him he saw the span of a bridge. To one side there were burning vehicles, to the other a smelly landfill site. The tarmac was slick with fuel and covered in shards of glass from broken windshields, spent ammo, blackened pieces of metal. Within seconds he was covered by huge black flies. He couldn't quite work out where he was or what they were supposed to be doing, but clearly something had happened here. He didn't realize it, but he was at the same trash dump where the tanks had rescued the soldiers from the 507th half an hour earlier. Whatever opposition there had been was now mostly gone. It looked as though the tanks had dealt with it.

He got his men to take cover, positioning them so their sectors of fire did not overlap. As a fire-team leader within Bravo's 1st Platoon, he was in charge of the Marine Corps's smallest combat unit. He had three other marines in his team. One carried an M249 automatic weapon, and the two others were armed with M16 rifles. He carried an M203—an M16 rifle with a 40mm grenade launcher attached under the barrel. His training at the School of Infantry at Camp Geiger in North Carolina had taught him that the fire team was always at the hard edge of any combat. As a fire-team leader he was responsible for keeping his guys together and working as a unit. He kept them low, their weapons scanning the fields for targets, each taking a sector of responsibility. They kept ammo discipline, not firing unless they had a target. Other marines from his company were out in the fields clearing buildings. Suddenly squad leaders started calling their fire teams back.

"Bravo 1st Platoon, back to the tracks."

Welch jumped back into the track and they were off. He was thrown first backward, then forward. It was all stop and start. One minute they would get the order to go, then they would have to pause. The AAV treads churned up the mud on the edge of the road. It looked as though it had rained here a few nights before. A lone cow chewed on the sparse vegetation, oblivious to the chaos around. Iraqis watched passively as they moved by. Welch could hear constant chatter on the radio. It didn't make much sense to him, but it sounded calm and purposeful.

"Tanks are refueling."

"This is Timberwolf. Sitrep, over."

"Small-arms fire from port and starboard. Nothing we can't handle. Over."

To his right, he could make out a road sign, half of it written in English: WELCOME TO NASIRIYAH. It put Neville Welch on edge. *Why was it written in English?* He thought it was a deliberate and cynical message to the Americans rolling toward the town. It wasn't a message of welcome. It was a message of death. *This is your burial spot.*

As if on cue, the patter of small-arms fire pinged off the side of Welch's track. It was coming from some huge oil tanks to the northeast, just over the span of the bridge.

"Keep pushing. Keep pushing."

Marines around him were now yelling at each other.

"See that green mosque thing with the onion-shaped dome? There are troops inside with small arms."

"Port side, port side. No, to the right. They're dressed as civilians. They've got a white flag but they've got AKs and they're not surrendering."

Welch saw the mosque a hundred meters from the road. To the side of the mosque was a small dirt berm. He saw an Iraqi stand up, put an RPG to his shoulder. Welch fired two rounds. The man didn't go down. The RPG shot out of its launcher. Several other marines from another track let out a burst of gunfire. The figure collapsed in the dirt. The RPG and its trail of white smoke spun wildly off into the distance. To the right of the mosque, a crowd of women and children seemed to be waving at them. Welch wasn't quite sure whether to wave back. And then the crowd parted and some men, dressed in black robes, stepped out between the women and let out a burst of AK fire. Welch and the other marines on his track shot back. He wasn't shocked. He was in an Arab country and knew that women and children were prepared to commit acts of suicide. *This isn't an environment of love. I'm not going to assume that people here love me. Am I going to get back home or am I going to let them send me back home?* He didn't have time to contemplate whether they had good intentions. The rules of engagement were clear and had been drummed into Welch during training. They shouldn't fire indiscriminately. That would exact a heavy toll on the civilian population. But for Welch, the reality was more complicated. *If they are out in the street, they mean to do me harm. If they mean to do me harm, they are a target.* All his focus went on protecting himself, his marines, and their vehicles. He let out another burst of gunfire.

It was how he'd been trained at Boot Camp. For twelve weeks at Parris Island, South Carolina, he'd been shouted at, manipulated, indoctrinated. He didn't mind. He understood that the Marine Corps was preparing him to react to fire, to carry out a mission without question, to develop teamwork, to confront imminent death, to sacrifice himself for fellow marines. *You don't escape Parris Island without experiencing sacrifice.* Some recruits found it difficult to cope. Welch didn't. *If you have the eyes to see why you are doing these things, you understand.* He welcomed the uniformity, the incessant drills, the movement as one mass. He'd seen the smoke pit, a twenty-foot-by-twenty-foot sandbox, where those marines who couldn't conform were made to exercise at a rate that made their hearts want to drop out. Push-ups, jumps, squats—sometimes all day and all night. He understood that the drill instructors had to transform belligerent young men who had grown up answering back to figures of authority into marines who would accept orders without question. Welch understood, and he complied.

A couple of kilometers behind Corporal Welch, Lieutenant Colonel Grabowski received a call on the radio from Captain Tim Newland, the Bravo Company Commander.

"This is Mustang 6. Sir, we are on the Euphrates Bridge."

Grabowski knew he couldn't be there yet. He could see from the icon on his Blue Force Tracker that Bravo Company had only just arrived at the railway bridge. They were still a couple of kilometers south of the Euphrates.

"Mustang 6, this is Timberwolf. Check your map again."

Newland's Blue Force Tracker had broken down. The Blue Force Tracker worked perfectly in the Humvees, but for some reason it didn't work very effectively with the power output in the tracks. Newland was relying on DCT, a satellite tracking system that related position directly to a map grid. And the maps he had didn't show up very clearly that there was a railroad bridge south of the Euphrates Bridge.

"Timberwolf, this is Mustang 6. Sir, you're right, we're continuing to push."

Captain Newland, in the track just behind Corporal Welch, ordered Bravo across the railway bridge. Suddenly a cry went up.

"We've got tanks. We've got tanks."

The CAAT vehicles that had been flanking Bravo Company on its approach to the bridge pushed forward. As they reached the highest point of the span, the CAAT marines saw two enemy T-55 tanks dug in on either side. The air erupted in a hail of machine-gun fire. Working their .50-caliber machine guns from their Humvees, the marines sent rounds tearing into the dug-in positions, scattering Iraqi fighters in all directions. Some collapsed in the dirt, others took cover behind trenches. Sergeant Edward Palaciaes spotted more dug-in tanks on both sides of the bridge. Their turrets weren't moving and they were probably so antiquated that they were unmanned, nothing more than machine-gun bunkers. But in Palaciaes's eyes they were Iraqi tanks, and he wanted to kill them. As the machine gunners showered the area with suppressing fire, Sergeant Palaciaes and Corporal Josh McCall fired off TOW missile after TOW missile, keeping the crosshairs on the tanks and watching them explode into huge fireballs. Palaciaes was in heaven. The Tube-launched, Optically-tracked, Wire command-link guided antitank missile was an expensive piece of equipment. Palaciaes didn't get to fire too many of them in training. *This is one helluva exciting thing.*

Iraqi fighters were running around in the fields by the bridge, firing at them from both the east and west sides. A fog of thick acrid smoke from the U.S. Army vehicles, which were still in flames, swept across the area, obscuring the marines' vision.

Palaciaes scanned the horizon for more tanks. The turret of a dug-in T-55, hidden by mounds of earth, turned toward him. The small two-lane bridge was too crowded with CAAT vehicles. His driver maneuvered his vehicle away from the three other Humvees on the bridge. The backblast on a TOW can stretch up to a hundred meters and could easily kill a man. Looking behind him to make sure he was clear, he took a shot. It hit the turret of the T-55, sending a ball of dirt and twisted metal into the air.

The sound of loud cheering and laughing came over the radio.

"Five T-55s engaged and killed."

Lieutenant Colonel Grabowski, a couple of hundred meters south of the railway bridge, could see the CAAT teams on the span of the bridge ahead of him firing their TOW missiles. He was shocked that they had come into contact with tanks so early on. *They've got tanks. There's more to this mission than we've been aware of. This is supposed to be a walk in the park. This is not how it is supposed to be.* His own tanks were still back being refueled. He knew that he was now on a timeline and he had to get the battalion moving. But he didn't want to go any farther into the city without the M1A1 Abrams. He got hold of Major Sosa.

"Hey, if we don't get tanks up here we are not going any farther."

Once again Grabowski got on the radio to his XO, Major Jeff Tuggle. This time he showed his frustration.

"I need those tanks up here as soon as possible. Tell them to get their asses up here."

"Roger, boss, I'm working on it."

All of a sudden there was a huge boom. A hot storm of dirt and rocks blew toward them. *They've hit one of our amtracks.* Grabowski feared the worst.

"What the heck was that?"

The battalion gunner replied.

"That's a Javelin."

It was the first time his battalion had fired a Javelin in combat, and although they were a couple hundred meters away, he was surprised at the strength of the backblast that sent hot air, dirt, and packaging from the missile hurtling toward them. He looked up to see the gunner and his loader hollering and high-fiving with excitement.

"I guess they hit what they were aiming for."

He was proud of them. They were doing what they had trained to do. Locate, close with, and destroy the bad guys.

For the fourth time, Grabowski got back on the net and asked Major Tuggle where those tanks were. All of a sudden, he heard a rumble and felt the ground shake. Through the thick black smoke still pouring from the burning U.S. Army vehicles appeared the outline of four M1A1 tanks. They roared through his position toward the bridge. He called Captain Newland of Bravo Company. He wanted to get them "Oscar Mike," or "on the move."

"Mustang 6, you've got your tanks. We need to get you moving."

"Roger that, sir."

"Let me know when you are Oscar Mike."

Grabowski knew that to meet Natonski's deadline he had to go for those bridges.

9

Major Peeples and his tanks had driven about ten kilometers south to get to the refueling point at the rear of the battalion's column. He was pleased with the way the movement had gone so far. His team had performed well, and they were jubilant and high on the adrenaline of battle. He wanted to get the tanks refueled quickly, but there was no great hurry. He knew that the battalion was planning to establish a defense south of the city. He then presumed there would be a huddle before a decision was made on whether to go for the bridges. It was a principle that even the most junior marines were taught. *The attacker controls the clock.* The only thing he regretted was that he hadn't had time to conduct a proper handover with the commander of Bravo Company, Captain Tim Newland, now that Bravo had taken over as the lead element.

He saw a flurry of activity around the fuel truck. That's when he had a bad feeling. He had eleven tanks, each requiring five hundred gallons of fuel. One of the support staff came up to him.

"We've only got fourteen hundred gallons of fuel left to give out."

Peeples quickly did the calculation. It meant that each of the tanks was not going to get much more than a hundred gallons. That would only get them an extra 120 or so kilometers. There was worse to come. They'd been having problems with spare parts for the pumps and some of the pumps weren't working. Now Peeples discovered that none of the pumps worked. The tanks would have to be gravity fed, and there was only one hose.

Nearby, Captain Scott Dyer had answered the question that had been bugging him for years. *How will I fare in combat?* He was pleased with the answer. They had rescued American soldiers and none of his crew were injured. Now he wanted a much-needed leak. It came out like a torrent, forming a huge puddle. *I'm pissing like a racehorse.* He was so exhausted from the fight that he inadvertently trod in it and was irritated to find that the mixture clumped to his boots.

Milling around the hospital tracks at the rear of the column near the refueling point were some of the rescued soldiers from the 507th. Dyer ran over to one of them, a staff sergeant, to find out more about what the Army convoy had been through. The picture the soldier painted of the city was not at all what he had been led to believe. Dyer realized that the intelligence they had been fed for the past few months was all wrong. Waiting for them in the city were not crowds of cheering Iraqis, ready to shower them with flowers for taking on Saddam. The soldier talked of fortified positions, of machine-gun bunkers lining the streets, of thousands of armed Iraqis swamping the streets, ready to attack the invaders. He painted the area to the north, around the Saddam Canal Bridge as swampy, treacherous, and not trafficable by tank. *This is brilliant battlefield intelligence.* It dawned on Dyer that their whole strategy was built on wrong assumptions. *I've got to get this information to the lead units.*

Dyer ran over to the main battalion command post where the XO, Major Tuggle, was coordinating logistics for the battalion from his C7 command track. Major Tuggle was the backstop for Grabowski at the forward command post. That was the quickest, most reliable way of feeding the battalion commander information. Dyer tried to explain what the soldier had told him, but Tuggle didn't seem to take much notice of what he was saying. He was preoccupied with something else.

"Bravo is in contact and needs the tanks."

Dyer looked at him. He saw from his face that he was desperately try-ing to conceal worry and stress. *Tuggle knows that everybody's ass is in a crack.*

"We've just got a call from Bravo. They are in contact and need the tanks back up there as soon as possible."

Captain Dyer was confused. *Why the hell are they in contact?* Then it struck him that the battalion must have started the attack without them.

"What the hell is going on? Why didn't you tell us that they were going to attack?"

Dyer thought that Tuggle gave him a strange, almost apologetic look.

"It's too late. It's done. You need to get up there and help those boys."

Dyer could not believe it. They had planned the maneuver for months on ship and in Kuwait. They had gone through it over and over again. Tanks were central to the success of the mission. Team Tank was going to take a po-sition on the south side of the Euphrates Bridge and provide a base of fire to support Alpha Company's seizure of it. Then Bravo, reinforced with the other four tanks, would go around to the east of the city to take the northern bridge with Charlie Company. Team Tank would then make their way up to the northern bridge to support its seizure. It had been endlessly talked about and rehearsed, and he felt confident that they all knew what they were doing. But that mission had been downgraded to a "be prepared to" mission. And now it seemed that Bravo Company had begun the attack without them.

Major Peeples was monitoring the refueling process when Major Tuggle ran up to him.

"Bill, we need those tanks up there as soon as possible."

Like Dyer, Peeples didn't understand the urgency. *Why the hurry?* Peeples knew they had been told that they were going to get into a block-ing position south of the city along the interchange between Route 7 and Route 8. Then a decision would be made as to who, if anyone, would actu-ally seize the bridges. Clearly, something had changed.

With only one hose, it was taking fifteen minutes to give each tank a hundred gallons. Peeples cut short the refueling for the four tanks from 2nd Platoon that were supposed to be with Bravo Company. He'd given them the four tanks that were in the best condition because they would be the farthest away from the rest of the tank company and would find it harder to get backup support. He yelled to Gunnery Sergeant Randy Howard, his 2nd Platoon commander.

"You need to get the hell up there."

The four tanks from 2nd Platoon had roared off up the road. To make sure he wasn't missing something, Peeples checked again where his reserve position was to be after the rest of his tanks finished refueling. He was right. They were supposed to be in a location just south of the Euphrates Bridge. *What the heck then did they need those tanks for so quickly?*

With the loss of the tanks from 2nd Platoon, his Team Tank was now down to seven tanks. Captain Thompson's 1st Platoon had three tanks, Captain Cubas's 3rd Platoon had two tanks, and he and Captain Dyer, the HQ element, had two tanks.

10

Captain Dan Wittnam was in the TC's hatch of his Charlie Company command track, fourth from the front of his column of vehicles. Just in front of him was Alpha Company. He knew that the change in the order of the column meant that the CAAT vehicles and Bravo Company were out in front by the railroad bridge. From the radio reports, he could tell that they were in contact with tanks and machine-gun fire. He pictured again the map of the city and the satellite images that he had pored over for months. It was how the modern Marine Corps taught the art of combat. *Visualize the battlefield, visualize potential problems, and visualize how to solve them.* They were taught to run a mental video of the battlefield through their heads so when it came to the real thing they could predict how the battle would unfold, how to react, and where and when was the best place to make a move. And the more you mentally downloaded those maps and images, the more efficiently you could control your battle. *Make the enemy fight your fight. Don't get suckered into reacting and fighting his fight.* General Mattis had sent a prebattle message to his marines before they crossed the line of departure: *"Be the hunter, not the hunted."*

Wittnam was feeling confident in his abilities. He was well versed in the military principle of Commander's Intent. It was drummed into him when he was a young marine, and from the first day of training he had drummed it into the marines under his command. Know what the commander wants to achieve at the end of the day and put all your efforts into achieving that aim. It appeared in all the Marine Corps warfighting documents. *"Commander's Intent is the commander's vision of what he intends to have happen to the enemy."* It was a doctrine that gave everyone, from company commanders down to the grunt on the ground, a role in decision making, enabling them to act in a changing environment in the absence of additional orders.

"Palehorse 6, this is Palehorse 1. We are receiving sporadic gunfire from buildings to the left of our position. Nothing we can't handle, over."

It was Lieutenant Scott Swantner, leader of 1st Platoon, Charlie Company, letting him know what was going on. Wittnam was pleased that his platoon leaders were giving him information about enemy activity. His marines were trained to be as clear as possible about where it was coming from and its strength. What you didn't want to do, though, is clog the airways or give too much information that wouldn't be of any use to anyone.

"Roger that. Keep your eye on it."

Behind Wittnam's track in the hatch of Charlie 208 was Lieutenant Ben Reid, Charlie's FiST leader. He was monitoring the radio when he heard that the CAAT team had encountered tanks at the railway bridge. He heard the battalion staff coordinating the fight up ahead and the cheers as the CAAT team launched some TOWs at enemy tanks.

He got hold of his artillery forward observer, Fred Pokorney.

"This is pretty impressive. Battalion is doing pretty good at controlling the engagements."

The amount of communications on the net was increasing with every minute that went by. Reid now realized that there was a real fight up ahead by the railway bridge. F/A-18 Hornets streaked by, shooting up stuff in the tree line. Over the battalion net there was a confused chat about the red smoke in the air.

"What is that red smoke and where is it coming from?"

Reid knew that it was the trail of the Zuni rockets fired by the Cobras at the tree line. He tried to get comms with battalion to find out what the helos were engaging and what their frequencies were. He felt frustrated that he wasn't able to let his company commander, Dan Wittnam, know what the fire support situation was. He wasn't at the front line, but nevertheless he felt control of the fight slipping away from him.

And then came an order from the battalion commander that confused him. It was just before noon.

"We got to take those bridges. Alpha, take the southern bridge. Charlie, take the northern bridge. If we don't take those bridges now, regiment will give our mission to LAR."

Reid spoke with Pokorney to check that he'd heard correctly. He didn't like the sound of the order. It was hasty and rushed, and somehow that hastiness was passed on down the radio. And what did it mean that they are going to give the mission to the Light Armored Reconnaissance units? Was it some sort of threat to get them moving?

"Hey, he's not projecting a whole lot of confidence in the way he gave that order."

It gave him a bad feeling. He felt that an element of panic had just been introduced. One minute they were planning to establish a defense to the south of the city, and then out of the blue they were going to carry out the "be prepared to" mission and take the bridges. Suddenly, the battalion net he was monitoring went crazy. *The net has just gone to shit. Everyone is stepping on each other. They're all talking at the same time.* He heard intermittent chatter and recognized who was talking from their call signs, but he found it hard to build up a coherent picture of what was going on.

"Hey, Timberwolf, this is Badger, be advised we've got two enemy tanks that we're engaging."

"Roger that."

"We've destroyed these tanks."

"I've got enemy infantry at my position."

"Where are we supposed to be?"

"Alpha, what is your position?"

"Small-arms fire from the left and the right."

First Lieutenant Conor Tracy, the vehicle commander of AAV Charlie 204, also heard the order over the radio. He could hear from the chatter over the company radio that the order had spread confusion throughout Charlie Company.

"Are we really going up there?"

"I am not sure what he said. What do you think he said?"

"I'm not sure. I think we're going to go in."

The movement forward had been carried out deliberately and methodically. Suddenly, it had turned into a rush. What worried Tracy more than the rapid escalation in the speed of the movement was that they still didn't have tanks with them. He felt it was suicide to go into an urban environment without tanks. They had planned to seize the bridges in a certain order and with tanks in front. It seemed now that things had changed. *What's going on? We're in the wrong order and there are no tanks up ahead.*

The marines from his track were dismounted, clearing buildings to the east. He realized that regardless of whether they had tanks or not, the order had been given to move into the city. And speed was vital. *We've got to get going.*

In the driver's seat of 201, Lance Corporal Edward Castleberry was also surprised by the battalion commander's order.

"Push, push, push. We don't want to lose this fight to LAR."

Castleberry was momentarily thrown by the tone of the radio message. *Who the hell cares who fights the battle?*

In the TC's hatch behind him, Lieutenant Swantner popped his head out and looked for his platoon. Adrenaline was now pumping, and Castleberry heard him yell at the top of his voice.

"Back in the tracks. We're moving. We're moving."

Private First Class Robinson was pulling security by the side of the road when he heard the order. He noticed an urgency in Swantner's voice that hadn't been there before. His earlier lethargy was disappearing. He felt his heart pumping. They all piled back into the track. For the past few hours he had been almost numb to the continuous stop, start, dismount, mount-up routine. He'd done it all in a daze. But now there was something about the way everyone was acting that made Robinson think that this was for real. As they pulled out onto the hardball road, he picked up bits from the radio but couldn't understand what it all meant. Amid all the noise and crackle he had trouble putting it all together.

"Army stuck in the city . . . heavy casualties . . . we're going in . . . say again . . . where are the tanks? . . . keep pushing, keep pushing . . . we're going to take the bridges."

He thought for a moment. *This isn't how it's supposed to be. This is weird.* He was expecting a fragmentary order, something just to let them all know what was going on. One last briefing. Anything to prepare them for what they were going to do. He knew that several options had been planned. But the latest order they had received the night before was that they were going to set up a defensive position south of the city and go into the city the next day. *Has that changed? Are we going to go right into the city?* Whatever they were doing, it seemed as though there just wasn't time to go through the plan. AAV 201 started to move off real quick. Ahead he saw flames and smoke and helos pounding positions in the city. He heard loud explosions above the roar of the amtrack. Minutes earlier the marines in his track had been talking about which girls they were going to hook up with back home. Now it went kind of quiet. Looking out over the flat, barren landscape he suddenly longed for the sights and sounds of home: the waves rolling onto Santa Cruz's beaches, the smells from the beachfront food stalls, the yelling and screaming from the Giant Dipper roller coaster on the boardwalk. There was no turning back. They were heading right into the action.

II

AMBUSH ALLEY

1230–1600 Hours

1

Gunnery Sergeant Randy Howard, commander of 2nd Platoon, Company A, 8th Tank Battalion, led his four tanks at full speed back from the refueling point, up and over the railway bridge to rejoin Bravo Company. Second Platoon tanks had been assigned to Bravo Company to "mech" them up into Team Mech, a mechanized unit with an armored punch, for their attack into the city. The other tanks from his company were still back in the rear refueling. As Howard crested the railway bridge, he saw the smoking T-55 tanks that the CAAT vehicles had shot up moments earlier. He was shocked at how the day had quickly escalated into a series of violent firefights.

The CAAT vehicles and Bravo's AAVs parted to let Howard's tanks come through to the head of the column. Captain Newland, the Bravo Company commander, was waiting for him. He was anxious to get moving toward the Euphrates Bridge. There was a quick discussion, then Howard jumped back on his tank and led the column the two kilometers or so from the railway bridge to the Euphrates. Behind him were the CAAT vehicles, Bravo's AAVs, and the forward command element. But it was Gunnery Sergeant Howard and his four tanks that were the tip of the spear. He passed through some sort of palm tree grove and then, up ahead, he saw at last the plain concrete bridge span with a slight rise as it crossed the Euphrates River. As the tanks rumbled across the bridge, he went through his mission again. He could see the mouth of Ambush Alley, the route that went from the foot of the Euphrates Bridge to the northern bridge over the canal. He knew that he had to avoid that route by looking for a road to the right, one that would take them through the eastern part of the city.

Howard had joined the Marines relatively late in life. He was thirty-three when he walked into the recruiting office. The recruiter had said he was too old and suggested he joined the reserves. He knew he wasn't going to run around with the grunts so he looked for a different Military Occupational Speciality. *I'm not going to hump a pack around at my age.* He chose to be a tanker. Right out of tank school, he'd been sent to fight in Desert Storm. Now, fourteen years later and having spent one weekend a month and two weeks per year training at Fort Knox in Kentucky, he was once again in combat.

It was 1245. Howard saw the edge of the city and Ambush Alley cutting right through it. As he dropped into the city from the bridge, he looked to the right for a turn to take him through the city outskirts. But all he saw was a wide, open, dusty expanse of land. It was not how he'd imagined it from the maps. He saw no roads off to the east of Ambush Alley. He didn't realize it, but to turn east, he first had to turn west and then double back on himself toward the river to get on the road that headed east, along the Euphrates. The only option he saw from his position was to move north along Ambush Alley. As he got closer, he saw that the mouth of Ambush Alley was a wide four-lane highway, crisscrossed with telegraph and power poles, and with a concrete strip down the middle. The city looked to him like a mass of gray, low-rise buildings, haphazardly laid out in a way that seemed to bear no resemblance to the straight, well-defined lines on his map. A dusty haze covered the whole city, making it even harder to distinguish between its various features. It looked like the sort of place you might get lost in and never find your way out from. He listened for instructions on the radio, but the radio was silent. All of a sudden he felt alone. With no order to the contrary from Captain Newland, he pushed forward.

It was the muzzle flashes he saw first. They were bursts of light from windows, roofs, and bunkers dug in by the side of the road. Then he felt a few rounds whiz by his head. He saw black-robed Iraqis running from one building to another. Then another group darted across the street in front of him. More appeared in an alleyway to his left. A "technical," a white pickup with a gun mounted in the back, poked its nose out of an alleyway to the side of him. Howard traversed the turret and shot it on the run with the main gun.

Two tanks behind, in *Death Mobile,* Gunnery Sergeant George Insko, the 2nd Platoon sergeant, scanned the area on the left side of the road. Through his sights, he saw a game of soccer in progress on a dusty field. He watched as one by one, the group of men stopped playing and looked up in surprise at the tanks on the road. Then, in one rush, they all charged toward him. *Why are they trying to rush unarmed at a tank?* Out of the corner of his eye he saw that they were running toward a stash of weapons near a building only twenty feet away. The marines in the tanks let out a spray of fire from the coax, scattering the group and knocking some of them to the ground. Those who survived just picked themselves up and reached cover by running into a passage between some buildings. From the roof of a mosque, a machine gun opened up on them. There was an MPAT round in the chamber of the main gun. Insko was not supposed to fire at places of worship unless he identified them as a legitimate target. With a huge *boom,* the roof of the mosque crumbled, spilling body parts out into the street below.

Randy Howard, at the head of the column, was about three blocks into Ambush Alley wondering what the hell they were getting into when his radio crackled into action.

"This is Mustang 6. Make a right when you can. Repeat, make a right."

It was the Bravo Company commander, Captain Tim Newland. He was worried that Howard was going to lead his tanks and the rest of Bravo Company straight up Ambush Alley. Howard found an opening to his right.

"Driver. Hard right. Hard right."

He was glad to be off the main highway in the shelter of buildings. They were two-story-high cinder-block structures, closely packed around a network of paved and unpaved streets and alleys, some no wider than twenty meters. In front of many houses were courtyards enclosed by three-meter-high walls. He weaved his way through the streets on the east side of the city, hoping to get to the large open area he'd seen on the map. The streets were so narrow that the side of his tank scraped walls and telephone poles. *We've got to be careful that we don't hit some high-tension cables and electrocute ourselves.* Figures ran in and out of buildings ahead of him. Cars and trucks quickly disappeared each time he emerged from around a corner. He saw muzzle flashes from windows and roofs, but the sound of gunfire was muted by the roar of his M1A1. In gaps between the houses, he saw pools of green, stagnant water. The area was littered with junk and mud puddles. The paved streets gave way to what looked like hard-packed mud roads. He was about eighty meters ahead of the rest of the convoy and had just emerged into a wide-open area when he felt the tank grind to a halt. *Why have we stopped?* Then suddenly his driver spoke to him through the headset.

"Gunny, we're stuck."

Howard looked around him. He felt his tank slowly shift and realized with horror that he was sinking. It was one of the most shocking feelings he'd ever had. He just couldn't quite believe it. His M1A1 tank just kept sinking until the treads were almost completely covered in mud.

"What the fuck?"

Iraqis, some in uniform, were now running through the streets toward him. Some were preparing grenades as they ran. *They are going to overrun me.* He pulled his pistol out. His driver tried to work his way out of the mud but the treads just dug in even deeper. *This is it. This might be the end of me.*

"We've got another tank stuck."

He knew that his wingman, Staff Sergeant Dominic Dillon, was coming up behind him. For some days the turret power on Dillon's tank had been malfunctioning and the only way to work the turret was to turn the turret by the manual hand crank. Fortunately, the main guns on both tanks were still functioning. He looked back and now saw that Dillon's tank, thirty meters or so behind him, was also floundering in mud. Neither of the tanks was going anywhere. The well-planned maneuver was turning into a chaotic debacle. Howard yelled into his headset.

"Watch out for anything. Kill whatever you can. Just keep them off us."

The third tank, Gunnery Sergeant Insko's *Death Mobile*, came around the corner. Insko had heard the yelling over the radio and knew that the other tanks were stuck. He tried to take extra care, maneuvering over what he was sure was hard-packed mud. He couldn't believe it when he, too, ground to a halt, and watched in horror as his tank also started to sink. He jumped off the tank, but he tripped and landed with such force that he swallowed the mouthful of tobacco that he was chewing. For a few seconds he just lay there gagging and puking as rounds landed around him. *I've got to warn Harrell.*

Insko, whose civilian job was as a network engineer at the University of Kentucky, quickly got on the radio to Staff Sergeant Aaron Harrell, who commanded the fourth tank, and warned him to stay away. Twenty-eight-year-old Harrell, a shift manager at a CVS pharmacy, had had a mechanical failure and had set off a minute later than the other tanks. Fortunately, he had missed the initial turn and had made his way to the group of tanks by an alternative, safer route. The sight that greeted him shocked him. In his eight-year career as a tanker, Harrell had been involved in many recovery operations, but he had never seen tanks stuck like this. Three tanks were completely immobile in thick, squelching mud. They were buried up to the top of the treads. The stink was awful. Harrell saw that what he thought was hard mud was just a thin layer of hard crust concealing a bog of watery mud and sewage. *What do we do now?*

Corporal Neville Welch was posting air security in a track near the front of Bravo's column as they followed the M1A1 tanks across the bridge. *This is it.* He felt the marines inside the track below him tense up with anxiety. He scanned the horizon and kept up his mantra. *I'm not going to be hit. That's not my way of doing business.* It was a refrain he'd used since they crossed the Line of Departure in Kuwait. *We are not here to interview people. We are here to kill Iraqis. We're here to get the message to Baghdad that this is a reality. And I'm coming back alive.* It was the same harsh determination that had got him out of Guyana into college in the United States and had made him plunge into the serious business of studying hard to get his degree. Some of the other marines saw the mission as a great adventure. Welch didn't. From day one, he had not had a humorous moment. He knew a guy named Elik who had picked up a discarded Iraqi RPG and fooled around with it. His entire face got lit up. No, this was serious, and he wasn't going to take anything for granted. And when it was all over, he would know that he had made his contribution. Even though he still spoke with a Caribbean accent, nobody would be able to claim to be more American than he was.

The bridge was a plain two-lane span with a low barrier on either side. As they crossed it, Welch felt a chill. *They might blow the bridge. It might be booby-trapped.* He was acutely aware of his own nervousness and shouted down to the marines in the belly of the track.

"Get your asses up here and provide more firepower."

Sandbags lined the top of the hatch to give rifle support and to slow down incoming rounds. Inside, some marines were nervously flicking through their one copy of *FHM* magazine or eating MREs from the two boxes that they kept with them. Anything to distract from nerves and anxiety.

Inside one of the tracks behind Welch, another Bravo infantryman, Lance Corporal Leslie Walden, nervously fingered his M16. His emotions were all mixed up and his stomach was churning. He heard rounds smacking against the side of the track and the marines up in the hatches firing back. He'd read all the intel briefs and knew what was supposed to happen once they got to Nasiriyah, but somehow it didn't seem to match the reality of being in the rear of a track and being shot at. He had no idea what was around the next corner. *At some stage, I'm going to have to get out of this track and face what is waiting for me outside.*

As the convoy came over the bridge, a large, smiling portrait of Saddam Hussein came into view on the right-hand side. Some marines on air security reached for their disposable cameras and clicked away. Neville Welch was glad that at last they were doing something concrete. The drive up had been so long, boring, and featureless. But now the air was thick with nervous excitement. They had reached a town, they were seeing things they hadn't seen before, they were going into battle. The odd crackle of gunfire rang out from the opposite bank. Welch couldn't tell where it was coming from. Whoever was firing at them seemed to be poor marksmen. Somehow they managed to miss seriously hitting any of the twenty vehicles in the long, lumbering column.

The convoy came off the bridge and Welch saw in front of him a wide, dusty four-lane highway dotted with telephone poles and power lines. On either side were large open areas that gave way to a labyrinth of two- and three-story buildings stretching into the center of town. Figures were swarming up ahead of them. About two hundred meters along the road, the Bravo convoy turned to the right into an area of low mud brick houses, separated by large algae-covered pools of mud. As the convoy of tracks passed, Welch saw Iraqis standing by the side of the road looking up at him, almost nonchalantly, as though it was the most normal thing in the world.

Some of the kids started waving at the convoy as it weaved between the houses. The marines in back of the track, M16s and pistols at the ready, waved back.

Suddenly, out of nowhere, a burst of gunfire cracked through the air above Welch's head. Marines ducked into the amtrack, dropping their pistols and coming back up with their M16s. The .50-caliber machine gunner on the amtrack let out a short burst at the windows of one of the mud brick houses, tearing chunks from the building. The convoy kept moving. Marines who had been waving at the kids seconds before were now raking gunfire into the surrounding buildings.

A cry went up.

"Tanks are stuck, tanks are stuck. We can't move."

"We're sinking. We're fucking sinking."

As Welch's track turned a corner into a large open area, he saw a pathetic sight. Three tanks and one AAV were half-submerged and floundering helplessly in pools of mud. The tank commanders were yelling their heads off, urging the drivers, with a stream of obscenities, to hit the gas. The treads just whirled uselessly through the soft, wet ground, unable to get a grip and digging even bigger holes. Welch shuddered with disbelief. Tanks were such a major part of the battalion's strength and security. They provided massive firepower, offered security and protection. To see them go down like that was bewildering. Welch felt a shock wave of panic pass through the whole company.

Following behind the tanks, the CAAT vehicles, and Bravo Company, the two tracks and Humvees of the forward command post containing Lieutenant Colonel Grabowski, Major David Sosa, and part of the battalion command staff, crossed the long span of the Euphrates Bridge.

"There is no turning back now. We are committed." In planning meetings, Grabowski had talked about "going into the bowels of hell." It didn't feel so different. *God knows what's waiting for us on the other side of the bridge.* An RPG skipped across the road, narrowly missing the vehicle in front. Rounds whizzed overhead, but he was so busy coordinating the movement on the radio that he hardly noticed. His vehicle crested the span and headed toward the entrance to the city. Now he could see that the lead tanker, a kilometer or so in front of him, had missed the first turn toward the east and was heading up Ambush Alley. He was just about to call Captain Newland to find out what was going on when he saw the tanker take the next road to the east. *At least he's heading east. That's not so bad.* He saw the convoy turn into a narrow labyrinth of small alleys and roads with power lines overhead.

Grabowski had tried for days to get aerial overflights of the eastern half of the city to find out what the terrain was like. He and his staff had never managed to build up a convincing picture. From the maps, it looked as though they would be able to find a way through the eastern part of the city to an open area from where they could head north to the canal bridge.

But as he came down the span of the bridge into Ambush Alley it looked very different, more open than how he'd imagined it from the maps. There was a flow of information coming to him across the net from Bravo Company and the C7 command track. Some commanders traveled in the C7 command track, but Grabowski preferred the freedom of a Humvee. He found it easier to see what was going on from the front seat of a light mobile Humvee rather than from the back of a windowless track. Besides, they always seemed to have problems with comms in the C7. He knew, though, that at some stage he would have to stop and set up a proper forward CP. It was difficult to communicate when constantly on the move. He was just turning to the east when the radio call came through.

"The tanks are stuck. We've got tanks down."

Tanks stuck. What does that mean? He recognized that something had gone wrong, but at that moment it didn't really make much sense. He followed the convoy through the streets and alleys of a poor, ragged neighborhood where the buildings were tumbling down and roads petered out into little more than bumpy dirt tracks. As he came around a corner, next to two houses in front of an open area, he saw his command-and-control vehicle, the C7, which contained the battalion's staff and communications equipment, sink up to its axles in deep mud. It happened so quickly that he saw it almost drop down to its belly until mud covered the treads.

The battalion net was just going crazy.

"We've lost another tank."

"Now another one has gone down."

"We're losing our Humvee."

Grabowski's movement forward had been completely halted. He jumped out of the Humvee and ran over to the C7. The driver was working the treads trying to get the C7 out, but it was just sinking further into the bog. He could now see that what looked like hard mud was in fact a thin crust of dirt covering pools of slimy mud. *This is not a good situation.*

"Timberwolf, this is Mustang 6. We are now receiving small-arms fire. Several vehicles are stuck."

It was the Bravo Company commander, Captain Tim Newland. He was only a few hundred yards away on a parallel street. *What sort of mess are we in?*

Two Iraqis in uniform were lying dead in the dirt. At first Grabowski thought his marines had shot some cops, but Chief Warrant Officer David Dunfee, the gunner, looked at the uniforms and confirmed that they were military. He was already looking through their pockets for maps and documents that might be useful later.

The level of incoming fire was increasing. Grabowski was nearly deaf in one ear and couldn't hear the rounds whizzing past his head. He was too focused on how they were going to get out of there. Dunfee yelled at him.

"Hey, sir, you need to get the fuck down."

Grabowski looked around at his young marines. *There are a lot of scared Marines out there, and I'm one of them.* They were running around disoriented and confused. *Jesus Christ. If we have guys starting to panic we're going to have a real problem on our hands.*

Corporal Welch was torn away from the terrible sight of seeing the tanks slowly sinking further into the bog by the yell of the marines around him.

"Get out. Everybody get out. Everybody OUT."

It was SOP to get out as quickly as possible when a track went down.

The ramp on his track lowered and dazed marines scrambled out, their M16s swiveling. They were running in all directions, some of them bumping into each other. Their confused sergeants and lieutenants were trying to organize them into some sort of defensive perimeter to keep the tanks and Humvees from being overwhelmed by the enemy. Welch had done plenty of training in Military Operations on Urban Terrain, but now, out in this alien environment, he was lost. MOUT had taught him about fighting in cities, about street plans—radial, ray, rectangular, and combined street patterns—about how to stay alive in urban terrain and keep situational awareness. But the area in front of him seemed to have no pattern. Paved streets turned into dirt tracks and rectangular blocks of buildings gave way to wide-open spaces dotted with green, slimy water holes. He was third man from the front and tried to exert some sort of control over his fire team.

"Jones, you got the front. Manah, you got the rear. Nguyen, keep your eyes open."

He wanted to put Jones with his M16 in front as point man. His weapon was light, and he could react quickly. It sounded cruel, but they were taught to put the inexperienced and youngest at the front. If he was shot, those with more experience and bigger weapons would still have a chance. But a good point man could save lives.

"Jones, keep eyeballing what's ahead of you.

"Watch your weapon. Keep your rifle pointed away from marines."

Welch wanted each member of his team to have a clear field of fire. He'd been taught how easy it was to shoot each other accidentally in combat. He wanted to keep them all together and alert.

"Watch out for incoming."

They skirted a wall and went to the right. To his horror, he realized he'd led them straight into a dead end. Figures in black scurried on the roofs overhead. Muzzle flashes exploded from windows. Fire rained down on them from all sides. Welch's team pressed themselves into doorways and gaps in the walls and returned fire. It was like the training they did in the specially constructed town at Camp Lejeune.

"Hajjis on the roof to your right."

He saw marines fall to the ground around him as they tried to protect the tanks. *Shit's not going right. This is chaos.* He watched in disbelief as a tanker, the man who had all of the M1A1's enormous combat power under his control, climbed on the turret of his tank and uselessly fired a 9 mm pistol at Iraqis on the rooftops. He had imagined losing a track or a tank to enemy fire, an RPG or something, *but not to the earth.* Some of the dismounted marines were wading through the mud, trying vainly to stop the tracks, tanks, and Humvees from sinking further. One marine was up to his waist attaching a towrope to the track's underbelly. When he started sinking, other marines had to run over and pull him out. An amtrack pulled up alongside and took up the slack of the towrope. As it took the strain, that one, too, churned uselessly in the mud and began to sink.

Am I going to get home and see my wife or am I going to become a statistic? There was not enough time to ponder or contemplate. He had a quiet word with God and began again his mantra. *I am not going to get killed. I am going to get home and chill out.*

He went into action, firing down alleyways, onto rooftops, through windows. He went back to his training. *You gotta keep firing, keep taking cover, keep seeking concealment, you gotta keep putting rounds downrange. Maintain your situational awareness. No time to think of anything else.* They were in a bad position, exposed and in the open. They were inviting a firefight. He saw rounds go off all around him. A shot rang out, another from his rear, more from the rooftops. He went back to the basics of his infantry training and the mission of a marine rifle platoon—*"to locate, close with, and destroy the enemy by fire and maneuver."* In his mind, he laid down a challenge to those who were trying to kill him. *If you got it, bring it on, or we'll take it to you.*

Lance Corporal Leslie Walden was providing security down an alleyway across the street. With him in the narrow alley were about ten other marines, trying to find a way to push forward through the mazelike streets. On the roof opposite he saw a couple of Iraqi soldiers moving around as though they were trying to get in position.

"We got hajjis on the roof over here."

Walden let out a burst of suppressive fire, and the whole squad tried to find their way out of the alley. As he rounded a corner, he glanced back over his shoulder to see the outline of a man with an RPG on his shoulder aiming straight toward him. *Holy shit. He's gonna shoot.* Walden remained frozen to the spot as the ominous dark shape of the missile came hurtling toward him trailing a plume of white smoke.

"Oh shit."

The RPG passed by him and exploded on the ground ten feet away, picking him off the ground and hurling him into a wall. For several seconds he remained slumped on the ground. A group of marines ran over to him and hauled him away.

"Walden. Can you hear me? Are you okay?"

Groggily, Walden opened his eyes. He patted himself down, checked for broken bones and blood, tried to shrug off the ringing in his ears, and continued the fight.

Corporal Welch saw his buddy Walden fly through the air and sink to the ground. He thought at first that he was dead. The heaviness of despair momentarily came over him. As soon as he'd realized that the battalion was going into the city without a full complement of tanks, he'd had a bad feeling. He crouched behind a wall, trying to catch his breath and keep at bay the sense of panic that was beginning to surge up inside him. *This is a suicide mission.*

Major David Sosa, traveling alongside Grabowski, tried to get a handle on the mess they were in. He could hardly take in the sight of three of his tanks mired in thick mud. They represented a huge loss of firepower and protection. Just in front of them two Humvees were almost upended in the bog. His driver slowed down and steered away to avoid getting caught himself. He turned back to see the C7 and P7 command tracks rapidly sinking up to their axles. Sosa looked at the C7 and was horrified. The track contained all their comms equipment. *My God. We've lost command and control of this fight.*

His radio was squawking with the sound of panicked marines, all trying to talk on the net at once. He felt a shudder of panic, as if everything was collapsing around them. *If we are in this sort of mess, what on earth is going on with the other companies?*

2

A couple of kilometers south of the Euphrates River, Alpha Company's commander, Captain Mike Brooks, waited for the tail end of Bravo Company to pass through his position. As the last of Bravo's AAVs and Humvees roared past him and over the bridge, he reached for the radio.

"Let's move on out."

Alpha Company's three lead tracks, filled with marines from 1st Platoon under Second Lieutenant Matt Carr, bounced onto the road followed by Brooks, fourth in line in the command track A304. Eight other tracks filled with marines from 2nd and 3rd Platoons and two Humvees brought up the rear. Brooks felt a rush of adrenaline revive his tired and aching body. He looked around the track. With him in the command track was the FiST team—artillery and mortar forward observers to provide fire support, the FAC or forward air controller to call in air strikes, a couple of radio operators, and a young AAV crew. His company packed a formidable punch. Sitting across from him was a journalist from the London *Sunday Times*. He didn't really mind having him there. It was a good thing that the public could get to read about how the marines served their country. He was more worried about letting rip with a string of swear words. What was peculiar was that the embedded journalists seemed to have had more combat experience than the marines. The British journalist with him had even been asked to hold classes for the marines about life in a combat zone.

Brooks had spent weeks on ship rehearsing this maneuver, but although they had changed the order in which the companies would attack the bridge, it didn't seem to matter. Things were going to plan, just like a well-executed football play. He felt comfortable and in control. From his position at the heart of the column, he could see what 1st Platoon was doing and was ready to help them out if they got into trouble. He could also issue orders to the marines behind. As his convoy approached the bridge, Brooks heard the *tink, tink* of small-arms fire hitting the track's aluminum frame. And then, out of nowhere, there was a *whoosh* as an RPG, fired from the far bank, shot across the road in front of them.

In the tracks behind, marines from 2nd Platoon were crouched in the darkness, swaying with fatigue in the belly of the track as they rumbled toward the bridge. There was the *ping* of metal hitting metal. To those inside it sounded like the popping of popcorn. Most of them had never heard the sound of rounds hitting the outside of their track.

"What's that?"

Lance Corporal Christopher Rigolato was on air security, standing on one of the benches with his torso out of the roof hatch, when the bullets started hitting the track. At first he couldn't hear anything above the noise of the track's diesel engine, but then he caught the unmistakable crack of a bullet as it whizzed past his head. He heard explosions, maybe mortars, off to the side.

"What's going on up there? What can you see? We can't see. Tell us what's going on."

From inside the track, marines demanded to know what was happening. Rigolato could tell their questions were tinged with panic. But Rigolato couldn't see what was going on, either. The thick black smoke from one of the tanks that the CAAT platoon had killed earlier was blowing right across the road and into his face, and he could hardly see where they were going, let alone who was shooting at them. Every time a cloud of dust blew past, he had to duck to avoid it and immediately lost situational awareness. He tried to tell them about the smoke, the noise, the explosions, the RPG that just flew down the road in front of them, leaving a plume of white smoke, but it was all happening so fast that he couldn't get the words out. The black smoke parted and Rigolato found they were on the bridge, crossing the wide expanse of the Euphrates. The flowing river and palm tree–lined banks were a shock to his eyes after days of nothing but desert and scrub. Another RPG whooshed past and he was tossed from side to side as his AAV swerved to avoid the rocket. Up ahead, it looked as though the road was on fire. Flaming vehicles pouring out thick smoke littered the entrance to the city. *It looks like all the war movies I've ever watched, but now I'm in the middle of one.*

Two tracks ahead of Rigolato, Captain Brooks was trying to get his bearings. He was coming off the bridge into the city, but somehow none of it looked as he imagined it from the maps. He looked for the wide expanse of road running northwest through the city that he'd expected to find as soon as he crossed the bridge, but he couldn't see it. He saw muzzle flashes from the buildings ahead of him. *This isn't the welcome we were expecting.* He pressed forward, deeper into the city, and found what he was looking for—an open area of road to his left that gave him a clear view into the heart of the city. The wide-open space reminded him of the Mall in Washington, D.C. There were two-story cinder-block houses on either side with a mosque and a large mural of Saddam on the left-hand side. He was in a good strategic position at the junction of the road heading northwest and at the entrance to what some marines had named Ambush Alley, the main road heading north to the canal bridge. He looked back toward the Euphrates Bridge and was startled at how far he was from it. *We must have come five hundred meters into the city.* It was much farther than he'd planned. *I hope we don't get isolated here.*

In the tracks behind, marines from 2nd Platoon were getting nervous. Beads of sweat trickled down their faces. They nervously fingered their rifles and let out a string of expletives as each new explosion rocked their vehicles. Lance Corporal Jacob Anderson felt a gnawing anxiety eating away inside him. For hours they'd been sitting in the darkness, in the same position, next to the same guys, wondering what was going to happen next. He really had no idea what he was getting himself into. Now he just wanted to get out into the open, even if it meant running into a firefight. *Nothing in training has prepared me for this.*

"Get ready to dismount—ramp opening."

The tracks wheeled around and came to a halt, back-to-back in a defensive position. The hydraulic rear ramps slowly dropped, letting light flood across the marines inside. Anderson fought with the others to scramble out. As the marines came tumbling out, it was chaos. Blinking in the sunlight, Anderson ran in all directions, disorientated, looking for cover as he'd been trained. Gunfire echoed all around.

"Dismount."

"Get over here."

"Get the fuck down."

Sergeants and lieutenants were shouting out orders. Cobras and Hueys were clattering overhead. Mortar crashed into the dust around him. There was fear, excitement, and the rush of adrenaline all mixed up together. He tried to work out where he was. He saw the river behind him, the wide road running into the city. He looked for his fellow squad members, but all he could see was a blur of running bodies. *This is like a video game. But I'm in it.*

As soon as the ramp on his track dropped, Lance Corporal Christopher Rigolato headed for the cover of a wall. An RPG smashed into the telephone pole above his head. Rigolato felt overwhelmed with confusion.

"Move over here."

"Move, move. Let's go."

"We're moving to the other side of the road."

It was his platoon commander yelling at them. Rigolato and most of 2nd Platoon were just north of the bridge on the west side of the four-lane highway he knew as Ambush Alley. It looked a long way to the other side, maybe fifty meters. There was no cover. It was just a wide-open expanse of road. When the order came, he gripped his M16, jumped over a metal barrier, put his head down, and ran as bursts of machine-gun and small-arms fire erupted all around him.

Lance Corporal Dante Reece, with the rest of 3rd Squad alongside him, tried to cross the road after him. Reece was struggling to get his heavy squad automatic weapon across the metal barrier. They had just gotten halfway across the road when an RPG came flying out of a building from the north, whizzed toward them, and passed right through the middle of the squad. It had missed him by inches. Reece looked at the others in surprise. Sweat and dirt stained their faces. Reece couldn't take it in. He felt he was in denial. He tried to pull himself together. *This is for real. This is for real.* But he still wasn't sure if this really was happening.

Anderson followed them across the road at a sprint.

"Anderson, over here."

Gratefully, he dived behind a mound of earth, pleased to be back with his squad again. With Lance Corporal Van Gipson he formed a line along a berm, covering the southern flank toward the river. Incoming rounds started hitting the ground around them, sending up dirt as they cracked by. Anderson turned to Gipson with wide eyes and they both rolled down into the ditch, laughing. Some reacted to fear by sweating and trembling. Anderson and Gipson laughed uncontrollably.

"They're actually shooting at us."

The two of them lay in the ditch panting with elation. Then seconds later, reality set in.

What happens if I get shot? For the first time, Anderson was scared. He didn't have time to linger on his fear. *If it's my time, it's my time.*

From the TC's hatch Brooks watched his marines dismount and scatter into a 180-degree perimeter. He was heartened at the way they reacted. He'd seen many of them in action at the combined arms exercise over the summer when they'd practiced as a helo-borne company. Several had struggled through training, getting things badly wrong because they were either out of shape, lazy, or just slow. He knew some of them had checkered backgrounds, were troublemakers, and carried a whole lot of baggage with them. Now, amid the flying metal, the explosions, and the swirling dust, he saw all that stuff go away. Individually, they were nothing special, but when they came together they were amazing. They were moving together, reacting to what was going on around them, taking the initiative.

There was a coherence, which gave him an enormous sense of pride. He was surprised that the marines who had struggled with training were now the ones who seemed to be taking control.

With all the noise and chaos, Brooks couldn't actually see who was firing at them. He had a good view up the road into the city, but there was no sign of tanks, artillery, or mortars. He didn't see anyone in uniform. *But something was going on.* He pulled out his binoculars. Figures appeared in the alleyways ahead of him, on roofs, in windows, and then melted into the background. The situation felt sinister. He couldn't put his finger on it, but it reminded him of the opening scenes of the movie *Black Hawk Down.* The figures didn't appear to be armed, but there was something about them that put him on edge. In the distance, he saw white pickup trucks and orange-and-white taxis congregating in the middle of the highway and then careering off down side streets. One taxi filled with young men and flying a white flag came hurtling toward them before screaming into a side alleyway. *Something is about to happen.* He wondered whether the white pickups were *technicals,* improvised fighting vehicles that had been used with success against U.S. forces by irregular fighters in Afghanistan and Somalia.

He looked back to check that the rest of Alpha Company had made it across the bridge and that they had it secured. Then he called the battalion commander. It was 1315.

"Timberwolf, this is Tomahawk 6. We've seized the Euphrates Bridge."

He wanted to be more exact.

"Timberwolf, this is Tomahawk 6. We have secured the bridge, but we are coming under increasingly heavy fire."

He got on the radio to his platoon commanders, who had now taken up position on either side of the road, just north of the bridge.

"Keep your eyes on those people."

His marines had spent months training for legitimate target identification. They didn't want to fire on unarmed civilians, so they had been taught to zero in on hands to look for signs of weapons. He got back on the radio.

"Hey, if you see an Iraqi with a weapon, then we need to take care of it and we need to kill that Iraqi."

The rate of fire was increasing, but it was still something they could easily cope with. There was a brief lull, and then he sensed that it was about to happen. *It's going to boil over.*

When it came, it reminded him of one of those light dimmer switches that is suddenly turned up. All at once RPGs and small-arms fire rained down on them from all sides. Small 60 mm commando mortars were coming in on them from the gaps between houses. To the north, east, and west he saw Iraqis dressed in black running out of alleys, dropping to one knee, and firing off round after round of grenades. Muzzle flashes lit up windows, mortars threw up splashes of rocks and dirt around him, and the sound of rounds cracked just yards from his head. *Oh Lord. What have we got ourselves into?*

3

To the north and east of Alpha's position, on the east side of Ambush Alley, Lieutenant Colonel Grabowski was trying to deal with the chaos unleashed by so many vehicles floundering in the mud bog. Some marines were already out of their vehicles, waist deep in mud, trying to attach towropes. Others were lying in small depressions in the ground, behind mounds, or against walls providing the tankers and trackers with some protection so they could get on with their job. Keeping well away from the mud bog, Grabowski ran to the rear hatch of the C7, which was already half submerged. He couldn't get too close. Standing a couple of meters away from it, he looked into the rear hatch where his fire support–coordination center team was frantically working away at calling in air support, mortar, and artillery fire for the battalion. He yelled into the back of the track.

"Have you got comms?"

His air officer made a slashing movement with his hand.

"Sir, I haven't had comms since we entered the city."

"Well, keep working on it."

The C7 was pushed up against a two-story house. Grabowski wondered whether that was masking transmissions from the PRC-119 radio. It worked on line of sight and was limited to a range of twenty-five kilometers. Any obstructions could block the transmission. The area was also crisscrossed with overhead high-voltage power lines. He wondered whether that was causing electromagnetic interference with the high frequencies of their VHF radios. Thankfully, no one had yet suffered an electric shock from their antennas hitting the power lines. All units had been told to get off the radio when they got close to high-tension lines.

How are we going to get those tanks out? Grabowski knew that the tank company's combat trains had some M88 tank retrievers with them. Doctrinally, the 88s follow in trace of the tank company, but because one of the 88s was towing a broken tank, Grabowski had ordered the combat trains to the rear so that they wouldn't slow the battalion's movement. Now he realized that they were dozens of kilometers from where they needed to be. He got on the radio to Captain William Blanchard, the AAV company commander. Until he got those 88s up, he couldn't get those tanks out. *If I don't get those tanks out, I can't push forward.*

There were now some seven vehicles floundering in the mud. As one of the tracks tried to pull another track free, it also became caught. One of the CAAT Humvees tried to ram another of the Humvees to push it out. It knocked the Humvee free, only to sink into the mud bog itself. A group of Iraqi civilians stood on their doorstoops and watched the marines helplessly running around trying to free the tanks, Humvees, and tracks.

Staff Sergeant Harrell, the CVS pharmacy shift manager, had maneuvered his tank close enough to Staff Sergeant Insko's tank, *Death Mobile*, to reach it with one of his inch-and-a-quarter-thick steel tow cables. He jumped off his tank, ran around to the rear of Insko's tank, and dug away at the mud with his hands in an attempt to get to the attachment points. Just when he thought he could attach the cable, the mud flowed back into the space he had just cleared. Two attempts ended with broken cables and hooks. Finally, he managed to connect one end of the cable to the front of his tank and the other to the rear of Insko's tank. Slowly, his driver reversed away from the mud and pulled Insko's tank clear. Now free from the bog, Staff Sergeant Insko maneuvered *Death Mobile* around a corner to support the rest of the platoon. He had nearly reached Staff Sergeant Dillon's tank when Insko felt *Death Mobile* jolt. Once again, his tank slowly started to sink back in the mud.

Nothing was going right. Harrell kept back a wave of panic. *We're stranded.* The sound of the helicopters flying overhead, pushing back the encroaching Iraqis, reassured him. The *boom* of a main tank round reverberated around the maze of streets and alleys. It was a warning shot to any enemy that tried to get too close.

Corporal Neville Welch, the fire team leader with Bravo Company, now had a clearer vision of the layout of the eastern part of the city. It was set out in a grid pattern of sorts. He'd begun to recognize which streets were likely to be dead ends. His squad leader had ordered him to take his fire team and start expanding the perimeter farther into the city to keep the Iraqi fighters away from the mired tanks. Using walls and vehicles as cover, his four-man team gradually pushed farther out from the tanks, keeping a couple of meters apart so they didn't provide an easy target for the Iraqis shooting at them from the roofs and windows. The marines were taught to turn defense into offense. *The harder you hit the enemy on the battlefield, the more protection you will have. Catch the enemy off guard and you'll lessen his chances of interfering with what you want to do.*

"Jones. Get your head out of your ass."

He tried to keep his team alert. None of them had slept much, and he was aware that he had to keep talking to them, encouraging them, and watching for anyone lagging behind.

"Nguyen. Keep up and stay close."

He demanded fire discipline. The Iraqis were firing at random. He kept his shots down to ten to twelve rounds per minute. He only squeezed the trigger when he had selected his target. Exceeding that rate was a waste of ammo.

Slowly, some order appeared out of the chaos. Fire teams were working within their squads, and soon the squads were working within their platoons.

"First Squad, secure the right flank. Second Squad, you take the rear. Third Squad, you take the left flank."

The barrage of rounds that had greeted them when they first arrived was calming down. Welch and the other infantry marines had pushed the security perimeter well away from the tanks and kept any Iraqi fighters at bay. Crouched behind a wall, M16s and M203 grenade launchers pointing at windows and roofs, Welch and his fire team maintained a precarious peace and waited for their squad leader to give them their next order.

4

As Bravo Company and Alpha Company had moved out to cross the bridge, Charlie's twelve tracks and three Humvees had pulled out from the fields and onto the road behind them. At the head of the column were the three tracks of Second Lieutenant Mike Seely's 3rd Platoon, followed by Captain Wittnam and Lieutenant Tracy in the command track with Lieutenant Reid and the fire support team's track just behind. First and 2nd Platoons followed the FiST track with the Hummers, one equipped with Avenger missiles for air defense, and the first sergeant's medevac track brought up the rear. The original plan called for Charlie to keep close to Bravo Company so that they, too, were protected by the tank platoon assigned to Bravo. But the last-minute change of order meant that Alpha Company was sandwiched between the two companies, leaving Charlie exposed at the rear.

In back of track 201, sixth in line, Private First Class Casey Robinson still wasn't sure where they were going. *That's the trouble with being a grunt. Nobody tells you anything.* Information was handed out on a need-to-know basis. *Apparently I don't need to know.* When he joined the USMC, he thought they would be treated well, given some respect, but after two years he knew that as a grunt, he was the lowest of the low, the bottom of the barrel. Many of his brothers in arms were from broken homes, had police records, and were condemned to live out shitty little lives. Some of them were aware, deep inside, that joining the marines was their chance to make something of their lives. Others didn't want to make it. Robinson was one of those who didn't yet know. He knew he performed excellently in the field. But there was something in him that wanted to destroy and rebel against all he'd achieved. He was proud of being a grunt, proud of being hard, proud of being a rebel, proud of getting into bar fights. Every fight he'd been in was a badge of honor. Only grunts understood. The POGUES didn't have the balls.

He adjusted the barrel of his squad automatic weapon, pointing the M249 out toward the fields on the west side of the road. With him, pulling air security from the hatch, was his team leader, Corporal Wentzel. All the other marines were inside the track, keeping their heads down.

He knew that the other companies had set off some minutes before, and he'd seen the CAAT vehicles roll ahead of them. He expected to see them in the distance. But they had all taken off so fast that all he could see ahead was an open road.

He tried to listen to the snatches of information on the radio.

"Sitrep . . . squad-size element . . . out in the open, west of main MSR. Small arms. Basic infantry."

"Receiving mortar fire from inside the city."

"Gunfire one hundred meters north of railway bridge. West of MSR."

So much information was being passed over the net that he had trouble taking it in. He wasn't a radio operator, but he could tell that there was too much talking on the radio. As the amtracks sped toward the railway bridge, he noticed a new urgency to the radio transmissions. *Something bad is going off.* Without knowing how, he picked up from the transmissions that things were beginning to spin out of control. There was very little he could do. He didn't know much more than that he was in Iraq and the marines were on their way to Baghdad. The higher-ups said they were there to liberate the Iraqi people. But Private First Class Robinson didn't give a shit about that. He would struggle to write a high school essay about Iraq or its people. He hadn't a clue about Shias and Sunnis. All he cared about right now was getting out of the track, firing his weapon, and staying alive.

Ahead of him, to the side of the highway, he saw the charred, smoking hulks of some trucks. Shards of glass from the peppered windshields littered the highway; a mangled gas mask, a lone helmet, and some spent ammo lay in pools of blood. Robinson had no idea that they were U.S. Army trucks. Others in the tracks who had heard the radio transmissions knew exactly whose trucks they were.

"Get up here and look what happened to the friggin' Army."

Twenty marines fought to pop their heads out of the hatches. They let out a collective whistle.

"The Army fucked up again."

They laughed uneasily.

Captain Wittnam, in the fourth track from the front, also saw the railway bridge and, at its foot, the burned-out 507th Army vehicles. *Whoa. They've had a tough time.* He thought about telling his platoon commanders more of what he knew of the 507th, but he didn't want to distract them. He wanted his men to think that things were going well. He needed them focused on their mission to take the bridges. Panic was a virus that replicated itself at speed. Under certain conditions, one small setback can quickly accelerate into a military disaster. That was not going to happen with his company.

One by one, as the Charlie AAVs pushed northward, marines posting air security saw the burned-up smoking vehicles. Lieutenant Reid, in the fifth track, looked over his shoulder and saw some crashed Humvees and two U.S. Army trucks with flames pouring out of the trailers. *What the fuck?*

He got Lieutenant Pokorney on the radio.

"Fred, do you see that? Holy shit, man, that's an Army truck. What the fuck is going on?"

He looked in disbelief at the windshields riddled with bullet holes and the flames licking the canvas covers. He couldn't resist taking out his camera and snapping a couple of pictures.

At the rear of the column in track 211, Lance Corporal Thomas Quirk and the rest of 3rd Platoon were celebrating Lance Corporal James Prince's birthday. Quirk thought he was a goofy sort of guy, but it was good fun singing to him, and everybody in the track joined in a tuneless chorus.

"Happy birthday to you. Happy birthday to you. Happy birthday, dear Prince . . ."

It was something to do. They'd given up playing cards inside the track because it was too crowded. They couldn't play outside because there was too much wind blowing around. They had a few porno mags floating around, but they'd all read them five or six times and were sick of them. Anyway, now that they were moving, rather than sitting in tents in Kuwait with nothing to do, they were all numb to the thrill of flicking through pages of naked girls or reading out the porno stories to each other. Quirk hadn't had sex for three months. He'd been seeing a girl on and off for ten years, and just before he'd gone to Iraq he'd traveled to New York to spend the night with her in her apartment in the Bronx. It was sort of a loose relationship, but they felt really comfortable with each other. She'd already written to him, but each time he started a letter to send back to her he'd crumpled it up. He could never quite put down what he really wanted to tell her. Sometimes he felt there was too much to say. Other times he felt there wasn't enough.

Marines around him took a sharp intake of breath. Thomas Quirk looked up at the commotion. Ahead of him he saw the burned-up 507th convoy. Marines were crawling all over the vehicles, trying to rescue some of the equipment, pulling off machine guns and spare parts before the flames got too high. Some vehicles were already lost. *My God. The Army fucked up badly.* But the charred and mangled Army vehicles were too much to take in. There was too much destruction, too much blood on the road. *This place is fucked up.* It didn't click that this was a real situation, that this was here and now. *It's like seeing your name on a winning lottery ticket and having to look at it three times before you are like, Oh, okay. I guess this is for real.*

Quirk couldn't quell the agitation he was feeling. He started praying. The day had been so exhilarating and his adrenaline was pumping so madly that his head had begun to spin.

"Dear Lord, give me strength for the day ahead . . ."

He'd often prayed to himself during training exercises, to get through the next drill, to complete the next run.

". . . give me a calm heart and clear mind . . ."

Toward the front of the column, First Lieutenant Conor Tracy, in the gunner's hatch of track 204, was just coming up to the railroad bridge when he heard Mike Seely of 3rd Platoon on the company net.

"This is Palehorse 3. Be advised that we've got something wrong with our track. We're trying to fix it. If it's not fixed in three minutes, we're going to execute the bump plan."

Track 209 was down. Tracy was the AAV platoon commander. Those tracks were his responsibility. He wanted all his tracks with him, but he knew that he couldn't hold up the attack. If he didn't fix 209, he would have to "bump" the marines from that track into some of the other tracks. The whole of Charlie Company halted while AAV crewmen tried to get it going again. Each time they thought they'd sorted the problem out, it would break down again. *What are we going to do now with track 209?* He glanced around at the strange situation in which he found himself: trying to fix a track on a dusty highway in Iraq. *What a poor, sad place this is.* He was reminded of his first impressions of Iraq when he crossed over from Kuwait. The first sign of life he'd seen were a few miserable mud huts with a scrawny, weather-beaten bedouin crouched on his heels, tending a scraggly looking herd of goats.

"Hey, Palehorse 6, this is Palehorse 3, we've got to execute our bump plan."

Twenty Marines from the deadlined track 209 dismounted and clambered into tracks 210 and 211. Quirk wasn't pleased. His track, 211, was already pretty full. He and nine other marines clambered out of the hatch and onto the roof of the track to make room for the new marines. He took out a can of Copenhagen to take a wad of tobacco. *We're just about to go into the city. Maybe it's not such a good idea.* Copenhagen tobacco was being traded among the marines for $40 a can. He didn't want to lose it.

In the delay to get 3rd Platoon going again, 1st Platoon had taken the lead. Captain Wittnam's voice came back over the company net.

"All Palehorse units, be advised that Palehorse 1 will take the lead. I say again, Palehorse 1 will take up the lead."

Charlie Company headed toward the Euphrates in a different configuration from the original plan. They were down to eleven tracks with 1st Platoon in the lead, followed by 2nd and 3rd Platoons, with the first sergeant's medevac track and three Humvees bringing up the rear. This configuration meant that Private First Class Casey Robinson, in track 201, was at the very front of the column. There were some twenty other marines with him, including Corporal Jake Worthington, Corporal John Wentzel, Sergeant William Schaefer in the AAV commander's hatch manning the Mark 19 and the .50 cal, and Lieutenant Scott Swantner in the troop commander's hatch. From his position posting air security through one of the AAV's open hatches, Robinson could just make out 201's driver, Lance Corporal Edward Castleberry. Even though Castleberry was a tracker, Robinson enjoyed his company. He had a mad, chaotic irreverence about him that he could relate to. He found some of the other trackers too geeky, too hung up on the boring mechanics of their vehicles. *Castleberry is a good guy. We'll look out for each other.*

Clutching the bow-shaped steering wheel of 201, Lance Corporal Edward Castleberry was too preoccupied to think of anything except catching up with the rest of the battalion. He'd seen Alpha's and Bravo's tracks disappear off into the distance, and he knew that he had to stay close to them. But the breakdown of 209 had delayed them. Castleberry had the driver's hatch open at a thirty-degree angle so he could look through it rather than through the bulletproof vision block, which limited his visibility. He gunned the track and set off at full speed toward the Euphrates Bridge. On one side of the road he saw the turret of an Iraqi T-55 tank. The marines ahead seemed to have taken care of it because it was pretty beaten up. *Holy moly.* He thanked God that he hadn't been in front. All through training it had been drummed into him what damage a T-55 could do to his vulnerable track and its thin aluminum skin.

Castleberry was from Mount Vernon, near Seattle, Washington. He had a reputation among his fellow trackers of being unpredictable, a bit of a rebel. It probably had something to do with his childhood. As a kid, he'd had a strained relationship with his parents, and at sixteen he'd moved out to live with a friend. His mother was superreligious. His dad, it seemed to him, hated God and spent most of his time fishing and doing his own thing. So Castleberry took off by himself. He'd been thrown out of school so many times for missing classes and for getting into fights that the state system wouldn't have him back. That's how he ended up in and out of jail. *I was a punk kid who thought the most important thing was to be cool.* Now, looking back, he could see what an asshole he was. *I would have been fed up with myself.* He didn't really know how it happened, but suddenly he stopped smoking dope, got a job, and put himself through a private high school to get a diploma. He began to have civil conversations with his parents and got a succession of well-paid jobs. Not as well paid as his brother, though. He was always quite jealous of his brother. His brother dyed his hair green and wore sandals and hippie shirts, but he still managed to earn very good money working at Microsoft. Edward Castleberry was much more into manual jobs. He was working for $27.50 an hour laying cables in the Seafirst skyscraper in Seattle when someone shouted to him to get down from the building because a plane had been flown into the World Trade Center in New York. He'd taken the elevator down to the lobby to see what the fuss was about. Then, on the TV monitors, he saw the second plane crash into the tower. It spurred him into action. The next day, he went to the Marine Corps recruiting station and signed on. It took him a month to leave for recruit training because of his criminal history. There was nothing that serious: a few misdemeanor charges and one felony for breaking and entering. He'd had to go to the Military Entrance Processing Center and talk to the Marine colonel there to convince him. He couldn't remember what he'd said, but it had worked. On October 15, he was in San Diego at recruit training. That was a blast. Most of the time he got into trouble for laughing. He'd never met so many stupid people before he joined the Marine Corps. *I don't know what sort of fucked-up education they had, but they were retards.* Some of them were so scared of asking the drill instructor if they could go to the bathroom that they would piss their pants. That's what would set him off.

"If you think it's so funny, then you can do some push-ups, too."

That would set him off even more, and he would laugh as he did the push-ups. He could cope with the mental stuff. He'd been to jail before, so he knew what respect and discipline was. And he was in great shape, so the physical stuff was easy. *I treated the whole of the Boot Camp thing like a game.*

Choosing his MOS—military occupational specialty—wasn't difficult. A friend of his had signed up as an amtracker and got stationed in Hawaii. He seemed to spend most of his time surfing the beaches.

"Whatever you do, don't sign up as an infantryman."

He'd done a lot of snowboarding and body boarding and was good with mechanical stuff, so he signed up to be an amtracker. In the end, he didn't get to Hawaii. Instead, he was sent to Camp Lejeune. It was okay. He loved the camaraderie and enjoyed messing about with the tracks. The thing he didn't like was the way the grunts thought of themselves as better than the trackers. They always taunted the trackers, calling them POGUES, people other than grunts, and saying that the infantry was the backbone of the Marine Corps. He always hated that because he saw the same amount of combat that they did. *I have to bring them to the fucking fight.* Castleberry always had a reply.

"If it wasn't for us trackers you'd be walking twenty-five miles with a pack on your back, you goddamn Earthpigs."

He also called them Dirtpeople because they painted on their silly camo faces and ran around in the dirt. But his favorite was Crunchies. *It's the sound they make when you run them over.*

Castleberry, like most trackers, saw himself as different from the other marines. Trackers even had their own individual call signs to set them apart. First Lieutenant Conor Tracy was Whaler because he wanted to bring the Whalers hockey team back to Hartford, Connecticut. Gunnery Sergeant David Myers was Taz, like the Tasmanian Devil of cartoon fame. Sergeant Matthew Beaver was Rotty because he was six feet seven inches and his life outside the Marine Corps revolved around breeding rottweilers. Corporal Nicholas Elliot was Axel because he did a mean Axel Rose impression. And Sergeant William Schaefer was Eight Ball. No one knew why.

In Kuwait, trackers and grunts didn't always train together because the trackers had to spend so much time maintaining their vehicles. The heat and sand caused an endless stream of mechanical failures. The tracks were their homes. They rode in them, ate in them, and slept in them. That's why it would send Castleberry into a rage when the grunts messed up his vehicle.

"Push, push, push."

It was Captain Wittnam's voice on the radio, urging Castleberry on to catch up with the rest of the battalion. His eyes were focused on the road ahead of him. Castleberry saw the rise in the span of the Euphrates Bridge. At any moment, he expected to see Alpha Company's tracks whipping up dust in front of him. But there was nothing. All he heard over the roar of the engine were snatches of confused and urgent radio transmissions and the occasional *ping* against the side of the track. *Is that someone shooting at us?* From his driver's seat, he remembered hearing discussions about tanks having to refuel, but he assumed they were now back in action and offering the line companies fire support. He felt safer when the tanks were in front because they were like bullet sponges and attracted fire away from his vulnerable vehicle. Now, as he began to cross the bridge, he realized that there was nothing between him and the city. *Holy shit. There are no tanks. This is for real.*

Three tracks behind, in track 204, Wittnam saw Alpha Company under fire on the far side of the Euphrates Bridge. As his track crossed the span, he got a better view of Alpha's marines dismounting from their tracks and taking up positions behind walls and dirt mounds. After weeks in the desert and days traveling across an empty landscape, it was a jolt to take in the sight of a swarming city. It looked as though it was teeming with fury. And he was going into the heart of it. As he reached the downside of the bridge span, the convoy stopped. From their respective hatches, both Wittnam and Tracy scanned the east side of the road ahead of them. They knew that the marines of Bravo Company were supposed to be in front of them, heading around to the east of the city. But there was no sign of them. Although the mechanical failure to the track had delayed them, Wittnam was still expecting to catch the tail end of the Bravo convoy. He tried to call Lieutenant Colonel Grabowski at the battalion forward CP. There was so much chatter that he couldn't break through.

Shots rang out overhead. They whizzed, rather than cracked. The closer the round was, the louder the crack as it whipped past. Wittnam was grateful that the Iraqis seemed to be such poor marksmen. But he couldn't stay where he was parked up there by the bridge. His 176 marines were sitting ducks. Wittnam had seconds to make up his mind. He couldn't see any sign of Bravo. Alpha had penetrated farther into the city than the original plan called for. *Maybe Alpha is having an easy time of it and the defense of the town is crumbling? Maybe Bravo has not gone around to the east? Maybe Tim Newland has rushed his company straight up the MSR to the northern bridge?* He knew that the main supply route that led straight to the northern bridge had been christened Ambush Alley by some of the marines on the ship on the way over. He couldn't remember who had coined it first, but he knew he had kind of laughed about it in Kuwait. It had been portrayed as an urban canyon where defending forces could set up positions and blast away at any attacking forces. He knew that no infantrymen would want to go down it.

But he also recalled the doctrine of Commander's Intent. *Know what the commander wants to achieve and, in a confused situation, do what you can to make it happen.* The battalion commander's aim was to seize the northern bridge. The regiment's motto was "Keep Moving." The shortest route through the city to the northern bridge was along that 4.6-kilometer stretch of Ambush Alley. *Maybe it won't be as bad as they had all imagined.* He got on the radio again to try and find out which route Bravo Company had taken. There was no reply. Time was running out. He had to make a decision. He was acutely aware that his next move would have a crucial impact on the course of the battle for the bridges. *What should I do?* He reached for the radio and called all of his units.

"All Palehorse units. Keep moving along the MSR to the northern bridge."

Lieutenant Reid, behind Wittnam in track 208, surveyed the scene from the span of the bridge. *What's going on?* He recalled the briefing he had been given by those higher up and which he in turn had communicated to his Weapons Platoon sergeant, Staff Sergeant Philip Jordan. They would establish a defensive position south of the city with a be prepared to mission to seize the southern and northern bridges. He remembered that the tanks would establish a support-by-fire position south of the Euphrates while Alpha took the bridge. Then Bravo and its tanks would cross the bridge, move around to the east, and establish a support-by-fire position at the northern canal bridge while Charlie seized that bridge. Now nothing seemed to be happening as they'd planned.

He couldn't see any trace of Bravo Company, the CAAT, or the forward CP. He saw that Alpha was in some sort of firefight at the foot of the Euphrates Bridge. He knew that they couldn't stay exposed on the bridge for long.

"We're going to move along the MSR."

It was Captain Wittnam on the radio. He sounded quite calm. He was telling them that they were going to go for the northern bridge through the heart of the city. Reid had never called it Ambush Alley, but he certainly remembered it as the road that they had talked about avoiding at all costs while on ship.

He didn't see it as a warning signal. He wasn't afraid. He had a lot of confidence in Wittnam. They were Americans. They had a load of firepower. They had Cobras flying overhead. *The hajjis might blow off a few rounds to save their manhood but that will pretty much be the extent of it. They're not going to want to mess with us. They know we can kick their ass.*

At the front of Charlie Company, the driver of track 201, Lance Corporal Castleberry, waited for an order. Stretching ahead of him was the four-lane highway of Ambush Alley that led to the northern bridge. There were people and trucks moving about in the middle of the road up ahead. To his left and right, he saw Iraqis climbing over roofs and balconies, appearing at windows and then vanishing again. He saw white flags being waved from rooftops. He saw ghostly black-clad figures running through the alleyways.

To his right, manning the track's up-gun system, was the AAV vehicle commander, Sergeant William Schaefer. He, too, knew that they were supposed to head to the east to link up with Bravo Company. He looked up at the road ahead of him. *My God, there are hundreds of hajjis running around out there.* Suddenly, out of nowhere, a round whizzed over his head. He felt the air snap in front of him. It was close. *My God, they're shooting at me.*

Then, over the radio, he heard the transmission from Captain Wittnam ordering them to push forward.

"This place is hot. We've got to keep moving."

Schaefer thought he'd heard wrong. Track 201 was at the head of the convoy. There were no tanks and no tracks from Bravo in front of him. That wasn't in the original plan. The tanks were supposed to be there to protect the vulnerable tracks. He wanted to make sure that he didn't do anything stupid. He got on the radio.

"Say again."

It was his platoon commander, Lieutenant Tracy, who answered.

"We've got to keep moving and pushing."

"Roger. We're going to push."

He checked to make sure that his platoon sergeant, Gunnery Sergeant Myers, bringing up the rear of the column, was up and ready. He didn't want to go tearing off alone. Then he got back on the radio and, using his call sign, made sure that everyone knew that track 201 was on the move.

"Eight Ball, Oscar Mike."

With that order, Schaefer's driver, Lance Corporal Castleberry, revved up the AAV's 525-horsepower engine and gunned the track into the city. *I'm just going to haul ass.* Ahead of him, Schaefer saw Iraqis running across the streets and trucks maneuvering back and forth. It was like going into a beehive. And then it started. At first it was just a few *dinks* on the side of the track. Then they just got louder and more insistent. Schaefer, manning the .50 cal, sent bursts of automatic fire into the buildings ahead. Scott Swantner, the infantry platoon commander who was fairly new to the Marine Corps, was sitting right next to him, his rifle by his side. He heard Schaefer yell at him over the sound of the AAV's engine and the incoming rounds.

"Hey, sir, don't you think it would be a good idea if you started shooting?"

Robinson, posting air security in track 201, was still real hazy about the plan. Somewhere in his head, he knew that they were supposed to be following Bravo, but he couldn't see them. He also remembered that in Kuwait, their platoon commander, Lieutenant Swantner, had mentioned something about avoiding a route called Ambush Alley. They had all looked at each other in bemusement, but they wrote it down in their notebooks. And now they were taking off at speed, and from what he could make out, they were heading right down the road they were supposed to avoid.

Groups of Iraqis were running across the road ahead of them. He wanted to look behind him to make sure the other tracks were following, but knew that he mustn't. He had to keep his eyes on his area of responsibility—the left side of the road.

"Where did these friggin' hajjis come from?"

Suddenly, the world around Casey Robinson exploded. Shots came in from every angle, bullets whooshed overhead. It was like hitting a firestorm.

Robinson went into shock. He shut down. It was as though he wasn't there. It was in slow motion. Then suddenly, something clicked. He felt a round whiz past, and he just started firing.

"Fuck, they're firing at us."

"Well, shoot back, you asshole."

There were two-story houses on either side of them. To his right side, the houses were set back only a few meters. On the left, the houses were set back fifty to one hundred meters with a scrubby and dusty wasteland in between the houses and the road. He now saw that there were Iraqis stretched out all along the highway, some standing in doorways by houses or crouched behind sandbagged positions against walls, while others were lying in ditches in the wasteland area or running across the road in front of him. He had never shot live ammo at human beings before, and he had never imagined that this was how he would have to do it. He could see the people he was shooting at. Some of them were only meters away from him. There were no soldiers or military vehicles to shoot at. Some were women and children.

He let out a burst from his M249 at a group of people firing at him from an alleyway. He saw some of them drop. He picked targets in front of him, but by the time he had let off a few rounds his track had sped past and he missed them. He moved on to the next target. Training just took over. He didn't think. *Look for targets and fire. Look for targets and fire.*

"Wentzel, to your right, to your right. One hundred meters to your right."

Yelling, he pointed to a crowd of people in a square on the west side of the road. Most of them were scattering, but as they split they revealed an Iraqi dressed in black, firing from the hip with an AK-47. He saw Wentzel fire the M203 grenade launcher, which arced in the air and landed in the middle of the fleeing crowd. Pieces of rocks, debris, and people flew into the air.

There were white flags fluttering from a window. As he passed, the white flags were whipped away and he saw muzzle flashes from the same place. *What the fuck is going on?* He saw more white flags ahead. This time he fired right into the windows. He tried to take aim at the groups of people huddled in doorways, but it was hard to tell who was the enemy. Some were women and children who just seemed to stare in amazement at the convoy as it hurtled past, rounds whistling up and down the street. Robinson looked again. He couldn't believe it. He swore that was a kid firing an AK-47 at him. Just as he got ready to fire back, the kid ducked into a doorway. *Fuck, I've got to fire at anything that might be a threat.*

The noise level had reached a terrifying pitch. Rounds were pounding on top of them. From the hatch, he now worked his fifteen-pound squad automatic weapon almost continually, spraying hundreds of rounds a minute into the houses along the street. He saw a muzzle flash from a window, then a roof, then a balcony. He just let it rip. He was so focused on looking for new targets that he hardly glanced at the masonry and glass that exploded from the buildings as he pounded them with his SAW.

Marines below were linking up his ammo and handing it up to him. Robinson got the feeling that they were almost jealous that he was doing all the shooting.

"RPG."

A smoking RPG flew right toward him and blew apart one of the packs attached to the outside of the amtrack.

"Get up here, someone."

Two marines poked their heads out of the hatch and returned fire. Robinson was glad that there were more of them firing from the hatch. When he turned back, though, they had ducked down again. Someone else poked his head up and then quickly ducked down. Then no one dared put his head up. He knew that the men inside the track were terrified.

Fuck. How come I'm not getting hit? Iraqis on the balconies above him were just sticking their AKs over the small parapet walls and firing wildly at the column of vehicles. *They can't shoot for shit.*

All the same, he started to sink lower and lower into the hatch to keep out of the way of the rounds that were ricocheting off the track. The marines below had gone quiet, apart from that goofball Milter trying to be funny.

"I hope you've taken your malaria pills."

Some marines laughed uneasily. Robinson didn't think it was that funny, but in spite of the anxiety he felt he couldn't help smiling.

Schaefer, in the gun turret of 201, flipped back and forth between the .50 cal and the Mark 19 grenade launcher. He was having trouble seeing what was going on. The sight on his guns was blown and he had to keep half his torso out of the turret. He wasn't having a good time. *Combat's not as much fun as I thought it was going to be.*

"Sergeant, a hundred meters to your right."

Ahead of him was a sandbagged machine-gun pit on the corner of a two-story building overlooking the street. It was manned by three men in black robes. Castleberry maneuvered the track into position. Schaefer aimed the grenade launcher and fired.

Boom.

The grenade hit directly under the sandbags and exploded the position, making big holes in the building. Just as in the movies, Castleberry saw men being flung into the air and then limbs and pieces of flesh raining down into the street.

"Castleberry. RPG. Get out of the way."

The smoke trail of an RPG careered wildly, almost comically down the street toward them but passed by harmlessly. Castleberry saw what looked like a school bus come to a halt in the middle of the street ahead and off-load black-robed fighters with RPGs. Schaefer saw it, too, pressed the electric turret control button with his foot, and spun the turret to face them. He squeezed the trigger of his Mark 19. He watched the grenade loop in the air and hit the target. The bus jumped in the air and exploded. One of the fighters crept out from behind the wreckage, crouched on one knee, and aimed an RPG directly at the track. Schaefer flipped back to the .50 cal and let off a burst of fire that punched holes through the top half of the man's body.

"Fifty meters to the right. Hajji on the roof. Hajjis in the ditch by the road. Port side. Machine guns down alleyway. Hajjis coming from east."

Castleberry tried calling targets to the marines in the hatches, but there were just too many to call out. Through the driver's hatch, he saw Iraqis out in the open, shooting from the hip by the side of the road. It was against everything he'd ever been taught about infantry. *Friggin' hajjis. I could get shots off all day.* He kept his right hand on the bow-shaped steering wheel, and with his left he put his M203 out of the window and shot grenades at anyone he could see. Everyone around him was screaming and yelling, but he couldn't tell whether it was through fear or whether they were just having fun.

It seemed as though the whole town was out in the streets. Some were just watching; others standing with them were aiming AK-47s at them. Castleberry couldn't understand why there were so many kids running around in a war zone. *If you cared about your kids, why would you let them out like that?*

There's a gagglefuck of hajjis ahead. As he'd been trained to do, he stopped the track and turned into the fire so Schaefer could take them out with the .50 cal and the grenade launcher. On the radio, he heard the exasperated voice of his platoon commander, Lieutenant Tracy.

"Quit fucking stopping. Push, push, push."

In track 204, fourth in line, Captain Wittnam was shouting out targets for Tracy to take out with the up gun. There was a mass of Iraqis running across the street firing at them. *I just hope the column keeps moving.* Several of the regiment's AAVs had broken down in the two days since they left Kuwait. If one of them broke down now, it would create one hell of a problem. *What if one of them is hit by an RPG and immobilized?* He tried to think what they would do if they found themselves isolated and under fire in Ambush Alley. There was so much going on that he put the thought out of his mind.

Lieutenant Reid was behind Wittnam in track 208 with a mortar squad and his FiST. They were a couple of hundred meters into Ambush Alley before he heard the first sound of small-arms fire pinging off the side of the track. Like most of the marines, he couldn't quite believe that anyone was shooting at them. He saw the tracks ahead blasting away at something by the side of the road. Some Iraqis, dressed in the black robes of the fedayeen, were jumping over the rubble ahead of him, trying to escape the gunfire. He yelled at the vehicle commander, Corporal Elliot, sitting in his gun turret.

"Hey, Elliot, light those guys up."

Reid saw Elliot get on the net to ask his AAV platoon commander for permission to shoot. By the time he got an answer, the Iraqis had gone. Reid was livid.

"Hey, Elliot, the next time I tell you to fire on hajjis, if you don't fire, I'm gonna haul your ass out of there and I'm gonna get up there myself."

Reid was pissed that they'd never clearly sorted out their relationship with the trackers. Elliot, like all trackers, found it difficult to take commands from the infantry guys. During training they would say, "Hey, you don't break my track." The infantry guys would answer, "We don't want to break your shit, so we'll do it your way." It meant they had never really established the right relationship. For Reid, the right relationship was that they should do what he told them. Reid was the troop commander of that vehicle and, according to Marine doctrine, Elliot had to answer to him. It was as simple as that.

As they pushed forward, Reid looked behind him. He saw guys blasting away with their M16s from the hatches. He clutched at the pistol by his side. He didn't take it out. He wasn't going to waste his fifteen rounds going up Ambush Alley. He felt like General George Patton sitting up there in his hatch, watching his marines unleashing so much firepower. *We are invincible.*

"I'm hit. I'm fucking hit."

It was Lieutenant Pokorney on the intercom. Reid looked back and saw him sprawled on the deck of the track. He was clutching his right arm, but it wasn't bleeding. Pokorney scrambled to his feet. Reid thought it must have been a round that had ricocheted off the track.

"It hurts like hell, but I'm fine."

Pokorney pulled himself together, put his head up out of the hatch, took out his pistol, and continued scanning for targets.

The company net had come alive.

"RPG teams left and right."

"Enemy fire from roof to left."

"Keep pushing."

"RPG heading this way."

A barrage of RPGs swept past the convoy leaving a trail of thick white smoke. One thudded against the side of one of the tracks. The marines inside waited for the inevitable explosion. It never came. The grenade had impacted with the line of rucks strung up on the outside of the AAV and embedded itself.

Elliot, in 208's gun hatch, was thrown out of his seat as his driver, Lance Corporal Noel Trevino, executed a stagger drill, weaving from side to side to avoid the RPGs that were now whooshing across the road.

"Whoa."

Something sped past Elliot's head, whipping up a blast of concussion and heat. *I wonder if today's my day. I wonder if I'm gonna make it or not. Well, there's nothing I can do about it.* He didn't feel anything at all and was almost apologetic at being so passive. *What a bland reaction to being shot at.*

At the rear of the column track 211, packed with some marines who had off-loaded from 209, followed the convoy into Ambush Alley. Thomas Quirk was one of nine marines lying on the top of the track. He had expected combat to be different. He was expecting it to be like a Hollywood movie. Right before they went in, they would stop just before the bridge, break the mission down one last time, and get this giant pep talk. *That's what is gonna happen.* But it hadn't happened like that, and now Quirk realized they were rolling headfirst into a battle. His track had gunned it, picked up speed real fast, and now they were heading down Ambush Alley. Lieutenant Mike Seely, the platoon commander, yelled at the men.

"Nobody fires until I tell them to."

Firing? What's he talking about? That's when Quirk realized that this was it. This was combat. He was going to fire at real, live human beings. Then and there his mind-set just switched. Seely yelled at them, pointing to a window.

"AK-47."

Everybody just opened up. Quirk squeezed the trigger. It was his first combat shot. He didn't think about whether it was on target. He thought about how dangerous it was. He was on top of a track with nine other people, squashed between Seely and Sergeant John Maloney, trying to get off shots. *That's pretty close. I don't want to shoot one of our own guys.*

There was a blur of Iraqis in windows, on roofs, darting out from alleyways, in bunkers by the side of the road—and they were all shooting at him.

A round whizzed over his head. *Thank God these fucking bullets aren't hitting me.* He realized that the enemy fighters couldn't have been well trained. *With a few machine-guns bursts, they should be able to wipe all of us out.* Now he found himself doing everything as he had been taught in training. It was muscle memory. The drills had been learned so obsessively that it all just came to him then and there as if he'd known how to do it all his life.

"Changing magazines."

The men had laughed whenever they said it during training because it had seemed such a stupid thing to yell out during a real firefight. Now he just did it and understood its value. The guys next to him picked up their rate of fire, covering for him while he slammed in a new magazine.

"Machine-gun position behind the wall."

"Guys with AKs on the roof."

"RPG in the alleyway, nine o'clock."

Marines, some sitting on the shoulders of those inside the track, were lobbing M203 grenades over a wall, trying to hit a machine-gun post. They walked rounds onto the target. It was kind of guesswork, but there was too much going on to get an accurate reading off the sight.

"There's a motherfucking hajji on that wall. Shoot your fucking 203."

Quirk was yelling at the marine next to him to shoot into the dead space behind a wall. The guy didn't want to do it. He had clammed up.

"Shoot the motherfucker."

The marine just stared at him with a look that said, *I don't want to be here. I don't want to shoot people.*

"You're taking it like a pussy. Shoot at the hajji."

"I can't."

Quirk knew that the marine didn't want any part of it.

Right next to him, firing into the buildings on the left side of the road, another marine was working a M240G machine gun. It fired a large 7.62 mm round and was rattling so hard in Quirk's ears that he felt it was fucking them up. He switched over to the right side of the road. He saw hands and arms reach over the parapets of balconies and roofs above him and fire AK-47s without aiming them. In his fury, he wanted to kill all of them. He saw nothing of the street, the buildings, the tracks in front, the sky. Nothing existed for him except his weapon and the Iraqis he was trying to kill.

"Hajjis with RPGs port side."

"Kill those motherfucking ragheads."

"Keep fucking pushing."

Castleberry, driving at the head of the column in 201, could hardly keep the AAV straight as it swerved across the road, buffeted by rounds from all sides. Looking ahead, he now saw that the four lanes of Ambush Alley were about to turn into two lanes where the road hit the bridge across the northern canal. They were nearly at the end. They had nearly run the gauntlet. All of a sudden two guys jumped out from an alley fifty meters ahead of him, took a knee, and aimed RPGs right at him. *This is it. I'm a dead man.* Castleberry knew that an RPG could penetrate the hull of a track and mess everyone up inside. Castleberry almost screamed into the intercom.

"Sergeant, there is someone standing in the middle of the road. And he's shooting fucking rockets."

Schaefer was stung with annoyance. Castleberry was highly strung and nervous. In the year he'd been his section leader, he'd had to lead him constantly by the hand.

"Well, run him over, asshole."

Schaefer expected the Iraqi to move. *That hajji will get out of the way.*

Weaving the track from side to side, to make the track a harder target, Castleberry said his prayers and floored it. The Iraqi shot one grenade off. It headed toward the track and bounced off the concertina wire the marines had added to the angled front slope of their tracks and whooshed off to the side of the road. As the fighter reached down to pull out another rocket strapped to his leg, the second fedayeen prepared to fire his missile. Castleberry drove straight at him. The track shuddered as it knocked the man to the ground. Castleberry turned the track toward the body and ran right over him. He felt a bump as the treads went over the body.

Robinson, in the hatch of 201, saw the man being caught up in the treads. He heard a crunch. It was the nastiest sound he'd ever heard. The body was tossed free, spinning into the air in a messed-up, distorted shape. The legs were facing the wrong way, almost touching the head. He saw it all as a picture. He felt nothing. It was the weirdest thing. The amtrack lurched, but once the treads had churned out the mangled body, it leveled out. *These amtracks have got pretty good suspension.*

Castleberry headed for the bridge. As they crested it, Robinson wondered what was going to happen next. The maneuver had gone out of his head. *Is Bravo ahead of us?* He thought they might be on the other side of the bridge. But when he looked up, he saw nothing but an empty bridge with a wide, desolate expanse of land on the other side. That's when he realized that they had been the first ones through Ambush Alley. *Maybe that's why they attacked us like that.* He was dismissive, then angry, then confused. *Dumb-ass hajji ragheads. What the hell is going on? This wasn't the enemy we were expecting.*

Behind 201, the rest of the Charlie convoy now had the bridge in their sights. Sergeant Jose Torres was sitting in the rear of the overcrowded track C211. Marines from the overspill of track 209 were sitting on top of him. When he'd heard the AAV's engines gunning up to go down Ambush Alley, it had blown his mind. He'd expected the tanks to be with them. He heard the roar of the AAV's engine and a *ping ping* against the side of the track. He looked at the other marines in the AAV. They let out a collective "Whoa" and started laughing. From his position, in the belly of the track, he couldn't see much. There was a small peephole he could look through, but it offered such a narrow range of vision that it was not worth trying to angle his body into a position where he could see through it. By the time someone had shouted out a target, they had already sped by. He felt sick and nervous. The AAV was swaying from side to side. It was dark, noisy, and reeked of diesel. He had no idea what the outside world looked like. All he heard was marines up top yelling at each other. He almost wished that he, too, was up there. Down below, he felt small, vulnerable, and powerless.

Torres had wanted to be a marine ever since he could remember. He signed up on August 3, 1994. It was his junior year of high school. His mother thought he was crazy, but she knew that's what he wanted to do, so she supported him. In the end, he wasn't allowed to join till his senior year, so he had to go through the delayed-entry program for a year before he got to Boot Camp. He was the company's machine-gunner section leader. During his five years of training, he'd had plenty of practice but never fired a round in anger. Now he was looking forward to getting out there and doing his stuff. He'd had enough of endless hours sitting in this metal box. He looked at his watch. It was 1305. They'd loaded up at midnight and had driven for thirteen hours without getting out of the back of the track. He turned to the marines around him.

"Hey, you guys. Do you realize we've been in these tracks on a thirteen-hour movement?"

Directly above Torres, lying on the top of track 211, Quirk saw a black-robed fighter jump out from behind a house on the right side of the road and put the RPG to his shoulder. As he swung his rifle around to engage him, the Iraqi launched the grenade. He watched the missile fly toward the track and impact the side about three feet below him. The explosion lifted him up and knocked him on his back. For a second the world went black.

Inside, Torres was smoking a cigarette with Corporal Randy Glass when the RPG hit. The track was lifted up in the air. It was all in slow motion—a blinding flash, an ear-shattering explosion, a rush of hot air that seemed to suck away energy as it passed through the back of the track. Thick, black, acrid smoke filled the track's belly. Jose Torres first noticed that sound had been emptied of all its force as though everything echoed down a long tunnel. He heard a muffled shriek. There was a smell of burning flesh. People's legs were in other people's laps. His vision went all hazy and foggy.

When Quirk looked up from the top of the track, the black-robed figure was still standing there with the RPG launcher on his shoulder. Quirk walked rounds down the wall. *I'm gonna kill your ass.* The rounds smacked into the wall until they reached the man. The pitch of the rounds changed as they tore into him. The man shuddered, bounced, and collapsed into the dirt as track 211 sped past.

In the belly of the track, Torres screamed.

"My eyes, my eyes."

They were burning. It was like everything was hazy and in double vision. He tried to stand up to get a breath of clean air through the open hatches. It was chaos. He felt himself detaching from the scene, like some impartial observer watching the mayhem unfolding. He saw marines choking on the smoke, struggling to put on gas masks, a heaving tangle of limbs and torn clothing. Playing cards were floating in the whirling dust of smoke and debris. The RPG had hit right under the wheel well and sent pieces of hot metal ricocheting around the inside of the track at leg level.

"We've got to stop. We've got injured marines."

The driver, Sergeant Michael Bitz, slightly wounded and stunned from the explosion, slowed the track down to a crawl. Furiously, Seely banged on Bitz's Kevlar helmet.

"Go, go, go. We can't stop. We're out in the open. We've got to get to cover."

"We got a man down. We got a man down."

"Glass is dead."

Blood was pouring from Glass's leg as though it were pouring out of a faucet. A flap of skin was hanging off, revealing flesh and gristle throbbing in a bleeding mess. He was shaking, but he was breathing.

On top of the track, Quirk saw that Corporal Mike Mead was down, splayed out by the hatch, clutching a knife to his right leg. Quirk and Lance Corporal Donald J. Cline Jr. tried to tear off the MOPP suit around his right leg. It didn't look too bad, some kind of burn, but the skin wasn't blistering or bubbling over. At the same time, he noticed that the packs on the side of the track were on fire.

"Get some water up here. Get some fucking water up here. The packs are on fire."

He had no idea that anyone inside the track was hurt.

"Why is nobody fucking helping me? We need some fucking water."

Lance Corporal Jordan Fitzgerald handed up a canteen.

"You asshole. What the fuck am I going to do with a canteen? Give me a fucking Ka-bar so I can cut these packs off."

Quirk wanted the traditional Marine fighting knife. It had an incredibly tough and sharp edge that could punch through a quarter. Instead, Fitzgerald handed him an M16 bayonet. *You can't cut butter with these things.* Cline was real short, so Quirk grabbed him by the ankles and lowered him over the side to try to cut the packs off. They were moving again, and the air was feeding the flames. He knew that what they were doing was pointless. *We're not going to cut the packs off with this fucking bayonet. But what option do we have?*

"Pull me up, pull me up. It's burning my face."

The flames had begun to leap upward and singe Cline's face and hair. Quirk pulled him up.

"Did it burn my hair, did it burn my hair?"

He crossed himself. Still neither of them realized that just below them, in the belly of the track, marines were writhing around in a bloody smoking mess of limbs and debris.

"We are so fucking lucky that RPG didn't kill us. We were so fucking close to that thing."

Lieutenant Tracy, in the command track 204, had crossed the bridge and was herringboned to the east side of the road when he heard the radio call from Sergeant Beaver, 211's AAV commander.

"I'm hit, I'm hit."

He watched the track fly by. Thick black smoke poured out of the open hatches and flames were licking the marines' rucks attached to the outside of the AAV. There was screaming from inside. Like some growling, wounded beast, the track kept moving up and over the northern canal bridge, coming to a halt about two hundred meters on its northern side.

Sergeant Schaefer also heard Beaver on the radio.

"We have wounded."

Schaefer got Castleberry to pull toward a berm on the west side of the road to build up an armored coil, a hasty 360-degree defense. The tracks maneuvered around each other to face outward sheltering the marines in the middle of the coil and allowing the guns in the front of the tracks more shooting space.

Track 211 had stopped in the middle of the raised highway in an exposed position. Schaefer ran over to the track and pulled open the rear hatch. The fire was already spreading across the top of the track. Someone thrust Corporal Glass into Schaefer's arms. Schaefer went into shock. Glass's leg, tied with a rifle sling as a tourniquet, was a bleeding mess. Schaefer had never seen anybody so messed up. He just stood there for a second. *What the fuck do I do?* Nothing in training had prepared him for this. He dragged Glass away from the track and laid him by the side of the road out of the line of fire. It was a slap in the face. *We're Americans. This is not supposed to happen to us.*

He ran back to his track, furiously firing his M16 back toward the city. He was confused and out of control. *Motherfucking hajjis.*

Robinson saw Schaefer from the hatch of track 201. He saw him firing off rounds until he ran out of ammo. He then watched the frustrated tracker hurl his M16 onto the ground. Robinson couldn't understand what he was doing, throwing his rifle away like that. An infantryman is taught that the rifle is almost a part of him. It's like an extra limb. It could save his life. It has to be treated with care. *He's lost his head. What is he thinking? Why the hell is he doing that?*

Inside 211, Sergeant Torres was trying to feel where the burning, searing pain was coming from. He grabbed his leg. He felt solid flesh, but it was wet and dripping blood. His desert boot was red and glistening. It looked as though a tiger's claw had ripped through it.

"Open the goddamn loading ramp."

"It won't open."

"Just get those marines out of there."

He felt someone grab his arm from the top of the open hatch. At the same time, someone still inside grabbed his other arm and tried to pull him down.

"Don't leave me. I can't breathe."

A hand grabbed him and yanked him through the back hatch into the sunlight and onto the side of the road. He gulped a lungful of clean air. He let himself be carried into a ditch a few meters from the track. Within moments a Navy corpsman, a Marine Corps combat medic trained by the Navy, was at his side. It was HM3 Robert Richie. He pulled bandages out of his combat lifesaver MOLLE bag.

"You're gonna be fine. But you got real bad shrapnel wounds to your right leg."

Next to him, a twenty-two-year-old Navy corpsman, HM3 Luis Fonseca, worked on Glass, assessing the injuries to his leg. He gave him some morphine and wrote the time it was given, 1327 M, in black ink on his forehead. The corpsmen were sprinting between the wounded, who were laid out in a line in the ditch. There were five of them, all with lumps of flesh missing below their knees. The RPG had hit the side of the track and set off a secondary explosion inside it, scattering chunks of hot metal under the track's benches where the marines were sitting.

Quirk, still on the top of 211, looked down into the hatch and thought about getting out by going into the track and out of the back hatch like he usually did. Fitzgerald was with him.

"No, just jump off the fucking track. Jump off the top."

It was over ten feet to the ground. They were loaded down with their deuce gear, the pouches holding their magazines and their grenades, their asspacks with flashlights and some food, flak jackets, and Kevlar helmets. They were carrying over thirty pounds of equipment. They both took a running jump over the burning packs and landed in the dirt. Fitzgerald screamed out in pain.

"I've broken my fucking ankle."

Quirk realized what a dumb thing they had just done. *If we hadn't had a million pounds of adrenaline rushing through us, we would have never made the jump.*

Quirk heard screaming and gurgling from the men in the ditches around him. It was the sound of pure pain as marines were pulled out of the track. He never thought he would ever hear those kinds of noises. Now he knew it was a sound that he would never forget. He looked at them lined up on the ground, a bloody, screaming mound of pulsating blood and flesh with a smoking AAV as a backdrop. *This is like a scene from a horror movie. It's a fucking bleeding mess.* The marines with whom he'd spent a year partying, yelping and hollering at war movies, going to strip clubs, and training for the peak of physical fitness were now a bloody mess of pale flesh, their faces scared and wide-eyed with pain. For a moment his mind just froze up, overcome by the awe of what he was looking at. *This wasn't part of the plan. This is fucking wrong.*

Quirk didn't know what to do. Lieutenant Seely shouted at them to get over to a berm on the east side of the road and provide security. Quirk sprinted over there and dived into the dirt, glad to be doing something. Rounds were whizzing over his head, but he had no idea where they were coming from. *Where do we shoot? What is going to happen?*

Lance Corporal Trevino, driving track 208, brought it to a halt about 125 meters to the north of the bridge and herringboned on the east side of the road near 204, the command track. Lieutenant Ben Reid crawled out of the command hatch, threw his Kevlar helmet and maps on the ground, and jumped down after them. *This is a pretty big drop. I'm in combat, I'm in the air without thinking, and I'm going to break a leg. What a stupid way to get hurt.* The landing was hard, but safe. He ran around to the back of the hatch and banged on the rear ramp, frustrated that it seemed to take so long to drop.

Second Lieutenant Fred Pokorney, the artillery forward observer, was one of the first out followed by mortarman Corporal David Johns. Reid was anxious to get the battalion's 81 mm mortar platoon and the "arty" or artillery batteries way back on the southern side of the Euphrates up and firing. He didn't know where the mortar platoon had set up, but he feared they would be out of range. He knew they couldn't reach much more than 5,700 meters.

"Fred, get comm up and let arty know our position. Help Corporal Johns with the 81s. I'm going to get the 60s up and firing."

As FiST leader, Reid's job was to coordinate fire support for the company, making sure that Charlie had available to them the full force of the Marines combat power. In his immediate team, he had an artillery forward observer who could call in strikes from the rear batteries and a marine who could call in 81 mm mortar strikes. He did not have a FAC with him, but he could relay requests for airpower through the battalion's FSCC, the fire support coordination center. Reid's job was to decide what fire support he needed and to deconflict the area by calling in artillery, mortars, and airpower at different times and onto different targets so they worked in sync. He had to make sure that the weapons systems were directed at enemy positions and didn't hit each other, or friendly troops. It was the "big sky, little bullet" theory. Yes, there was lots of space up there and the bullets were small, but all it would take was one of those bullets to hit a Marine aircraft and it could cause a friendly fire incident. It was nerve-racking stuff, but when it worked it was like watching the intricate movements of a ballet.

Reid had gotten in a lot of practice at the combined arms exercises at Twentynine Palms over the previous summer. He'd tasted how chaotic communications could be and how time-consuming it was to call in fires. At CAX, it sometimes took forty minutes from working out where and how he was going to use his fire support to the moment the rounds were sent downrange. He had to draw the gun target lines and the final attack headings for the airpower, pass it on the firenets to the fire support coordination center, and request an ETA for the incoming fire. In training, there was always a well-scripted scenario, and they already knew where the threat was going to come from. He felt that they hadn't done as well as they could have at CAX, but it was valuable experience. He knew it was more difficult in combat when he might not have the luxury of knowing where the attack was coming from or what he needed to target first.

He ran over to where his three 60 mm mortar squads were getting together their equipment. Out of the corner of his eye, he saw Seely's track, 211, still on the highway and in flames from the burning packs and the ammo inside. He didn't know that anyone had been injured. A couple of marines were on top of the AAV vainly trying to cut the packs free. Reid shouted over to his platoon sergeant, Staff Sergeant Philip Jordan.

"Get those dumb-asses off the fucking track. Tell them to just leave the burning packs."

Now he found that his fears about identifying targets and coming up with the right combined arms package in combat were justified. He tried to get a sense of where the enemy positions were located. About every minute or so an RPG would whistle over his head, landing to the east of his position. Then small-arms fire would crisscross from what seemed like the west, south, and north. It wasn't heavy incoming fire, but it was confusing because he couldn't identify where it was coming from. He saw a white building complex to the north and recognized it as a military compound marked 44 on his map. That's where he would start.

He needed to get the three 60 mm mortars up and firing. The marines called them 60 mike mike. They could fire shells up to 3,490 meters. On impact, they would kill anything within a radius of about 15 to 25 meters. If he could take out the enemy fighting positions, the infantry squads could maneuver into killing range. They didn't have time to dig foxholes. He got the mortar crews to lay down the baseplates on the east side of the road. They attached the barrel and bipod, fixed the sight, and got ready to drop the first round of mortars. Months of practice had gotten the procedure down to a fine art. They took only minutes.

Reid took out his wiz wheel, a chart which told him how much propellant he needed for the round to hit the target and what elevation the mortar needed to be set on. He began to issue firing orders.

"Line it up on the fucking big-ass white building. Charge 1. Elevation 1420."

A marine pulled off the safety pin and dropped a round into the barrel. Reid didn't even watch as the round soared toward the building. He was already yelling orders at Corporal Manny Espinoza for the next round.

"You just keep firing up that military compound."

Fred Pokorney grabbed him.

"We've got no comms. We've got no communications. I don't know if it's a transmitting problem or whether we are out of range."

"Well, keep working on it. Until we get comms, we can't get any arty."

Reid lay down on the road and looked for some targets. He put some dots on his maps. He really needed those comms so that they could get some artillery rounds on those targets. Fred was the arty expert. Reid was there to give guidance and to deconflict the area by making sure that he didn't have weapons systems or aircraft interfering with each other, but Fred Pokorney had to do his job.

"Fred, put fire on these two points. I don't care how you do it, use the work-around nets. Those grids aren't perfect, so you need to do your arty shit to refine them a bit. If you need me, I'll be with the 60s over there. They are all we've got right now."

Reid pulled one of the mortar squads out of action and redirected their fires away from the compound to the north and got them to fire to the west, where there was a big berm with Iraqis and their vehicles in exposed positions. Reid was concerned about mortar ammunition. They had only packed out with ninety high-explosive rounds, thirty illumination rounds to light up the landscape, and thirty white phosphorous rounds that explode on impact and burn white hot. He was going through his combat load pretty fast.

Jordan ran up to him and lay down on the road next to him.

"Torres is wounded."

"What the fuck?"

Reid couldn't believe it. Torres was one of his most experienced machine gunners and his section leader. Reid had deliberately put him in charge of a young section. There was a lot of punch in his Weapons Platoon. But the M240G machine guns were the backbone of the company's firepower. To hear that Torres was down was a massive blow. Jordan saw the look of horror on Reid's face and tried to soothe him.

"He's bad, but not that bad."

Reid still couldn't quite compute what Jordan was telling him and carried on looking at him in disbelief.

"Sir, it's all right. I already killed two or three of their guys, so now we're even. So what do you want to do?"

Reid had only been in the battalion for two years and was grateful for Jordan's experience. Jordan, a native Texan whose home was now in Enfield, Connecticut, was forty-two and had been in the Marine Corps for twelve years. He had served in Panama, Bosnia, and during the Gulf War. The younger marines looked to him to make sure everything was okay. If he was worried, they should be worried. But when Reid looked at Jordan, he seemed to be taking it in his stride. No. It was more than that. He seemed to be having a good time. He suspected that Jordan had told his marines to take care of him. Whenever he got off a track, he always found that one of the marines had already pulled off his pack. When he got back in again, he would find that his pack was already loaded. They would even save their chili and macaroni MREs for him because they knew he hated the other choices. The marines in his platoon took care of their lieutenant.

"Hey, we need to redirect any machine guns we can find and get them faced back toward the city to the southwest."

Jordan sprinted across the road to sort out the machine guns. Reid was lying on the elevated roadside near his three mortars. He could see 1st Platoon on the other side of the road but had no idea where 2nd and 3rd were located. Reid was not sure whether everyone had made it across the canal.

Through his binoculars, he saw teams of black-robed fighters with rocket-propelled grenades out to the west. They ran out of some buildings about six hundred meters away and lobbed RGP rounds toward them. None of them were accurate. They must have just pointed the things up in the air and hoped for the best. Kentucky windage, Reid called it. He told his mortars to aim toward them and helped them out by taking an M16, propping it up in the dirt as a makeshift aiming stake.

"Elevation 1242. Charge two. Fire two rounds."

By firing two rounds, he could be sure that the explosions he was seeing were his rather than a random hit. He watched them land and made his corrections.

"Right two. Drop one."

Once on target, his mortarmen turned the traversing handwheel one turn after each round and fired a can of eight rounds. It allowed his mortar squad leaders, Corporals Patrick Nixon and Jose Garibay and Lance Corporal Joshua Stickney, to cover a wider area. Reid stood up to get a better view to the west.

Pokorney rushed over to him and tackled him to the ground.

"You stupid fucker. You're going to get us all killed."

Reid looked up at the sky and noticed for the first time that hot metal was whizzing around from every direction. He'd had such tunnel vision, focusing on his mortars, that he hadn't noticed the increase in gunfire. *Fuck. We really are getting shot at.*

Lance Corporal Michael Williams, who carried Reid's radio, handed him the handset.

"Sir, Lieutenant Swantner is calling you on the radio."

Reid heard the urgency in the 1st Platoon commander's voice.

"Palehorse 4, this is 1. We're taking mortar fire. Do something about it."

Reid was frustrated. What did Swantner think Reid's men were doing?

"We've got all three mortars putting rounds downrange. That's all we've got right now. Comm to battalion is down right now."

He really needed the 81 mm mortars or artillery. They had a wider killing radius of thirty-five to fifty meters. But they were all to the south, and the FiST had not yet managed to get communication with them. Reid had four radios at his disposal, but he couldn't get anyone up on them. *If we can get hold of the forward command post or Bravo, we can relay everything to the artillery batteries through them.* He didn't think about using the radios on the track. There was just too much going on. In any case, the tracks weren't set to the firenet frequencies, and they would have had to spend time plugging in new frequencies. *We'll just have to work with the 60 mm mortars and keep working out the comms.* Reid shouted at Garibay.

"Pick up your shit and bring your crew. We're going to move your position sixty meters to the south." As the small group ran south, Reid looked back to find Jordan running along behind with two more cans of ammo. He began to feel even better. *This is working. Things are working out.*

From the top of track 201, Casey Robinson had watched the drama of the burning track 211. He saw marines scrambling out of the track and hitting the dirt. Thick black smoke poured from its hatches and floated over the wide expanse of desolate wasteland into a cloudless sky.

Below him, in the driver's compartment, Edward Castleberry lowered the ramp. It was the sign he gave for the 1st Platoon marines in the rear to dismount and to start doing their infantry stuff. As a tracker, he had to stay with his vehicle, ready to maneuver it in case the track was targeted. Sergeant Schaefer, the AAV commander, stayed with him to provide supporting fires from the track's up-gun system. A third tracker, Lance Corporal Kyle Smith, who looked after the crew compartment, passed up ammo.

Robinson and the twenty marines in back of 201 tumbled down the ramp, disorientated. Many of them had been cooped up inside the track for hours and struggled to run without their legs collapsing from under them. A round snapped past Robinson's head, followed by the whistle of what he thought were incoming mortars. The missile exploded about fifteen meters away, shaking the ground around him. Another one came over.

Bam. Bam. Bam.

It was a terrifying, awesome thud. *So that's what live mortars sound like.* It went quiet again. He ran out into the mud fields and launched himself into the dirt behind some low berms. It would have to do for the moment while he worked out where everyone was. Other marines from his squad jumped breathlessly into the ditch beside him, glancing at each other anxiously. They were wearing kneepads, already ripped and battered from diving onto the hard, stony ground.

He needed to get situational awareness. To his left, on the south side of the canal, were the low buildings of the city. Occasional bursts of gunfire came from that direction. Straight ahead, looking west, were long flat mud fields, dotted with a few huts and brick buildings. To his right, in the north, was a large white building that he guessed was the military complex they'd been told about. Behind him, to the east, was the road they'd just driven along. It was raised, so he couldn't see what was on the other side, but he guessed the landscape was similar to the scrubby expanse in front of him. He went back to a basic lesson on infantry skills. *When you can accomplish it, get into an offensive position.* The aim was to take the fight to the Iraqis.

"Let's push forward."

Someone yelled that they should head out toward the canal to expand the security perimeter. It seemed like a good idea. They split into squads of twelve marines. One squad covered while the other leapfrogged them in bounds, just as they had done in training. Then they took cover and provided covering fire for the first squad to leapfrog them. They moved forward, running through a muddy landscape crisscrossed with ditches and mounds, toward the canal, getting closer to where the fire was coming from. Robinson realized he was doing things without even thinking. And the marines around him were doing the same. All that mind-numbing training was paying off.

"Go, go. First squad, go."

Up ahead of him, running along the banks of the canal, he saw black-robed figures getting in positions to fight.

Captain Wittnam was about two hundred meters on the north side of the Saddam Canal Bridge when he turned to see the smoking track 211 grind to a halt in the middle of the road on the bridge's north side. He saw marines jump out the back. There were flames licking its sides, but it was still mobile and it didn't look too serious.

He had expected to see Bravo and the forward CP once he crossed the bridge, but there was no sign of them. He now realized his decision to move straight up Ambush Alley was based on the mistaken assumption that it was the route that Bravo had also taken. To the north and east was flat, muddy scrubland. To the west and south, toward and beyond the Saddam Canal Bridge, it was swampy, crisscrossed with smaller irrigation canals. It was reasonably good cover. Parallel to the road heading north there were small berms and ditches on both the east and west sides. He was surprised that the terrain on either side of the road was so uneven. From the maps and satellite photos, it had looked as though they would be able to maneuver their tanks and tracks over it. Now he realized it was impassable to most of his heavy vehicles. His marines had used the ground well and were set up in firing lines behind the berms. He grabbed the radio handset and called back on the main battalion tactical net with his position at the 39 northing.

"Timberwolf 6. This is Palehorse 6. I am on the bridge."

There was no reply. He looked at the bridge's plain, concrete span and couldn't believe that this was what they were fighting for. He repeated the coordinates of his position. It still wasn't clear if Lieutenant Colonel Grabowski had got the information. There was too much chatter on the radio. Everyone was trying to talk at once. He jumped out of the track and set about trying to organize his marines into a defense. He knew from Intel that there were two Iraqi brigades to the north of his position. They'd been told that one was an Iraqi commando brigade and the other was part of the 23rd Infantry Brigade. And they might have tanks. *They mustn't be allowed to come back in and reinforce the city.* He would have to fight on two fronts: protecting the bridge from an attack from the north, and making sure that no one could seize it from the south. He was worried about the possibility of taking on Iraqi tanks, but looking around at the barren landscape he felt that for the moment, at least, there was no imminent threat. The level of incoming fire was only a few rounds per minute. *It won't be long before Bravo gets up here to reinforce us.*

5

Lieutenant Colonel Rick Grabowski and the staff from his forward command post were trying to work out exactly how many vehicles were stuck in the mud in the streets on the east side of the city. The latest toll was three tanks, three Humvees, and three AAVs, including the C7, the battalion's forward command vehicle, which contained all the radios and electronics for command and control. But it was hard keeping count. Several times a track managed to haul itself free, only to get caught in another mud bog. The AAVs that were on solid ground couldn't get close enough to tow out the sinking vehicles without themselves sinking into the mud. The towropes were not long enough. The marines had trained for almost every eventuality. But none of them had trained for this.

Thirty minutes ago, Grabowski had set off with such optimism across the Euphrates Bridge. Now he found himself under fire and unable to go anywhere.

Fedayeen fighters appeared at the entrances to alleyways, on roofs, and in the windows of houses, trying to get close enough to attack the stricken vehicles. The CAAT Humvees equipped with TOW missiles and heavy machine guns were weaving in and out of the alleyways shooting at any potential threat, trying to keep the encroaching crowds away from their perimeter. The tanks could still traverse their turrets and fire their main guns. As soon as any technical got too close, the tanks' gunners would fire an MPAT round and obliterate it.

Under fire, Grabowski was still trying to get communications with his subordinate units. The radio operators in the C7 were having difficulties receiving and sending radio messages. The two-story houses they were bumped up against were masking the VHF signals. Even in his Humvee, he couldn't get a consistent signal among the labyrinth of houses.

"Can't we get the goddamn comms up?"

He was desperate to contact Charlie Company. He had been trying to speak to Captain Wittnam ever since they had got stuck some thirty minutes ago. He had no idea where Charlie was. He wanted to make sure that Wittnam didn't send his company around to the east as in the original plan. Otherwise, they too would get stuck in the same mud bog where his tanks and tracks were now floundering. *I've got to get through to him and stop him, otherwise it is going to get ugly. Then what would we do?* He heard snatches of panicked radio transmissions that seemed to suggest that Charlie Company was engaged in some fight with the enemy, but it was difficult to work out exactly where they were and what was going on. And just when he thought he was getting to grips with what was being said, the signal would cut out. *Where is Charlie Company?*

"Palehorse 6, this is Timberwolf 6."

"Palehorse 6, this is Timberwolf 6."

All he heard back was an incoherent mess of radio traffic. There were too many people talking at once and no one made any sense. It was like a basketball court where a dozen people were shooting into the same basket and knocking each other out of the way.

He reckoned that some of the younger kids were so nervous that they were "hot miking"—occupying the net and cutting everyone out by keying in the handset even when they weren't talking.

Then he heard a brief transmission. He could only just make it out.

"Timberwolf 6. This is Palehorse 6. I am on the bridge."

Grabowski keyed in to talk back to Wittnam.

"Palehorse 6. This is Timberwolf 6. Which bridge are you on? Repeat. Which bridge are you on?"

The signal cut out. Grabowski's frustration was growing. It was his job to know where all his companies were. He couldn't direct the fighting unless he knew what was going on. *Which bridge is he on?*

He knew that the regimental commander, Colonel Bailey, was waiting for news that they'd taken the northern bridge. He'd already told him that they'd seized the southern bridge over the Euphrates. Bailey was now moving from the regimental CP several kilometers south of the Euphrates Bridge to the foot of the bridge itself. Grabowski hoped that he wouldn't want to come up any farther. *He has no business going farther.* He wanted to be left to get on with his job. *I don't want the regimental commander in the middle of all this shit.*

"Hey, sir."

It was the battalion fire support officer, responsible for fire support co-ordination. He had been monitoring the radios from the sinking C7.

"Charlie Company is on the second bridge."

Grabowski hit the hood of his Humvee with delight.

"Great. We have got both bridges."

He got straight on the radio to report the success to Bailey. He knew that his CO would be getting pressure from Brigadier General Natonski for news on how it was going.

"Viking 6, this is Timberwolf 6. We have now got both bridges."

Grabowski breathed easier. He was still in the shit, but things were looking up. *I have a marine rifle company on the north bridge and one on the south bridge, and there is nothing in that city that can push them off. All we need now is to get those tanks up there.*

Standing a few yards away, Major David Sosa, the battalion's operations of-ficer, was figuring out what their next move should be. The very heart of the battalion's decision-making process, the C7 command-and-control ve-hicle, was stuck in the mud. The forward command staff, including the in-telligence officer, the fire support officer, the forward air controller, and the battalion commander, had been forced to dismount to try to get their own comms up outside the C7. He almost didn't notice the fighting going on around him. It reminded him of being in a pool with his head under-water. When he was talking on the radio, there was only a faint muffled background sound. When he put the radio down, it was like coming up for air. He heard rounds whizzing over his head, smelled the stink of the muddy, stagnant water, saw marines crawling into ditches to reinforce the perimeter.

He watched Grabowski talking on the radio, trying to give out orders. Sosa wished that the battalion commander wouldn't spend so much time on the radio. He had a habit of talking at length, and just as he was getting to a crucial piece of information someone would key in and he would lose the comms. It was frustrating for everyone.

Charlie Company is on the bridge. How do we reinforce them? How do we support them? He couldn't just move companies around. Each of them had their own mission. He couldn't get hold of another battalion because that was tied to what the regiment as a whole was doing. And he couldn't talk to regimental headquarters because they kept losing communications. He was on the point of despair. The one good thing he could take from it was that Bravo's young infantry marines were keeping the enemy at bay. They were lying in ditches, behind walls, and in water holes, firing at any-one that got too close. Command and control at battalion level was break-ing down, but at the small-unit level the marines were doing exactly what they'd learned in training.

It was coming to decision time. Sosa realized that from where they were, the forward command couldn't coordinate the fight. *If we can't co-ordinate the fight, we're not doing what we need to do. Our whole mission in life is to coordinate the fight.* He turned to the battalion commander.

"We've got to do something. We can't just sit here."

Grabowski had already decided he was going to press on with the origi-nal mission by going for the northern bridge. They agreed to leave a small force to guard the stricken vehicles. The rest of Bravo's marines and the re-mainder of the battalion staff would continue to push their way north. *Hopefully, we can find a pause where we can get better comms.*

One of Bravo's infantrymen, Corporal Neville Welch, was lying in one of the alleyways with his fire team when he got the call to return to the track.

"The helos have found a way out. They'll lead us out of here. Back to the tracks."

Marines congregated around their vehicles, some causing confusion by clambering into the wrong tracks. Welch made sure he was up at the hatch scanning the rooftops. There were only two thoughts in his mind. *I'm going to kill, and I'm going to make sure that I'm going to stay alive.*

The convoy set off more tentatively than earlier in the day. Welch was nervous about heading off without the support of the tanks. The column of some ten vehicles snaked its way through the labyrinth of dusty streets and alleyways, trying to avoid the water holes that threatened to suck them back into the mud. Some marines ran alongside the tracks, providing security at road junctions. They ducked and crouched and weaved their way through the streets, staying close to each other, keeping their eyes looking left and right and up and down just as they'd learned during MOUT training. From the hatch, Welch saw that the marines on the ground looked nervous and vulnerable. He had no idea where they were heading, but he was glad they were on the move. The buildings around them provided some cover. At each junction, the column halted while the lead vehicle checked that it was safe to continue forward before punching through. The problem was that the resulting blockage in the column resulted in some vehicles halting in the middle of an intersection, dangerously exposed to fire coming from four directions.

"Keep the column moving, for fuck's sake."

Welch watched an officer jump out of his Humvee and sprint forward to the lead track.

"You gotta keep moving."

He saw white pickups mounted with machine guns and carrying RPG teams maneuvering in and out of the alleyways, charting the convoy's progress. They stayed hidden. Any time one of the technicals got out into the open, a marine in one of the AAVs would take it out with the .50 cal or the Mark 19 grenade launcher.

From the top of the track, Welch kept his eyes focused on the windows and alleyways in his sector of fire. Sometimes people waved at him. Sometimes they shot at him. It was crazy. *This is not the enemy we've been briefed about. They're not playing by the rules.* Everything he had learned about identifying hostile intent now seemed to go right out of the window. Welch had always believed that he would be able to get what he wanted through hard work and determination. It's what had got him out of Guyana and put him through college. But now he was disturbed by the realization that however determined, however well prepared he was, some things were just way out of his control. His convoy was making slow progress through a battlefield and an enemy that he did not understand. Even the maps seemed unable to offer him some measure of clarity. What looked like a straight road north to the bridge turned into a mess of dead ends, narrow alleyways, and dusty streets blocked with water holes, trash dumps, and irrigation canals.

6

Out in the fields to the east of the road by the northern bridge, Robinson tried to maintain his situational awareness. He was in an irrigation ditch, his legs sodden with water, some two hundred meters from the amtracks, within shooting range of the far bank of the canal. Up ahead, he saw fedayeen fighters crawling among the reeds and scrubland. What had started as the odd crack of gunfire had now increased to a hail of machine-gun and AK fire coming at them from around the bridge. Lying prone, he aimed and fired at anything that moved. Around him, he heard the sound of panic as rounds smacked into the ground and marines went down.

"I'm hit. I'm hit."

"Corpsman up. Corpsman up."

"He's been shot in the leg."

With no warning, the air around him started to explode. RPGs were flying toward them from every direction. Mortars were landing nearby. It mystified him how a mortar would land behind him and yet a person fifty meters in front of him would go down. *What a fucked up thing. How the fuck does that work?*

There was now fire coming at them from under the canal bridge. It seemed like it was raining down from all sides.

"Grenade."

Robinson watched as a missile slowly looped over his head and landed in a berm to the side. The explosion threw up dirt and stones and made his teeth and guts shudder. Marines were writhing in the fields around him. Some of them were beginning to freeze.

"Corpsman up."

He saw the Navy medics sprinting from marine to marine as they went down. But there were so many marines dropping that there were not enough corpsmen to go around. Robinson's heart sank. He had long imagined this moment: in combat, killing people and doing macho stuff in Force Recon. But this was for real, and he wasn't sure that he liked it.

Corporal Jake Worthington had set up his Javelin gun on the top of track 201. He had helped write the book for the battalion on the antitank weapon. Its unique targeting system meant that once fired at a tank, it would automatically come down on its target from above, where the armor was most vulnerable, rather than impact the thick armor on the side.

It had been a boyish, macho dream of his to be in combat. He had always wanted to know, when it came down to it, whether he was going to have more than the average life. *If it comes to kill or be killed, me against someone else, who's favored?* It was like a test. He was adopted as a baby and had never known his real parents. Maybe that had something to do with it. He needed some proof that he was favored, that he was loved. His adoptive parents had been real good to him, but they'd split up when he was young and he stayed with his adoptive mom. She'd bounced around a bit so he never really had a home. She was going on marriage number five. He'd been in Los Angeles, teaching kids with learning disabilities for his adoptive father's company, when he decided that it was time to test himself in combat. *The marines seem like hard-asses and they've got better uniforms.* That's why, some two years ago, he'd stepped into the Marine Corps recruiting office in Los Angeles.

"What can the Marines do for me?"

"Get the fuck out my office."

Worthington was taken aback.

"What?"

"Get the fuck out of my office."

Worthington went next door to the Army office and asked the same question. The recruiter was sitting there munching on a sandwich from Burger King with a piece of food sticking to his chin. Between mouthfuls of burger, the Army guy began to tell him how they could give him extra money for college and help him out with this and that, but Worthington just sat there wondering why the Marine recruiter had reacted like that.

As he was sitting there listening, the Marine recruiter poked his head around the door.

"Had enough yet?"

Worthington nodded.

"Well, come back around here. Now, then, why don't you try another question?"

"I suppose you want me to say what can I do for the Marines."

"Now that's what we're trying to get at."

Worthington signed on then and there for four years. As he signed, he couldn't help but smile. *Damn, I can't believe I fell for that trick.*

From his position on the top of the track, he scanned the horizon through the Javelin's CLU, the thermal imaging sighting system that could pick out tanks and other moving vehicles and personnel. He felt vulnerable and wished they had their own tanks with them. He knew that an Iraqi T-72 would be able to hit them from eighteen hundred meters away. None of his marines would be able to see that far. He felt the weight of responsibility. *It's up to me to take the tank out before it gets us.* At his side he had an M16, ready to fire on any Iraqis that Sergeant Schaefer wasn't getting.

Worthington had trained in the Weapons Company and was an expert in most weapon systems. He'd enjoyed training with the battalion, but what he couldn't understand was the battalion commander's passion for backbreaking humps. *Carrying a heavy machine gun and a TOW and all that heavy-assed bullshit on long humps is no fun. All you are doing is hurting marines and lowering morale.* He couldn't see why they didn't go on long hikes with just their packs.

Worthington sensed the level of incoming fire being ratcheted up. He heard the whistle of incoming artillery and mortars and watched the ground in front of him explode in splashes of dirt, each hit getting closer. *I'm going to get nailed. It will be steel on steel.* He leaped from the back of the track and lay down in the small depression in the dirt left by the AAV's treads. *This is ridiculous.* No way would the shallow ground protect him from the incoming rounds. He heard the radio squawking with the sound of marines in a panic. He low crawled, slithering on his belly back toward the road. The truth was that he didn't have a clue what to do next. His "A" gunner, Lance Corporal Brian Wenberg, the assistant gunner who helped him load the Javelin and identify targets, was at his side.

"Corporal. What are we doing?"

"I don't really know. Let's get back in the track."

The two of them low crawled back to the track to figure out what to do next.

Lance Corporal Thomas Quirk was still taking cover behind a berm in a ditch by the side of the road. None of the marines with him were in his fire team. His squad leader wasn't there. There was no one telling them what to do. All command structure had collapsed. They just did whatever seemed like a good idea at the time. There were rounds cracking and whizzing all around them.

"Where are those fucking rounds coming from?"

"They're coming from our own track."

Track 211 was no longer just in flames. The ammo inside was starting to cook off. Quirk was only fifty meters away when rounds inside the track punched through the skin of the AAV and whistled through the air in all directions. High-explosive rounds, demolitions, and rockets punched through the track and exploded in the air, scattering sharp, hot shrapnel all around. *Our own shit is firing at us.* Quirk looked on with disbelief. He had no idea what to do. *I can shoot hajjis, but what do I do with a smoking track? You can't kill a track.* As he'd done so often before, he began to pray to calm himself down. *Give me a calm head and a strong heart . . .*

Reid had led one of his three mortar squads toward the canal bridge, about sixty meters south of the other two mortars that were still firing toward the military compound to the north and enemy positions to the west. The volume of fire coming at them from the city was increasing, and Reid knew that he needed to get Corporal Garibay's squad firing to the south to shut it down. Reid asked Garibay for his wiz wheel. He had left his own with Corporal Espinoza. But Garibay didn't have one, either. *Fuck. We've left the wiz wheel behind.* He sent Private Jonathan Gifford back to get it. At the sight of Gifford scooting back to the original position to the north, bent double and zigzagging to avoid the rounds, he and Jordan burst out laughing. It was partly nerves. But it just looked so funny.

Reid used the road as defilade. Because it was raised, he and the mortar squad could tuck themselves up against it as cover. *They can't hit us here.* All the same, he watched as several RPG rounds, coming from the southwest, flew over his head, slow as day, and smacked into the dirt a hundred meters away. The world around him had shrunk to what was going on in the few meters around him. He wasn't sure where any of the other platoons were, or what Captain Wittnam was doing. He was focused on the marines on either side of him and getting those mortars up and firing.

Fred Pokorney, the artillery FO, came over and lay down next to Reid.

"I got some fire missions out."

"Roger that, Fred."

"You might want to get your head down."

Reid was confused. *Keep my head down? What the fuck is he talking about?* For a moment he thought that Pokorney meant that he had altered the targets and they were going to be closer than those he had marked earlier.

"Were those missions where I told to shoot?"

"Yeah."

"Well, that's okay. We're good to go."

Reid was pleased that somehow Pokorney had got those missions out. He must have finally got through on one of the nets. Any moment now the 1/10 artillery batteries, set up some ten kilometers away south of the Euphrates, would start shelling the targets he'd pinpointed. He wished the cannon cockers would hurry up. The terrifying thuds of incoming RPGs and mortars were increasing. And they were landing closer. He turned to look downrange. Out of nowhere there was an ear-piercing explosion behind him. It was as though an iron beam had been dropped from a forty-story building, slamming into concrete right next to him. A searing pain shot through his arm and the blast twisted him back toward the road. He looked down and saw nothing but dust. His first thought was of the Vietnam movie *Hamburger Hill,* when the platoon commander is talking on the radio and gets his arm blown off and doesn't even know it. He just keeps talking. *My arm has been blown off.* As the dust cleared, he saw his arm dangling uselessly next to him.

"My arm's fucking broken."

"That's too bad, sir."

It was the voice of Corporal Jorge Gonzalez who was sitting right behind him. There was something about his tone that made Reid think that something was badly wrong. Then it was Garibay, off to the right, who spoke.

"Sir, Buesing is dead."

Reid looked up and saw a big hole in Lance Corporal Brian Buesing's face. He was sitting Indian style, slumped forward but still upright. He was having body spasms and was gurgling as though trying to breathe. Reid didn't know what to do. *Do I take my pistol out and shoot him? What the fuck do I do?* He turned away. He couldn't deal with it. He glanced to his right at the six-foot-seven-inch gangly frame of Fred Pokorney stretched out on the road. Pokorney was thirty-one and the father of a two-and-a-half-year-old girl, Taylor. Next to him lay his weapons platoon sergeant, Philip Jordan, the marine who everyone looked up to and who, just a few moments ago, had seemed to be actually reveling in the sound, taste, and smell of combat. Reid ran over to him and rolled him over. The bone structure on his face was shattered. His body was crumpled. He looked like something out of a movie set. He let go and stared at the body. He looked again at Buesing and then went completely numb. He turned to Garibay, who was right there just staring up at him with the biggest eyes he'd ever seen. He was alive but he too had been hit.

"You keep everyone here. I'm going to get help."

Reid was up and running. He made it about twenty meters and then all of a sudden found himself lying on his face in the dirt. He didn't feel anything, but he knew he'd been hit. He saw a bunch of blood forming in a pool on the ground in front of him. His eye wouldn't open. It was all screwed up. *I've lost my eyeball.* He felt himself zoning out. *Man, I'm done. This is it. Do I just lay here? How does this work? How did this happen?* In the few seconds that he lay there so much went through his mind. He wondered what his wife, Susan, would do with the insurance money from his death. They'd only been married eight months when he left for Iraq. He had a rush of anxiety over what she would do with the $250,000 insurance money. *I hope she doesn't blow it.* He wondered whether he should get up or just die right there in the dirt.

For some reason, he struggled to his feet and went from tunnel vision with two eyes to tunnel vision with one eye. The only thing he saw was a track. He slumped toward it and crawled in the rear. Inside he saw Corporal Elliot and Lance Corporal Trevino. He thought they were breaking out ammo. Reid half screamed, half moaned at them.

"We got casualties. We need to get them evacuated. You get up on that fucking gun and I don't care what you shoot but if they are hajjis you fucking kill them."

Elliot had to look twice to take in the apparition. Reid's face was all torn up. There was just a bleeding mess where his eyes should be. There was blood coming out of every orifice. He almost laughed at the horror of it. *Oh my god.* It was the first time he had seen anyone like that.

Reid yelled again.

"We've got to get those guys out of here."

He stumbled back out of the track and looked to his left to find his other two mortars. He couldn't see anybody around. No one. *Where the fuck is everybody?* He felt more alone than he had ever felt before. Like a man lost in space. A man living alone on a distant planet. He guessed he'd been fighting for nearly an hour, but his understanding of the battle was minimal. He had little idea what was going on or who was shooting at them or from where they were shooting. He was a first lieutenant, but, in the heat of battle, his understanding was no more than that of a private or lance corporal. *I haven't been able to control anything greater than the handful of guys around me.*

From track 201, Castleberry had seen the incoming shells getting closer and closer to Reid's mortars. He saw a mortar squad frantically trying to target where the shells were coming from. He almost stopped breathing when he saw what looked like an enemy mortar score a direct hit. Pokorney's body flew toward him. He didn't immediately react. There was too much going on to take it in. *If we don't move these tracks, we're also going to get hit.* As the tracker, he was responsible for moving the vehicle away from danger. But he couldn't go anywhere. Robinson, Wenztel, and the rest of the infantry were still out in the fields. It was a rule that you never left without your infantry guys. *I hope we come up with something and get the hell out of here because those mortars will fuck us up.* Castleberry focused on calling out targets for Schaefer, who was working the .50 cal in the turret of the track. He saw Iraqis running in and out of huts and shacks in the fields around him. They seemed to be collecting RPGs and AK-47s that had been stored there. *Holy shit. The hajjis are getting closer.*

Captain Dan Wittnam was still expecting, at any moment, to see the tanks and amtracks of Bravo Company hurtling over the bridge. He scanned the horizon, waiting to hear the throb of a large force on the move. *Where the hell are they?* His own position was sinking into confusion as fire rained down on them from all sides. They were now taking heavy machine-gun fire from both inside the city and from the north. There was small-arms fire from some huts to the east and from a swampy area to the west. RPGs, heavy rounds from recoilless rifles, mortars, and artillery shells were raining down on them from every direction. His AAVs were fanned out over a quarter-mile area a couple of hundred meters to the north of the Saddam Canal Bridge, mostly sheltered behind large dirt berms. Each time Wittnam and Lieutenant Conor Tracy, the AAV platoon commander, tried to get the tracks to move away from the mortar fire, artillery would bracket in on them. Wittnam realized that they'd fallen into a kill sack. The enemy had expected them to go for the northern bridge and had surrounded them with artillery and mortar positions. Their every move was being watched and targeted. What was worrying was the sheer volume of incoming fire. It was the key to any firefight. If Charlie couldn't match the volume of incoming, they would be overrun. He now wondered whether it had been a mistake not to prep the battlefield beforehand. Normally, prior to an engagement, the commanders would have sent in aircraft and artillery rounds to bomb the defenders before the ground forces arrived. He knew that they had not done it at Nasiriyah because they wanted to limit collateral damage. In any case, they had not been expecting a big fight. But now he believed that they really did need to get some artillery fire hitting the area of the city to the southwest of the canal bridge. That's where most of the fire was coming from. He grabbed the radio handset again. It was just a babble of confused radio transmissions. Until he knew where Bravo, Alpha, and the forward CP were, he couldn't risk calling in artillery strikes.

He rolled back to the company net and heard the news of mounting casualties. He ran over to the destroyed mortar position. A few moments earlier he had had been admiring how fast and furiously they had been going at it with the mortars. He had just complimented Reid on his work.

"We are winning."

Now he saw the lifeless bodies of four of his marines. He knew that they had been killed instantly. Staff Sergeant Philip Jordan, a decorated veteran from the first Gulf war, lay there in the dirt. He rolled over another body and saw the face of one of the mortar crew, twenty-year-old Corporal Jorge Gonzalez from Los Angeles. A few days earlier, he'd congratulated Gonzalez because he had learned that his wife had just given birth to their first child, Alonso. He saw the battered body of Second Lieutenant Fred Pokorney, who, after thirteen years of service, was going to be promoted later that day. He was going to shake his hand as soon as the bridges were taken. He saw twenty-year-old Lance Corporal Brian Buesing from Cedar Key, Florida, lying in the dirt. Buesing's grandfather had been a marine mortarman and Silver Star winner in Korea. The scene now facing Wittnam took everything to a whole new level. At that moment, something in him died. They'd been under his command for a year. He'd trained them, he'd urged them on, he'd been responsible for them. He felt proud when they'd done well. Now his young marines were dead. He knew that not a day would pass when he wouldn't think about them. He knew then that every day he would feel a wrenching regret that he wasn't able to bring them all home.

Wittnam had to stop the defense from breaking down. He ran along the lines, seeking out his platoon commanders, encouraging them to keep their marines in the fight. Many of them looked scared and confused.

"Keep doing what you are doing. Consolidate your ammo. It's not going to be too long. Our job is to secure this bridge, and we're not gonna leave it."

He knew he had to remain calm and show his face. That was how the Marines had taught him leadership. That's what kept the marines around him fighting.

At First Sergeant Jose Henao's medevac track, the number of casualties was mounting. Henao, who had spent twenty-two of his forty-one years in the Marine Corps, was already taking care of the five wounded from track 211. One of the wounded brought to him was the machine gunner, Jose Torres. Torres couldn't walk. His right leg was hurting so badly that he couldn't put pressure on it and had to hop on his left leg. His ears were still ringing and his vision was still foggy. He was only half there. He felt that part of him was floating in the air, looking down as if in a dream. Someone lay him down in the track and sat on him to stop the bleeding. He realized now that there were braggarts and bullshitters who claimed to have been in battle but really didn't understand what war was about. War got into your nose, your eyes, your ears, your stomach. War got into your head. Soldiers who had fought in the American Civil War had a phrase for it. They called it "seeing the elephant."

Michael "Doc" Robinson, one of the Navy corpsman assigned to the marines, winced as he cut away the chemical suit around Torres's right leg. There were chunks of flesh missing. He checked his airway, his breathing, his pulse. He pulled out some bandages from his molle bag, the first aid kit that had everything he needed for a combat medical emergency.

"We're gonna fix you up all right."

"Don't worry about me, work on the others."

Doc Robinson saw that Torres was in a bad way. He was emotional but strong. *That's the closest thing to a hero I ever saw.* He wanted to reassure him as he worked on him. At the same time, he couldn't tell him that it was going to be fine because he didn't know that.

"Corpsman up, corpsman up."

Robinson was up and running again. He had a marine running alongside him for protection. Robinson only carried a 9 mm sidearm. He could carry more medical equipment if he wasn't weighed down with heavy weapons. There were several casualties now lining up for treatment. Each time he stabilized one patient, the cry "Corpsman up" would ring out and he'd be up and running again, his molle bag banging into his side. He was grateful that the marines were wearing flak jackets and helmets. Most of the wounds he was treating were the extremities: gunshot and shrapnel wounds to the leg, broken limbs. He could deal with those. Shots to the chest and head he could do very little about. Caked in mud and dust, a marine was down in the dirt, clutching his leg and yelling in agony.

"I'm all messed up, Doc. Help me, Doc, save me. Am I going to die?"

A rush of impatience went through "Doc" Robinson. He knew it must be painful and he wouldn't like to get shot, but it wasn't a bad wound. He paused and went through the ABC routine—airway, breathing, circulation. His finger swept the marine's mouth, checking if the airway was clear and that he was breathing. Then he took his pulse. He tried to calm the marine down.

"It's going to be all right. You're safe. We're going to bandage you up and get you out of here."

It wasn't just about doing the physical thing. Ninety percent of what he did was sort out the mental side of his wounded marines. He had to encourage them, persuade them to be strong. In the three months that he'd been deployed with them he'd gotten to know them all so quickly, much more quickly than in Camp Lejeune. It felt as though he'd known them for years. He felt his heart jump into his throat, seeing his marines down and hurting. He had to push the thought aside and get on with his job. *There's time to grieve later on. There's time to feel sorry for them later on. Now it's time to act, not time to cry.*

First Sergeant Henao made a call to the battalion's assistant operations officer, Captain Joel Hernley, who was in the C7 vehicle at the battalion main command post south of the Euphrates Bridge.

"We need a medevac. It's urgent. We need a helo. But we're in a hot LZ."

Hernley asked Henao for the grid coordinates.

"I'll get back to you."

As Henao got off the track to look at his map, something big hit the medevac track, shaking it mercilessly and smashing a hole in its side. Marines inside screamed and yelled. A marine shouted at Henao.

"We've got to get the wounded out of here. We've got to take them back down south."

Henao was momentarily stunned. *Take them back down south? That's suicide. It's too far. We're not doing that.* No way was he going to go back down Ambush Alley.

He felt panic set in around him. He tried to remain calm.

"We're not going to go south. We're going to get the marines out of the track."

Henao knew the caliber of the shells landing around him. For over twelve years he'd been a marine mortarman. He knew that they were being pounded by 60 mm and 82 mm shells. He watched in awe as an RPG smashed into the rear of his track. It bounced off and landed in the dirt. It was a dud. Marines grabbed the wounded, picking them up any way they could, and carried them to another track. The driver tried to get the track started to get them out of there, but the ignition wouldn't turn over. They were taken out of the AAV again and laid down in a ditch sheltered by the raised highway. Marines half carried, half dragged Corporal Glass and Sergeant Torres and flopped them down in the dirt. They were yelling and moaning, their faces contorted in pain.

Torres looked around him at the dirt and dust and blood and the debris of marine boots, torn strips of uniform, and shredded MRE packets. For a few brief moments, he didn't miss anyone. He didn't miss his wife, his two-year-old son, his friends. He didn't even feel lonely. That made him sad. He felt light-headed and sick. He closed his eyes.

Nearby, marines made more frantic calls for an air casualty evacuation. Wittnam got the radio operator to call for help. The voice through the field telephone came back.

"When was the last time you took fire and from what direction?"

"We're taking fire from all directions and we're taking it now."

The landing zone was too hot. No helicopter could land there. The number of dead and wounded was mounting. Wittnam knew he'd lost the four marines from his mortar section. A shell had also killed a crewman in 208, Corporal Kemaphoom Chanawongse, a twenty-two-year-old Thai immigrant from Connecticut, as he was doing an ammo run from one of the tracks. But calling in a helicopter might make the situation worse. Even if the helicopter did manage to land, there was little chance that it would get out again unscathed.

There is a golden hour when you can get those guys out of here. Arms and legs were just dangling by pieces of skin and flesh. They were pumping out blood. Wittnam was aware that if he didn't get them proper medical attention they were going to lose their limbs completely. Or they might die. Comm was still not working effectively. He tried again to call Timberwolf to find out when help was arriving. He felt frustrated and impotent. The greatest military force in the world could do absolutely nothing to save his marines.

7

At the foot of the Euphrates Bridge, as he looked along the streets that led into the heart of the city, Captain Mike Brooks of Alpha Company saw Iraqi fighters pressing in on them along multiple routes. He had been at the bridge for nearly an hour, and the noise level and the amount of incoming fire was getting steadily more fearsome.

Whoosh.

An RPG streaked over his shoulder. He saw more and more muzzle flashes from the windows of the houses to the west of him and what looked like waves of Iraqi fighters crossing through the alleyways ahead of him. It was as though the whole town had woken up and begun to join the fight. His map was highlighted with the location of no-fire areas, such as schools and mosques, where the marines were not supposed to shoot. But now he looked through his binoculars to see groups of men running into a large mosque ahead of him. When they came out again, they were carrying weapons. *They've stockpiled weapons and ammunition in the buildings surrounding the bridge. They were waiting for us.* All the rules of engagement about not firing on sensitive buildings were now crumbling in the confusion. It was the first time he had been in combat, and he was taken aback by the sensation of hearing and feeling pieces of hot metal flying through the air, just past his face.

He was anxious to get his FiST working. His marines were being targeted by a rain of fire from inside the city, and Brooks knew that it would stay like that until he managed to fight back with some serious weaponry. To his left he saw his 60 mm mortar section taking cover in some sort of trash ditch. They had unloaded their mortar pieces and were now working furiously to attach the barrels to the baseplates. Within minutes, they dropped their first rounds on a blue building to the right where most of the Iraqi fire seemed to be coming from. The mortars were set on delay. They rocketed from the tube, smashed into the building, and erupted inside, shaking the walls and knocking the glass from the windows.

He looked around at his AAVs. They were all in a good position. They'd been able to pull in behind a solid five-foot-high wall that gave them cover. It was almost as though it had been built as a defense. From the AAVs' turrets, gunners fired their Mark 19 40 mm automatic grenade launchers. As the grenades impacted the ground, they punched holes in houses, destroyed sandbagged Iraqi positions, and tore apart anything within five meters of where they landed.

He had two platoons of infantry dispersed around the foot of the bridge, with one platoon further north tasked with securing the mouth of Ambush Alley. His young marines, lying in fighting holes and taking cover behind walls, were picking off Iraqis whenever they fired from windows or emerged from doorways to launch their RPGs. Brooks was grateful that his marines had such superior marksmanship skills. He also felt proud that they seemed to be working so well as small units, converting what they had learned in training into real combat awareness.

At their position a few hundred meters north of the Euphrates Bridge on the east side of Ambush Alley, Sergeant Frank Walker, Lance Corporal Christopher Rigolato, and Lance Corporal Dante Reece of Alpha's 2nd Platoon were behind a berm trying to work out what was going on. Rounds were whizzing over their heads from the labyrinthine alleyways ahead and behind them. Hueys and Cobras were firing into a line of houses on the opposite side of the road. *This is chaotic and confusing, but exhilarating.* Rigolato's training had taken over. *It's just like a rifle range except they're shooting back at us.*

Whoosh.

An RPG spiraled toward them and over their heads. Marines were yelling at each other.

"Get over here. No, this way. Watch your southern flank."

"RPG."

"Sniper at three o'clock."

Even though they'd trained for war, none of them was prepared for the reality of it. They were shooting into the city, but the amount of fire coming at them just kept increasing. Rigolato felt the fog of war descend on him and his understanding of what was going on escape from his grasp. *There's nothing I can do to lay out a plan. I'm just going to have to roll with the punches.*

Through his binoculars, Brooks saw the bizarre sight of a man with a child on his lap and his wife by his side sitting out on the door stoop watching the fight as if they'd come out to see a show. *Is that a commander observing the battle? Is he a forward observer pointing out our positions to the fighters? Is he using the child as insurance, believing that we won't shoot at him?* Brooks didn't open fire, but in the back of his mind he was wondering whether that was exactly what he should be doing.

He tried again to get comms. Sometimes it was crystal clear. Other times he could not get through, and all he picked up was the dialogue between the battalion's main command post and the forward CP.

"Timberwolf, this is Main. Sitrep over."

"Main, this is Timberwolf. Still taking fire from buildings around us. RPGs. Small-arms fire."

Brooks knew that these were conversations that needed to be held, but he had things that he had to pass over the net. There was so much chatter that he couldn't break in. *This is like waiting on an elevator that stops at every floor except mine.* He tried again.

"Timberwolf, this is Tomahawk 6. We are taking heavy fire on the bridge. I say again, heavy fire on the bridge. We need tank support."

Brooks waited for an acknowledgement. He was sending messages out but nothing was coming back. He had to assume that nobody could hear him. He couldn't understand why the tanks were taking so long to refuel. He glanced over again at the bridge, expecting to see the M1A1s rumbling toward him at any moment. There was nothing on the bridge. *Where are those tanks?*

For the moment, his weapon systems were keeping the enemy at bay. But he realized that the longer they were there, the more the level of incoming fire was increasing. His position was a good one. It enabled him to see right into the heart of the city. But it also meant that he was dangerously exposed to incoming fire from 360 degrees around them. Mortars, small-arms fire, and RPGs just kept coming. He felt that his young marines were edgy, and he didn't know for how long they would be able to withstand the onslaught. *It's only a matter of time before we take serious casualties.*

For a moment, he found his mind straying. *It's strange. After all that has gone on, I might end up dying in a shithole like this. It's not supposed to be playing out like this.* The U.S. Marines were supposed to be walking into Nasiriyah virtually unopposed. None of it was making sense. He didn't stay with the thought long. There were so many other things going on. *What should I do next? Is everyone doing what they are supposed to be doing?*

Once again he got on the radio to harass the battalion commander. This time he got through.

"Timberwolf, this is Tomahawk 6. We need those tanks. I'm not sure how long I can hold on here."

"Tomahawk 6, this is Timberwolf. We're working on it."

Brooks was fuming with frustration. *What I need are those damn tanks. Where the fuck are they?*

The Marine Corps had taught him in its warfighting books that "war is a clash between opposing human wills" and that to win it he had to shock and paralyze the enemy by "presenting him with multiple threats that overload his ability to respond or adapt." It wasn't working out like that. His military instinct told him that unless he had more firepower, they would be fighting along too many fronts and would soon be overrun.

8

At the refueling point several kilometers south of the Euphrates Bridge, Captain Scott Dyer, the XO of Team Tank, was still trying to gravity feed fuel into each tank. It seemed to be taking forever. While they waited, they pulled off the mine plows, a British invention that kept land mines from wrecking the front of the tanks, but which also slowed them down when they tried to move at speed. Four tanks, half refueled, had already gone back to meet up with Bravo Company. Now marines from the logistics train were focused on getting the other tanks refueled and ready for action. No one at the refueling point had any idea of the fight taking place for the bridges.

For the second time that day, Major Tuggle, the battalion's XO, came back in his track, driving at high speed, his head sticking out of the troop commander's hatch.

"What the hell are you guys still doing here? All units are in contact. We have to deploy the reserve. We need you to get all those tanks up there."

Dyer was astonished. *Deploy the reserve?* It was a phrase that meant a lot. Dyer knew that doctrinally the reserve is deployed at a critical juncture, at a decisive point on the battlefield, usually when the enemy has taken back some sort of control of the fight. The reserve is then deployed to break the enemy's tempo. Dyer was worried. *Maybe this means we are no longer in control of the clock. Maybe we are not in control of much else.*

"First it was Bravo in contact, and now you are saying that everyone is in contact. What the hell is going on?"

He could tell from Tuggle's face that this was serious. *There is a bunch of bad crap happening somewhere.* Dyer saw that Tuggle was trying to keep it in, but he was clearly struggling with raging emotions. His face was red and agitated. He was about to boil over. Dyer now understood that he and his tankers had been left out of the decision-making process yet again. *I can't believe that nobody has consulted us.* On the voyage over, various marines had told him that the battalion staff of 1st Battalion, 2nd Marines had a reputation for being reckless. Dyer had been told that at CAX the summer before, they had been criticized for rushing the HQ element through a breach too fast and needlessly endangering it when they could have stayed behind and commanded from a safe position with good overwatch to the rear. He had no idea whether it was true or not, and maybe it was sour grapes from other commands. But when he heard it, he had made a point of looking out for signs of carelessness.

Well, this is it. This is a prime example of hasty decision making. He got the feeling that Tuggle knew that this wasn't the best way of doing things but was not going to be publicly disloyal to his commander.

Which tanks can we send? Dyer saw that 1st Platoon were still struggling to get the mine plows off their tanks. The tanks from the HQ element were still being refueled. Tuggle was desperate, but Dyer didn't want to send all the tanks up there in such a disorganized fashion. A hasty decision might make the situation even more chaotic. He got hold of Captain Romeo Cubas, the commander of 3rd Platoon, whose tanks were partly refueled, and told him to take his unit and go and help Bravo Company.

Nearby Major Peeples was still trying to work the radio near the refueling point when he heard the roar of an M1A1 engine. He looked up to see Cubas jump suddenly into his tank and head north at full speed. *Where's he going?* He tried to stop him to find out what he was doing, but he'd already gone. Tuggle came up to him.

Private Casey Robinson
(*Courtesy of Private Casey Robinson*)

Major David Sosa, operations officer, 1/2 Marines. (*Courtesy of the author*)

Captain Mike Brooks, Alpha Company. (*Courtesy of the author*)

Lieutenant Conor Tracy,
AAV platoon commander.
(*Courtesy of the author*)

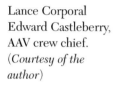

Sergeant William Shaefer,
AAV section leader.
(*Courtesy of the author*)

Lance Corporal
Edward Castleberry,
AAV crew chief.
(*Courtesy of the
author*)

Corporal Matthew Juska who was found alive in the destroyed AAV C206. (*Courtesy of the author*)

Tank Commander Major Bill Peeples, the day before attacking into Nasiriyah. (*Courtesy of Major Bill Peeples*)

Lieutenant Colonel Rick Grabowski (seated in Humvee) and Sergeant Major Arrick in Nasiriyah. (*Courtesy of CW04 David Dunfee*)

The welcome sign on the outskirts of Nasiriyah that so disturbed Corporal Neville Welch. (*Courtesy of Captain Romeo Cubas*)

Burning vehicles of the 507th Maintenance Company. (*Courtesy of CW04 David Dunfee*)

View of the bridge across the Euphrates, looking north. (*Courtesy of CW04 David Dunfee*)

Ambush Alley viewed from the southern bridge. (*Courtesy of CW04 David Dunfee*)

The Alamo—the house in Ambush Alley held by the Charlie Company Marines. (*Courtesy of CW04 David Dunfee*)

Gunnery Sergeant Greg Wright next to an Iraqi mural depicting 9/11. (*Courtesy of Gunnery Sergeant Randy Howard*)

Staff Sergeant Aaron Harrell pulling security by the mud bog. (*Courtesy of Gunnery Sergeant Randy Howard*)

A Bravo Company Humvee in an alleyway in eastern Nasiriyah. (*Courtesy of CW04 David Dunfee*)

Captain Cubas's tank stuck in the mud bog in eastern Nasiriyah. (*Courtesy of Gunnery Sergent Randy Howard*)

View from Charlie Company's position at the northern bridge. On the far left of the picture is the burning track 211, moments after it has been hit by an RPG in Ambush Alley.
(*U.S. Marine Corps photo*)

The dead and wounded from Charlie Company being evacuated from the northern bridge.
(*Courtesy of Major Eric Garcia*)

The ambulance carrying a top Iraqi commander that tried to head back into Nasiriyah on the night of March 23, 2003, before it was stopped by Captain Dyer and the crews of Team Tank.
(*Courtesy of Major Eric Garcia*)

Memorial service for Marines killed in Nasiriyah.
(*Courtesy of CW04 David Dunfee*)

"We need all your tanks up there. Now."

Peeples was just as confused as Dyer had been. He couldn't understand what the panic was about. It was then that Peeples finally understood that the battalion commander must have ordered the bridge seizure already. They'd done it without tank support. They'd done it without consulting him. *They've gone into the city without us.* He cut off refueling the last tanks and ordered what was left of his company to head north. He was down to five tanks—his own, Dyer's, and three from 1st Platoon. He wished he knew what was going on.

Peeples climbed in his tank, *Wild Bill,* and set off toward the city. Listening to the battalion net, he tried to work out where everyone was, but there was too much chatter and everybody was talking over everybody else. It was an incoherent mess of words.

"Where are you, Bravo Company?"

"Say again."

"We're taking fire from the north . . ."

"Timberwolf, this is . . ."

"Is that Alpha . . . Bravo . . . ?"

"We need those tanks."

"Where is Bravo Company?"

". . . fire from the northeast . . ."

"I can't get through to the battalion . . ."

"Palehorse 1?"

"Say again."

"We need air support at our position . . ."

I can't make hide or hair of what is going on. Peeples had helped plan the bridge seizure on ship. It had been meticulous and thorough. He was supposed to be at the Euphrates Bridge to offer support by fire before any of the infantry companies moved forward. Now he found himself bringing up the rear with no real understanding of where the companies were located. He guessed that Alpha must be at the Euphrates Bridge, and he'd picked up vague reports of Bravo and the forward command post being in the city, but he had no idea where Charlie Company was.

"Get the goddamn tank moving."

Something was wrong with *Wild Bill.* His driver, Corporal Michael McVey, sounded exasperated. He was frantically turning the M1A1's accelerator handles, nicknamed cadillacs, after the military manufacturer, Cadillac Gage. They worked just like the accelerator on a motorbike.

"I don't know what the hell is going on. I've got the cadillacs pulled back as far as possible."

"Shit."

Of all the friggin' times for the tank to go down. They'd had trouble with *Wild Bill* before, but Peeples thought the mechanics had fixed it. The heat sensor was malfunctioning and put the engine into emergency mode. It would only go five miles per hour. Peeples called back to what remained of 1st Platoon and switched tanks.

"Shit. Friggin' shit."

He scrambled for his maps and threw them into *Desert Knight,* one of 1st Platoon's tanks. *Shit. We've got to change the radio. Desert Knight's* radio was set up on the platoon net. He needed to be on the battalion net. Crewmen scurried around the tank for some minutes trying to get it sorted out.

"Let's go."

With the tanks from 3rd Platoon already on their way north, Peeples now only had four tanks with him as he headed toward the Euphrates. As they reached the railroad bridge, they saw some Iraqi T-55 tanks. One of the turrets was still moving. Peeples ordered the gunner to fire a SABOT round, a forty-five-pound armor-piercing projectile with stabilizing fins and a depleted uranium rod that could pierce and melt armor. *Boom.* The T-55 exploded in a fountain of metal and flames, its turret spinning wildly off into the distance. *It's toast.*

Next to him, in *Dark Side,* Dyer ordered his gunner, Corporal Bell, to engage three more tanks that looked as though they were still operational. There was a volley of small-arms rounds coming in at them from the fields around the bridge. Dyer replied with a burst from his coax. One of 1st Platoon's tanks was having difficulty firing its round. Dyer saw Staff Sergeant Samuel Swain dismount, run around to the front of the main gun, and shove a ramrod into the muzzle in an effort to clear the round. It wasn't pretty, but Dyer felt that for the third time that day his company was clicking.

He expected to see the battalion's vehicles at any moment, but the road ahead was empty. He was fuming. *They have attacked without us and nobody told us.* It was incomprehensible to him why anyone would charge into the city without tank support. And from what he could tell, they had done neither the blocking position to the south that they had discussed the night before, or the carefully choreographed movement to seize the bridges. *Where the hell are they?*

Dyer saw the span of the Euphrates Bridge ahead and smoke and debris billowing up in the city on the far side. *My God. This is apocalyptic.* The sky was dark from the thick black flames still burning around the broken U.S. Army vehicles. Shards of metal were flying through the air as the ammo inside the destroyed Iraqi tanks continued to cook off. Green and red tracers crisscrossed the smoky haze that enveloped them. And all the time they were getting closer to the city.

Dyer knew that, doctrinally, urban combat was seen as an infantryman's game. The accepted wisdom was that you don't bring tanks and armored vehicles into a city because they are vulnerable to a top-down attack. In an open field, tanks can spot and take out an enemy at a distance. In urban terrain, with so many obstacles, it's much harder to track soldiers and vehicles. That's why the tanks, in the original mission, were going to support the infantry in their seizure of the bridges from south of the Euphrates Bridge. This would be an infantry fight. Now, with his waist half out of the turret, he knew they were being sucked into an urban battle. He put the binoculars up to his eyes. He was shocked by what he saw. Alpha Company appeared to be pinned down at the foot of the bridge, and the level of fire directed at them seemed overwhelming. As he drove up to and across the bridge, he saw marines hunkered down behind walls and dug into ditches. AAVs were spread out on the road in front of him.

The streets ahead were teeming with vehicles and fighters on foot, and the air was thick with smoke and flying metal. *Jesus. It's like something out of a Hollywood movie.*

9

On the east side of Ambush Alley, the convoy of about ten Bravo Company vehicles, followed by the Humvees of what remained of the forward command staff, were still making their way northward, trying to get to the Saddam Canal Bridge through a labyrinth of roads and alleys. Each time they headed eastward to try to go around the outskirts of the city, they were blocked by irrigation canals and treacherous ground. Lieutenant Colonel Grabowski realized that they would have to give up on the idea of getting to the bridge by moving around through the east. They had come across an open area on the east side of Ambush Alley, about halfway between where the tanks were still stuck in the mud, two kilometers away to the south, and the northern bridge, two kilometers to the north. It was good for comms: There was more space and few walls or buildings to block the radio waves. Grabowski decided to pause there. *We're gonna stop here and circle the wagons till we find out what's going on.* Grabowski now managed to have a clear conversation with the regimental command post south of the Euphrates, but he had not heard anything from Captain Wittnam since Wittnam had called with news that Charlie Company had arrived at the northern bridge. He had no idea that Charlie was involved in a fight for its life.

Kneeling on the dusty ground, Grabowski and his staff formed a huddle and tried to figure out, on a makeshift terrain model, how they were going to get support to Alpha and Charlie. It was nearly 1400. Sosa and Grabowski knew where they had to be at the end of the day, but right now, they still had only a vague idea where each of the companies were and what was going on in their positions.

For Major Sosa, the impromptu planning meeting was frustrating. He hadn't expected to still be trying to figure out where everyone was at this point in the mission. There was information coming in on the battalion net, but none of it was clear. The battalion mortar platoon reported what they were doing, then Alpha stepped over them before they'd given out the full information, then Main keyed in to pass something over the net. Everyone was still trying to talk at the same time. What Sosa was understanding was that there was no longer one coherent battle being fought. *This is not one fight. There are several different fights going on at once.* He felt particularly resentful of the tank company. He still had no idea where all the tanks were. Major Peeples seemed to have his tanks here, there, and everywhere, and from what he could tell they didn't seem to be under his control.

Corporal Neville Welch and his fire team were pulling security for the battalion staff around the open area. The volume of fire passing over his head had lessened considerably, but every now and again he spotted an Iraqi fighter sticking his head from around a corner and letting loose with a poorly aimed volley of fire. Welch admired their bravery if not their intelligence. *Somehow they believe that they can carry on doing that and not get shot up.* His marines were focused on one building where there was suspicious activity. They saw a head pop out, let off a wildly aimed round, and disappear around the corner. The marines didn't fire back, but waited for the head to pop out again. When it did, his fire team let loose. He watched as the head jerked violently back and a body hit the ground.

On the other side of the open area, groups of people emerged from houses. They just stood and watched from afar. There were women and children just standing there gawking at him. Welch was perturbed. *I wish they'd get back inside.*

Circling above Grabowski's position, Cobra gunships were keeping any Iraqis at bay by making gun runs up and down the alleyways. Grabowski was grateful that the Marines had their own air support and that they had trained so thoroughly together during CAX in California's Mojave Desert the previous summer. Close air support could be a risky operation because pilots were engaging hostile targets right next to friendly forces. But it could be a powerful weapon. *When close air support works, it is something to behold.*

Within the battalion command, Grabowski had use of an air officer, an experienced pilot trained in the art of directing aircraft to target designated enemy positions. The air officer could call for helicopter or fixed-wing support. When the pilots were on station, the air officer would put them in contact with a forward air controller positioned with the frontline troops. Because the FAC was where the action was, he could give exact details of what the pilot was to target and how to target it without the pilot mistakenly hitting friendly forces.

The problem was that Grabowski only had two FACs to divide between the three frontline rifle companies. He'd given one to Alpha because they would be on the southern bridge, separated from the other two companies. The second FAC he'd given to Bravo because they would be the lead company. He didn't give Charlie a FAC. According to the original mission, Charlie would be located just behind Bravo until they pushed through, at the last moment, to take the northern bridge. At that point, the Bravo FAC would also be up by the northern bridge and would be able to control CAS, or close air support, for Charlie from then on. It was not an ideal situation, but there was no reason why it shouldn't work.

Two weeks before they had crossed into Iraq, Grabowski and his staff had been at a regimental staff meeting when they had been told that Type

3 CAS would be allowed. Rick Grabowski leaned over to a fellow commander.

"What is Type 3 CAS? I've never heard of that before."

No one seemed to know. After the meeting, Grabowski asked his air officer what Type 3 CAS was.

"I've got to get brushed up on it, sir. I'm not too sure myself."

"Well, get on it, because they are saying we can do it."

Grabowski knew what Type 1 CAS was. They had all practiced it many times. The forward air controller on the ground sees the enemy and makes contact with the pilot. He then talks the pilot onto the target and explains what to hit, the direction of approach for the attack, and how to egress the area. The key to Type 1 CAS was that the FAC saw the target and the aircraft with his own eyes. It therefore gave the pilot eyes on the ground so that he wouldn't mistakenly shoot up the wrong target. Type 2 CAS, which was less closely controlled, could be used when it was not possible for the FAC to acquire visual sighting of the aircraft because of bad weather or high altitude. It was more risky than Type 1, and Grabowski didn't like it. But when his air officer came back and explained what Type 3 CAS was, Grabowski was appalled. Type 3 CAS allowed a FAC to give the pilot a geographical area in which to operate, even when the FAC couldn't see the target or the aircraft. It was then up to the pilot to choose what to hit and how to hit it. It was not standard practice within the Marine Corps, although the Air Force did use it.

"We are not doing that. We have never practiced it."

Grabowski was vaguely aware that some of his marines thought he was too retentive and controlling. But he believed that not practicing something in training leads to mistakes in a war zone. He remembered as a young captain reading about a friendly fire incident during Desert Storm when an A-10 fired on a company of light armored vehicles, destroying two of them. The A-10 Thunderbolt was used by the USAF for ground-support missions. But it was notorious for mistakenly hitting friendlies. Because they were part of the Air Force and not the Marine Air Wing, A-10s did not have a good training history in the sort of CAS practiced by the Marines.

Grabowski's worst fear was that a pilot in the air, particularly an Air Force pilot with no history of working with the Marines, might mistake them for enemy forces.

Grabowski had it written in the operations order: "We will not authorize Type 3 CAS unless approved by the Battalion Commander." This meant that any request for a Type 3 CAS had to go through Grabowski himself.

10

As Bravo Company was making its way through the eastern edge of the city, and Charlie Company was crossing onto the northern bridge, two USAF A-10 Thunderbolts were flying several thousand feet above Nasiriyah on their way from Al Jaber Air Base in Kuwait toward Baghdad. They were heading for a grid location in southern Baghdad where they were to execute a bombing mission on unidentified targets. It was a clear day with a light wind. At the controls of the lead aircraft was an A-10 pilot with twelve years experience and twenty-two hundred flying hours under his belt. He was a major in the Pennsylvania Air National Guard, and his unit had been attached to the 332nd Air Expeditionary Wing for Operation Iraqi Freedom. Over the radio, he went by his call sign of Gyrate 73. He felt relaxed and calm and perfectly in control of his plane and his surroundings. This was his sixth mission in support of Operation Iraqi Freedom, and each mission had gone exactly as planned. There was no threat from the Iraqi air force. All its jets had been wiped out during Desert Storm and the first days of Iraqi Freedom. Gyrate 73 only had to resist the pressure of becoming too gung ho about the upcoming bombing mission to the south of Baghdad. The temptation to drop their bombs on any target was strong. *We're not going out there with our fangs hanging out. We're coming back with munitions if we don't have a target to hit. We're not just going to hit anything.*

His wingman, Gyrate 74, also a major in the Pennsylvania Air National Guard, had several years experience flying in Iraq. They included missions for Operation Southern Watch, enforcing the no-fly zone over the south of the country, which was imposed on Iraq at the end of the first Gulf war. While both pilots knew they were on a potential bomb run, they listened carefully to the chatter on the radio. They might get a change of bombing mission, or a call to provide emergency close air support for troops fighting on the ground.

The plane they were flying was nicknamed the "Warthog." The A-10 had an ugly, squat nose cone with antennae poking out in different directions from its frame. It carried five 100-pound bombs, high-explosive rockets, and Maverick and Sidewinder missiles. But what made it unique and fearsome was the twenty-two-foot-long, two-ton Avenger 30 mm Gatling gun, mounted on the underside of the nose. It was the most powerful gun ever mounted on an airplane. The seven revolving barrels fired thirty-nine hundred armor-piercing or high-explosive rounds per minute. The armor-piercing rounds, the size of milk bottles, contained a slug of depleted uranium that penetrated into armor, turning it into hot molten metal that ignited and burned. A-10 pilots liked to think of their plane as an aggressive, *down-and-dirty* type of aircraft that could fly in among the enemy, close enough so that the cannons could rip apart armored formations in minutes.

Thousands of feet below, traveling in the company command vehicle, was Bravo's forward air controller. His call sign was Mouth. He had been a FAC with 1st Battalion, 2nd Marines for over a year. He also had five years experience as a F/A-18 Hornet weapons information systems officer. He had been to combined arms exercises three times, once as a FAC. But this was his first time in combat. It had been a baptism of fire. All morning he had been calling in close air support from Apache and Cobra attack helicopters as 1/2 Marines had made their way up Route 7, across the railway bridge, onto the Euphrates Bridge, and into Nasiriyah. So far, though, the CAS had worked well. Even though he was weary from the battalion's fast march from Kuwait, he had managed to plot positions on his map, receive and send communications over two radios, maintain his awareness of the battlefield, and control the firepower of the helos. They had successfully taken out several tanks by the railroad bridge. He now had them hovering overhead, making sure that they provided supporting fire to the tanks that were still mired in the mud. He kept them close to Bravo's position. He didn't want them flying too far north, where they might get shot down.

Mouth felt he had close air support under control when he got a radio transmission from the battalion air officer, a hundred meters or so away at Grabowski's forward command post. The air officer's radio was broken. He was having difficulty communicating with regiment and the battalion main command post. He hardly had any situational awareness. The only person he could talk to was Mouth.

"Mouth, I need you to get on guard and get any air support you can find."

That was serious. Going *on guard* meant using the emergency channel to pick up whatever air support was in the area. And that meant using Air Force assets, too, rather than just the Marine planes and helos that he had trained with. He picked up the handset.

"On guard, on guard, on guard. This is Mouth in the vicinity of Nasiriyah. We have troops in contact and need immediate air support."

Several fixed-wing planes checked in with him, including what Mouth thought was a single A-10. He didn't have time to write down the correct call sign, but with the interference from the radio transmission he remembered it as Jenke 78. He consulted with Captain Tim Newland, Bravo's CO, to find out where the air support would be most effective. They agreed to send the aircraft north of the Saddam Canal Bridge, beyond the 3-8 grid line, to destroy enemy formations up there. Newland had told him that the battalion would be moving toward that bridge and they didn't want enemy reinforcements coming to meet them.

In the air, the two A-10 pilots, Gyrate 73 and his wingman, Gyrate 74, heard the on-guard call from Mouth and checked in with him. They listened as the Bravo FAC told them about the tanks stuck in the mud and the fight they were involved in down below.

"I need you to take out targets north of the canal bridge. That's the northern bridge on the eastern side of the city."

The A-10s flew in circles to the northeast of the city, trying to make sure that they knew where they were. Intel had briefed them that there was an antiaircraft threat in the area from Roland radar guided surface-to-air missiles. There was also a danger of SA-7 SAMs, small, handheld surface-to-air missiles, but so far there had been no sign of them. This was not a reconnaissance or patrol flight, like the ones they had done in the past. There was a real possibility of contact. The hairs on the back of the necks of both pilots were standing up as they heard Mouth directing them first toward the bridge at the Euphrates and then the Saddam Canal Bridge.

"I am between the two bridges, on the eastern side of the road."

Gyrate 73 called his wingman, circling overhead in a cover position. He wanted to make sure that they were talking about the same area.

"Gyrate 74, this is Gyrate 73. I'm not really sure what he's talking about."

"Let me take the tactical lead. I think I know where he is."

"Yeah, let's make sure we know what we're talking about."

Gyrate 74 swapped flying positions with Gyrate 73, and over the radio Gyrate 74 and Mouth went through the positions again. The A-10's specialty was getting close to where the action was. The pilots needed to get eyes on the target, rather than use remote-targeting systems. To do that, they needed to be *talked onto* the target. Mouth described the Euphrates Bridge, then told them to walk their eyes onto Ambush Alley and then onto the northern Saddam Canal Bridge. Gyrate 74 began to pick out the landmarks, following Mouth's description.

"Mouth, I think I know where you are. I got an open field where I'd like to put down a couple of rockets where I think is north of your position. Tell me if you see them."

Gyrate 74 fired a couple of phosphorous rockets to mark the area, but they didn't produce enough smoke and Mouth didn't see them.

The pilots picked up binoculars and scanned the landscape below for some other means of verifying their location. Then some helos came into view, flying across the canal from north to south. On the other side of the bridge, they saw a burning vehicle pouring out black smoke. Gyrate 73 assumed that the helos had just fired missiles on the vehicle.

"Mouth, do you see the helos and do you see the smoke?"

"Yes, I see the smoke. That is within our target area."

From the air, Gyrate 73 could now see other vehicles on the road. From 15,000 feet, through binoculars, there appeared to be eight or nine vehicles. Gyrate 74 thought they looked like dark pickup trucks. He was confident that they had correctly identified the target area. His battle-space awareness was growing with each second. They had practiced close air support over and over again so that they wouldn't hit friendlies. What had been missing from training were classes in identifying U.S. Marine Corps vehicles. The A-10 pilots thought that they had identified an enemy armored formation. What they didn't know was that the vehicles on the ground were Charlie's AAVs and that the smoke was from Charlie 211, the track that had been hit as it charged up Ambush Alley.

From his position on the ground south of the canal bridge, Mouth could see smoke rising to the north. He knew from talking to Captain Newland that there should be no friendly forces north of the 3-8 grid line running along the canal. Like the A-10 pilots, Mouth assumed the smoke was from an enemy vehicle. He called back to the pilot to confirm that the target area only contained enemy forces.

"No one is north of the 3-8 grid. There are no friendlies north of the canal."

It was 1355. Gyrate 73 now knew he had his targets. He made one final check on his map. He now told Mouth about the number of vehicles he could see below him. From his map, he confirmed that they were all north of the 3-8 grid line. *Okay. Nobody is north of the canal. Everything we are seeing, all the burning vehicles, they are north of the canal and north of the 3-8 grid line.*

Mouth got in touch with Captain Newland. He wanted to double-check that there were no friendly forces in the area. He was working off an aerial photo overlaid with grids. He knew from the plan that Bravo was supposed to be the lead unit. He got back to the pilot and put any gun runs on hold.

"Stand by while I check on the lead trace."

Newland again confirmed to Mouth that there were no friendly forces ahead of the 3-8 grid line.

At the northern bridge, just as the A-10s were circling overhead, Sergeant William Schaefer, manning the up-gun system of track 201, was trying to keep his fear and anxiety under control. He'd heard over the radio that the LZ was too hot for the helos to evacuate Charlie's wounded marines, yet with every minute that went by more of them were being brought to his track. He was beginning to panic. Their position was becoming increasingly fragile. If they didn't do something, they would be overwhelmed. He tried furiously to contact Lieutenant Tracy, his AAV platoon commander, on the radio, but he couldn't raise him. There was so much noise going on from incoming missiles that he didn't notice the sound of the A-10s flying overhead.

"I'm hit, I'm hit."

It was Axel, the call sign for Corporal Elliot, the vehicle commander of track 208. He was screaming in agony from a shrapnel wound to the neck, asking for help. Lance Corporal Castleberry, Schaefer's driver, also heard the screaming. They were both freaked. Schaefer radioed back to Elliot, "I'm coming for you." As he clicked out of the transmission he felt bad. *That's a blatant lie. I'm too busy to help him out.* Schaefer tried to contact Tracy again using their call signs.

"Whaler, this is Eight Ball. Can you hear me?"

There was just static on the radio. When Schaefer looked up from his gunsights, he couldn't see anyone. Everybody seemed to have disappeared. *I'm the oldest guy in the platoon. If Lieutenant Tracy is not around, I'm in charge.* At that moment, with chaos descending around him, he feared the worst. *Everyone else is dead. I am now the platoon commander.* The weight of the responsibility was terrible. He was terrified. *This sucks. We need to be more proactive. If we just sit here we're gonna get torn up.* He yelled to Castleberry.

"Drop the ramp."

Marines started yelling out.

"Back to the track."

"Let's go, let's go."

Private First Class Casey Robinson was still out in the mud fields on the west side of the road when he heard the cry go up.

"First squad back to the track."

He didn't know where the cry came from. Maybe Lance Corporal Roberto Sena, the radio operator, had received the call on his PRC-148 field radio. Or maybe his platoon commander, Lieutenant Scott Swantner, had called his squad leader. He had no idea how long they'd been out there. Maybe thirty minutes. Possibly an hour. Time had lost all meaning for him. He did know things were not good. *We're taking a hell of a beating.* He began to run back toward the track. He knew they were supposed to do it in a more coordinated fashion, covering each other while they were moving in bounds, but he no longer knew who he had with him. Some marines were injured. Others seemed not to be running with him, as if they were too scared to get out of the fighting holes they'd begun to dig for themselves. It was every marine for himself. Other members of his team seemed to be heading off toward the wrong track. He looked back and saw that Private First Class Gino Detone and Corporal Brad Richter had stayed out in the field. *This is confusing. This is not right.* He was grateful the enemy wasn't that smart. They led out a lot, firing aimlessly toward the marines, but then it would all go quiet. It gave him a bit more breathing space. He waited for a lull and then he ran, lugging his heavy M249 and ammo across the berms and ditches. The mud tried to suck him in, but long evenings working out at the gym, swimming in the pool, and surfing when he went home to California on liberty had given him the edge. Even with all his gear, his powerful legs pushed him easily across the muddy fields. When the firing started back up, he fell to the ground, listening in surprise to how loud and heavy his breathing sounded. He waited for a lull, picked up his weapon, and ran for the track.

Schaefer was yelling at them to get in. The track was being loaded up with wounded. Robinson peered inside. There were so many bodies in there that he couldn't work out how they could all fit in.

"Get in, we're moving. Get the fuck in."

As Robinson climbed up to the top of the track, a mortar slammed down next to him, tearing up the roof and sending metal flying into the open hatch. He could hear screams of pain from inside.

"I'm hit. I'm fucking hit."

Robinson stood on the roof and tried to pull the hatch shut. It stuck. He bent his knees, straightened his back, and pulled it again with all his strength. *The damn thing won't budge.*

"Let's fucking go. We've got to go."

Castleberry freaked out. Even though they were already overloaded, there were still people missing from 1st Squad. He knew that he was not supposed to go until he had everyone with him.

"Hold on, we've got more to load up."

Schaefer screamed back at him.

"They're on another fucking track. Let's go. We need to get out of here."

Neither Castleberry nor Schaefer heard the groaning of the A-10s as the planes began to circle lower overhead. There was too much noise going on right around them. Castleberry could hear people yelling over all of the four nets he was monitoring: battalion tac 1 and tac 2, the company net, and the AAV platoon frequency. He shouted at those still trying to come in through the back hatch.

"Just get the fuck in."

On the opposite side of the road, closer to the canal bridge, Lance Corporal Thomas Quirk was still lying in a ditch, sheltering from the incoming rounds. He looked around. There was no one from his fire team with him. Private First Class Gary Labarge jumped into the ditch carrying an M249 SAW. Quirk wondered why he wasn't firing it.

"I don't have any rounds. I got the weapon but no rounds."

"Holy shit."

Quirk ran down the lines, screaming at marines to pull out some magazines for him. The 249 normally used belt-fed ammunition, but you could also load it with 5.56 mm rounds from an M16 magazine. It was unorthodox, but it worked. Quirk threw the magazines at Labarge, who started loading them into the magazine well. At that moment they heard a new sound, the whistle of incoming missiles.

Vrrrrm. Vrmmm. Vrmmm.

Ever since he'd been a kid, he'd played these games where someone would imitate the whistle of an incoming shell and then it would explode and they'd fall to the ground like idiots. Now it was happening for real. *This is as scary as shit.*

VRRRMMMMM.

Quirk felt warm air shoot past his ear and heard a thud about five meters in front of him. *Holy shit.* He turned to Labarge.

"What the fuck was that?"

"You don't want to know, brother."

"Fuck the bullshit, what the fuck was it?"

"That was a mortar. It missed your head by about a foot and a half. It was a dud, thank God."

"Maybe we should get the fuck out of here."

The twelve marines in the ditch piled out. Using the road as defilade, they ran back south toward the bridge. Behind them, just as in the movies, rounds kicked up dust in their wake.

Dadadadadada. Dadadadada.

Then Quirk heard another noise. It was a growling, groaning noise from above. A noise he'd never heard before, a bit like a buzz saw.

"What's that fucking noise?"

"It's an A-10."

"What the fuck is an A-10?"

At the same time, a hundred meters or so north of Quirk's position, First Lieutenant Ben Reid, blood still running from his face, ran back to the location where his mortar squad had been hit. The bodies were still there, lying in pools of blood. Corporal Garibay hadn't moved. He was moaning and groaning like a kid with bellyache. Reid didn't stop to find out what was wrong with him.

"There will be a track coming over. You need to get these guys loaded up. I don't care how much it hurts. If I don't make it back to here, you need to get out of here and find the battalion aid station and get these guys help. I am going to grab some guys to help us out."

He went south to where he had seen a handful of marines lying prone in the dirt. There were mortars and RPGs flying through the air and thudding and exploding in the dirt around him, but he hardly noticed it anymore. *We're all fucking screwed up. We're screwed up.* He found some marines lying behind a berm and stumbled toward them. He fell, got up out of the dirt, and fell down again. He staggered to his feet, unaware of the rounds flying over his head. Finally, he reached some marines tucked up in a ditch against the east side of the road. It was Gunnery Sergeant Jerry Blackwell, Corporal Charles Wykstra, and a few others.

All Blackwell and Wykstra could see was a marine with a bleeding mess of a head stumbling toward them out of a thick cloud of black smoke.

"Who the fuck is that?"

"Gunny, it's Lieutenant Reid."

Wykstra and Blackwell pulled him to the ground and grabbed some bandages from their first-aid kit.

"Hey, Gunny, is my eyeball still in my head?"

Blackwell looked him over.

"I think it's still there. You look good."

"What the fuck is going on? We need to get out of this shit."

Reid did a quick sanity check on his own situation and realized that he'd been stumbling around without a Kevlar helmet or a gas mask. He'd lost his binos and his map. He didn't hear the plane overhead, but Blackwell did.

"There's an A-10 here now."

"That's good, Gunny. We need the help."

"No it's not. The A-10 is fucking coming at us."

Mouth, from his position on the eastern side of the city, south of the canal bridge, was now waiting for the A-10s to engage their targets. He knew that he couldn't control the close air support through Type 1 CAS. He could not see the enemy forces and was unable to satisfy the criteria for positively identifying targets. He did believe, though, that he had satisfied the requirements to safeguard incidents of friendly fire. The plan was that Bravo was always going to be the lead unit. He had checked with the company commander that they were still the lead unit. No one had overtaken them. Type 3 CAS would allow him to give the pilots a geographical area to target. The battalion commander, Lieutenant Colonel Grabowski, had stated that Type 3 CAS had to be cleared through him. Mouth was stressed. Comms with the battalion commander was virtually nonexistent. He didn't want to hold up the attack. *There is no time to find a clear channel to the battalion commander to explain the situation and then ask for approval for the fires.* He was worried that there were enemy forces congregating north of the canal about to head into the city to attack the marines there. *CAS is use it or lose it. It is flexible and lethal, but fleeting. If I don't act now, marines are going to die.* He decided that it was within his responsibility, through Commander's Intent, to authorize Type 3 CAS allowing the pilots to prosecute their own targets north of the canal.

Overhead, the A-10 pilots assumed that they were under the FAC's control and that Mouth had eyes on the target. They thought they were operating under Type 1 or 2 control. They got on the radio and asked Mouth for clearance to attack the targets.

Mouth, still operating from his track in the east of the city, was bemused. *Why are they asking for clearance?* Under Type 3 CAS, they were allowed to engage the targets as they thought fit. *I don't want to get involved in a discussion about close air support doctrine.* He decided to clear them hot so they would get on with the business of dropping their bombs and firing their rounds.

Gyrate 73 and 74 heard their clearance to engage. They wheeled around on a final east-west approach for a gun run on the vehicles below. It was a classic A-10 deployment. The pilots had their eyes on the target vehicles, and they knew their guns were extremely accurate and wouldn't cause collateral damage. They rolled the A-10s toward the road and lined up on their targets. Gyrate 73, followed by 74, swooped toward the target vehicles. The pilots flicked the triggers of their Gatling guns, unleashing whirling barrels that spewed out thousands of rounds. Both pilots felt a strong surge of energy as they let loose with the weapons. The power was so great that their jets shook as the guns went off, leaving a trail of gun gas blowing over their canopies. They watched as the rounds impacted the ground, tearing up everything in their path.

From his position in a ditch on the east side of the road, Reid looked up with his one good eye to see an A-10 roll in toward them. He watched as rounds from the 30 mm gun began to hit the ground about eighty-five meters to the northeast of where they were. Green sparks bounced off the ground, kicking up the dirt in a direct line toward their own tracks. Reid remembered that each track had been equipped with an orange panel to make friendly forces easier to identify from the air. The night before they left Camp Shoup, the company commanders had come by with orders from higher headquarters to take them off. They didn't want the tracks to have any panels on them unless they were green or tan.

Reid now watched with bewilderment as the rounds started to tear into their own tracks. *It's every man for himself.* Reid took off running to the east and didn't look back.

At track 201, Private First Class Casey Robinson, Corporal Jake Worthington, Sergeant William Schaefer, and Lance Corporal Edward Castleberry were all trying to take cover when the A-10s came in for their strafing run. Worthington first heard the rumble of something in the sky. Seconds later, he saw red sparks leap out of the top of one of the tracks herringboned nearby and more explosions coming in a line right toward them. As he rose to climb up through the hatch, he looked up and saw the underbelly of a plane with engines near the tail. He looked over at Lance Corporal Brian Wenberg.

"What the fuck was that? I thought we had air superiority. What's going on here?"

Seconds later, Worthington heard an ear-piercing explosion, like metal smashing on concrete, and leaped for cover. Robinson, still standing on the roof of the track, was thrown sideways. Schaefer felt a rush of air from below and was lifted out of his turret. Castleberry saw sparks bounce off the top of the track and something tear through the roof, cutting through the metal as if it were paper. The rounds tore up the ground around them.

Out in the fields, a group of marines were running toward track 201 trying to escape the mortar fire when one of them, the commander of 3rd Platoon, Second Lieutenant Mike Seely, heard a groaning noise overhead that he recognized. He had been strafed by an A-10 during Desert Storm. It was a low, loud growl he would never forget. With him was twenty-six-year-old Lance Corporal David Fribley, from the Florida town of Lee. It was the same Fribley that Lance Corporal Thomas Quirk thought was too nice to be a marine. Running alongside them was Lance Corporal Jared Martin, a twenty-nine-year-old former high school wrestler from Phoenix, Arizona. Martin saw a plane flying low toward them, moaning like some wounded beast out for revenge. He saw the ground up ahead being whipped up in dense clouds of sand. The rounds were heading straight for them. They willed themselves to get to the track. Heat and dirt kicked up all around. Seely felt something hit his side. Martin felt heat in his back. A piece of metal smacked Martin below the eye and blood streamed from his forehead. He looked down and saw his fingers hanging off.

"I've been hit."

"Man down."

Seely looked up to see Fribley lying in the dirt, almost broken in half, his flak jacket ripped from his body.

As one of the A-10s peeled off, Lieutenant Swantner, from the hatch of 201, saw a marine with blood pouring from his lower back and legs crawling toward him, trying to mouth the words "I can't walk." There was so much blood that he didn't recognize the marine. Swantner had only joined the company five months earlier. He had done pretty well to learn everyone's names on the ship over and in Camp Shoup, but he didn't know this guy. He threw off his helmet and jumped to the ground to try and pick the marine up.

Martin and Seely dragged Fribley's lifeless body to the rear of track 201. His helmet and the remains of his flak vest fell off. His clothes were shredded. As Martin tried to put him in the track, Castleberry felt another explosion. He looked back to see Fribley's back just blow out, pieces of flesh and guts fall off his body, onto Martin's face and Kevlar jacket.

On the other side of the road from track 201, Jose Torres was lying behind a mound, his leg still in agony from the RPG that had hit 211 as it was racing through Ambush Alley toward the northern bridge. With him was Captain Wittnam. They both heard the sound of a plane overhead. Wittnam had worked with A-10s during training. He recognized the sound. His first thought was *Thank God.* He was ecstatic that air support had come to help them out. Nearby, Lieutenant Tracy saw sparks fly up in the air. He, too, thought the A-10 was there to help them. *Man, that's kind of cool. It looks like a bunch of little sparklers on the Fourth of July.* Neither Wittnam nor Tracy looked up. But Torres did. He saw the A-10 bearing down toward him. Someone yelled out.

"Watch out."

It was all in slow motion. The rounds were kicking up dust and heading right for him.

"Oh my God."

At the last moment, he turned to avoid a direct hit. Torres felt a searing pain as burning metal tore through his left side.

Next to him, Wittnam was engulfed in a fountain of dirt and stones that erupted into his face. It was as if the entire world had turned black.

First Sergeant Jose Henao was on the west side of the road near the second mortar position, where they were still trying to pump out rounds to suppress the overwhelming amount of incoming fire. A marine yelled at him.

"First Sergeant. First Sergeant. We are in a shit sandwich."

"Yes, we are."

Everyone was yelling at him with news of someone who had been shot.

"I don't think the sergeant is going to make it."

Henao realized that he might not get out of this. *Man, I might get shot, too.* He thought of his wife and eight-month-old daughter. *I just want my little girl to see her dad again, that's all.*

As Henao got up and ran toward the bridge, he heard the sound of a plane. He looked up and saw it flying low toward him. He heard the groan of its gun and recognized it as the buzz of an A-10 on a gun run. As it kicked up rounds in front of him, he launched himself to the ground and covered his face. He looked up again and saw another A-10 firing terrifying bursts from its Gatling gun as it came in on its strafing run. As it passed, he looked up to see three marines lying next to him.

Corporal Matthew Juska, from Roxboro, North Carolina, was just reaching track 203, parked south of track 201, about three hundred meters to the north of the canal bridge when one of the A-10s made another gun run. There was so much noise around him that Juska didn't know what it was. He jumped into the track and pulled the hatch shut behind him. Corporal Randal Rosacker, a twenty-one-year-old machine gunner from San Diego, California, whose father was a Navy submariner, was already inside setting up his weapon to provide cover for marines darting across the road. Out of nowhere, Juska saw white sparks hit the top of the track. A blast of hot air swept through the track and blew the sides out. It was filled with 7.62 mm and 5.56 mm ammo on the left side and 40 mm grenades to the rear. He watched Rosacker's feet get swept out from under him as the blast lifted him up and dropped him back onto the deck of the track. Lance Corporal Bradley Seegert, posting air security in the hatch, felt his own arm burning. It was a hot, sticky mess. Hot metal fragments had shredded his triceps. The air swirled with dust, paper, and pieces of metal. There was debris everywhere. Juska didn't know about the A-10 overhead. He assumed they were being attacked by rockets. *They're tar-geting RPGs at us.*

Juska grabbed the marines with him and they poured out of the track and ran to a dirt mound. There was too much going on to think about what had happened to Rosacker. He didn't know that the blast had killed him in-stantly. Now more rounds rained down on the ditch where he'd taken cover.

"We've got to get out of here."

All around the northern bridge, it was chaos. Some marines popped off every bit of signaling pyrotechnics they could lay their hands on, sending green-and-red smoke into the air in an effort to get the A-10s off them. Tracks all around the northern bridge were being targeted. There were so many shells landing on and around the tracks that the marines couldn't tell whether they were being hit by the A-10, enemy artillery, or mortars. Wounded marines clambered into the back of any track they could find.

Lieutenant Mike Seely grabbed the radio handset and tried to call up battalion on the net. He screamed into his radio.

"Timberwolf, cease that damn A-10 fire. Cease fire. It's hitting friend-lies. Cease fire. Cease fire. You've got to turn off that air."

11

For nearly an hour, at the southern Euphrates Bridge, Alpha Company's com-mander, Captain Mike Brooks, had been nervously looking over his shoulder toward the river for signs of the tanks he'd been promised. The streets ahead were in turmoil. Iraqi gunmen were bounding from house to house, drawing closer to his battle positions. *The enemy is becoming more determined and better coordinated.* He almost felt the physical pressure of the encroaching enemy fire pushing in on the perimeter his marines had set up. *Where the hell are those tanks?* As he reached for the handset to get an update, he heard a deep rumble across the river and four tanks crested the bridge's span. The earth shook violently as they crushed the barrier separating the highway and moved up toward Brooks's frontline position. His heart leaped.

. . .

From the turret of *Desert Knight,* as he came down the span of the bridge into Nasiriyah, Major Peeples saw marines spread out around the foot of the bridge and into the city. Many were lying prone on the west side of the road, taking cover behind a long mud wall. Ahead, the mouth of Ambush Alley was teeming with military vehicles, taxis, trucks, and figures running from house to house. *How am I going to find the company commander?* He still couldn't quite believe that the battalion had just gone into the attack without them. He couldn't get anyone up on the battalion net. *Why is everyone still yammering away incoherently?* He looked out for an AAV with a diamond on it. It signified the company commander's vehicle. Just to the northwest of the bridge, he spotted it. As he jumped out of his tank, he saw Captain Brooks running toward him.

"What the hell is going on? What do you need?"

Brooks was so grateful to see him. In the middle of the road, with shots ringing around them, he pulled out a map and the two of them pored over it.

"I've got a platoon up to the north here and we're taking fire from buildings on the east of the road at about here. I want two tanks orientated that way to the north and another tank to the east."

"Roger that."

Peeples ran back to his tank and sent two of 1st Platoon's tanks a couple of hundred meters to the north. He told his XO, Captain Dyer, to take his tank, *Dark Side,* and face to the east. He rolled his tank forward and started shooting at some of the buildings on the west side. *This is not the way I thought we'd be fighting.* It was nondoctrinal warfare. Peeples's training had been about identifying and shooting targets a kilometer or so away. Now they were shooting at targets only a hundred meters away. He quickly switched his mind-set. This was close-quarter urban fighting. He saw muzzle flashes from windows and from bunkers.

Brooks's voice came over the radio.

"I want you to shoot the building with the blue door."

Peeples popped his head out of the turret. *There are three buildings with friggin' blue doors.*

"Gunner. MPAT." There was a frustrating pause while he tried to describe the target to his gunner.

"Shoot at all the fucking buildings with blue doors."

There was a huge boom, a massive fireball, and the first building just disintegrated. Methodically, the gunner traversed the turret, loaded another round, and fired the main gun.

In *Dark Side*, positioned just to the east of Peeples's tank, Dyer and his FAC, Major Hawkins, had managed to make radio contact with the tanks from 2nd Platoon. They had gone to help the 3rd Platoon tanks and the Bravo amtracks that were stuck on the east side of the city. Via messages relayed through Captain Thompson of 1st Platoon, Dyer now realized the full horror of their situation. At least three tanks were mired in mud and sewage in an area they were now referring to as *the shitbog*. Hawkins was on the radio and was speaking directly to the pilot of one of the helos flying overhead. The pilot painted a grim picture of waves of Iraqis trying to get at the mired vehicles. It was only the firepower of the Cobra gunships that was keeping them at bay. But now the pilots themselves were coming under attack from antiaircraft artillery fire.

"How does it look?"

"It looks okay, but we have to get them out of there."

Dyer had already called back to his tank leader, Gunnery Sergeant Greg Wright, to see if he could get the M88 tank retrievers moving north to help recover the tanks. There was little else he could do for the moment. *I've got to concentrate on the task in hand.* He needed to help Alpha's marines in securing the Euphrates Bridge. He yelled at his driver to maneuver his tank into position to give supporting fire. His tank was like a bullet magnet. As soon as it appeared on the scene, the Iraqis went for it, taking the gunfire away from the marines. All he could hear was a relentless *ping, ping, ping* as bullets bounced ineffectually off the thick armor of the Abrams.

"Driver. Hard left."

His driver, Lance Corporal Shirley, located in the driver's seat in the belly of the tank underneath the main gun, wasn't responding. He had been driving for thirteen hours and had only three hours of sleep the night before. Each time they stopped, he fell asleep in his seat. Dyer yelled at him again to wake him up.

"Driver. Hard left. Steady."

There were mud pools all around. He didn't want to get stuck like the others to the east.

"Gunner, we are going downhill. Raise the gun tube."

He saw waves of Iraqis running about ahead of him, darting in and out of buildings, preparing to attack the tank. He made a point of not calling them hajjis. He called them Baathists or fedayeen. He shouted at his driver to avoid the marines who had taken up positions all around him.

"There are grunts all over the ground, so be careful. I want you to pivot to the right. Okay, move forward, hard left."

He wanted to maneuver *Dark Side* ino a position where he could shoot long. He spotted machine-gun positions and bunkers. From what he could tell, Iraqi runners were resupplying the enemy's defensive positions with RPGs. Another round zipped past his head. He had never felt such clarity of thought. The adrenaline was flowing, his mind was clicking. *I am in the game.*

"See that wall? I want you to pull right up against that wall."

Dyer leaned out of the turret to make sure they didn't hit anything.

Gunfire poured down on them from roofs, windows, and behind buildings. Many of the marines on the ground around him were not shooting back. Maybe they were conserving ammo, but it was perplexing not to see them firing. Dyer worked on maneuvering his tank into a more effective position.

"Driver. Hang right, hard right, hard right. Steady. Go straight."

It was hard to identify who was a threat. No one seemed to be in uniform. Some civilians had weapons; others were just standing around, looking as though they had been pushed out into the streets and didn't know how to get away.

"Hard left. Now, now, now."

He turned to see a group of Iraqis with weapons run into a building in front of him.

"Gunner, coax, fire into that building."

His gunner, Corporal Bell, couldn't see which target he meant.

"Which building? I don't see anything."

"Fire a Z pattern through that whole building. There is at least a fire team in there."

The hum of the NBC system came on and the heavy machine gun mounted on the same axis as the main gun started chattering. Chunks of masonry exploded in the air as Bell fired first one way, then another. When he ceased fire it was eerily quiet. Nothing inside the building moved.

Dyer yelled down to the marines on the ground.

"Where do you need fire?"

One of the marines ran in front of the tank and fired two shots into a side alley. Dyer took it as a hint and fired the coax into the alleyway.

From the radio chatter, Dyer could hear that the battalion net was still clogged by everybody talking at once. And those who were talking shouldn't have been on it. Again he blamed it on Grabowski and Sosa. *They want too much control. This is what happens when every movement has to be authorized by them.* He wished the battalion command lived by a different maxim. *You keep the dogs of war on a leash until it starts, then you cut them loose.* He was both frustrated and relieved that he couldn't raise either Grabowski or Sosa on the net.

Suddenly, from around a corner of the same alleyway he had fired into earlier, an Iraqi with an RPG launcher on his shoulder popped out, took a knee, and fired. Dyer felt his heart freeze and drop into his chest. *Fuck me. I'm gonna die.* It was in freeze-frame. The gunner was rooted to the spot. Dyer stood still in his turret. The grenade spiraled toward him, trailing a snake of thick white smoke. He felt nauseous. *I'm gonna die.* In an instant it was over. The RPG flew past his head and exploded harmlessly behind him. The gunner disappeared around the corner. Dyer yelled at Bell.

"Gunner. Fire into that building."

The tank rocked back as a round exploded out of the muzzle and smashed into a corner of the building, spraying bricks and mortar into the alleyway. *I must have got him.*

The marines on the ground cheered and started pointing out targets. Iraqis were now trying to rush the tank on foot. He couldn't help but admire their bravery and their confidence in their ability to win. But they were stupid with it. *How on earth do they think they can take out a tank?*

Dyer worked between the main gun and the tank's coaxial machine gun. The coax punched big holes into the Iraqi fighters as they ran through the streets toward him. They would fall back and drop to the dirt. When he hit them with the main gun, they simply disintegrated. There was nothing left of them. With each *boom* of the main gun, marines would cheer and big grins would appear on their faces. Dyer noticed they got back to the fighting with renewed vigor. *It's like they've been given a shot in the arm.*

He now had a clearer view of how the Iraqis were managing to keep in the fight. Some of them were talking into cell phones and what he recognized as French-made infantry radios. He guessed they were target spotting for the mortar and the RPG teams and calling for taxis to drop off more fighters and ammo. *If only Special Forces had shut down the cell phone network.* He was relieved that he had ordered in extra ammo. In Kuwait, he had fought with the battalion staff, particularly the logistics officer, Captain Christopher Lynch, to get what he wanted. He knew that others in the staff had bitched about how much ammo he requested, but already he was eating through the main gun and the .50-cal rounds.

He had adopted a simple survival strategy when dealing with the battalion staff. *I have to work with these guys, but I don't have to like them.*

Captain Mike Brooks looked over toward the tankers. They weren't buttoned up; instead, they were out of their turrets manning their guns and looking for targets. Infantry sometimes looked down on tankers, but now Brooks had to admire their courage. They didn't often train with armored vehicles. But he could see their value. With each terrifying shot, the ground shook. It was awe inspiring. Whatever the tank targeted, the incoming fire from that position just stopped. Even the concussive force of each round going off seemed to wear down the energy with which the city's defenders were prepared to fight. He'd never understood what a difference a tank can make on the battlefield. For the first time in hours, he felt he was beginning to reassert some control.

12

Lieutenant Colonel Grabowski and his battalion staff were still in the open area just off to the east side of Ambush Alley, trying to build up a picture of the battlefield. Grabowski knew that Alpha was involved in a fight at the Euphrates Bridge. Captain Brooks had called him, wanting to know whether the tanks had finished refueling. He'd also received news that Charlie Company was now involved in some sort of firefight on the northern bridge. His staff had received worrying messages that Charlie had some casualties and needed a helo to medevac them out of there. But the landing zone was too hot and the medevac was canceled. The fight was tougher than he'd thought. But the next radio transmission he received took the battle to a new level. It was from a platoon commander with Charlie Company.

"Timberwolf. We've got air running on us. It's an A-10. Get them to call that A-10 off of us. For God's sake, sir, get them to stop."

There was so much going on that Grabowski couldn't grasp its impact. *How can there be an A-10 firing on our own marines?*

Moments later, the forward command post received another call.

"Cease that damn fire. Abort air, abort air."

It was the same voice again. Grabowski recognized it as that of Lieutenant Mike Seely, a Charlie Company platoon commander. Seely's voice was breaking under the strain. Grabowski knew Seely as a solid marine who had won a Purple Heart and a Bronze Star for his action during Desert Storm. He remembered that Seely had told him of one episode during the campaign where he had been run on by an A-10. If anyone knew what he was talking about, it would be Seely. He got on the regimental net.

"We've got friendly air running on us. You've got to turn it off."

A wave of frustration and helplessness swept over Grabowski. *Godamn. This is about as bad as it can get.*

13

Sergeant William Schaefer, in track 201, fighting with Charlie Company at the northern bridge, felt the battle spinning out of his control. Marines were being overwhelmed by enemy artillery, mortars, RPGs, and machine-gun fire, and now by friendly air. He still had no idea where his CO, Lieutenant Tracy, was, but he now saw other tracks desperately maneuvering on the road to get out of the way of the incoming rounds. He knew they had to move, too.

"Get in. We've got to get the fuck out of here."

Lance Corporal Jared Martin and the others were still struggling to push Fribley's lifeless body into the track through the small rear personnel hatch. Marines yelled and shouted in panic as they tried to wedge him in. They couldn't get him in. His head got caught on the frame of the hatch. They stripped off the remains of his Kevlar jacket and ripped off his chemical suit and his cammies down to his PT gear. His guts were coming out of his back. They pushed again. There was not much holding him together because his rib cage had been blown out. They crumpled him in half and pushed him in.

From inside the track, Corporal Worthington, still unsure as to exactly what had hit them moments earlier, saw the marines loading up a bulky, formless shape. He looked closer. It was a person. Martin stared at him.

"Fribley's dead."

Just as they closed the rear hatch, another shell rocked them, sending more shrapnel down the open top hatch.

Wenztel yelled in agony and clutched his shoulder.

"I'm hit, I'm hit."

On the roof of track 201, Private First Class Robinson was still trying to pull at the top hatch to close it. It wouldn't move.

"Close the hatch, close the fucking hatch."

"Just get in. We gotta get out of here. Get the fuck in."

Robinson ducked inside. Schaefer lodged himself into the AAV commander's seat. He ran a U.S. flag up the turret, hoping to ward off the A-10, which he could hear was still buzzing around. He was formulating his plan on the fly. He couldn't see Captain Wittnam or Lieutenant Tracy. The driver of track C205—which carried the injured twenty-year-old Corporal Randy Glass and Corporal Mike Mead, along with the young Navy corpsman, Luis Fonseca—had decided to take off across the Canal Bridge and head back down Ambush Alley without waiting for orders. Schaefer knew none of this. But he did know that they couldn't stay where they were. They were just getting shot up. He was going to take the track back down Ambush Alley toward Alpha's position. *We need to get out of here, and we need to get the wounded to the aid station.* He saw other tracks maneuvering around with the same idea. He sent out a message to the AAV commanders.

"Let's go. Watch for the flag."

Schaefer didn't know how many tracks would follow him, but he saw that Corporal Elliot in 208—which was carrying several wounded, including much of the mortar crew—was in front and was already taking off and heading back south. He wondered whether the other tracks with him knew what he had decided to do. He had a horrible moment of doubt. *I hope I was clear enough with my instructions.* He ordered Castleberry to get moving.

Castleberry gunned up 201's engine and went into full combat lock. He closed his hatch and got back on the road. In front, lying in the dirt, were the remains of Lieutenant Pokorney. He made sure he steered around the lifeless body. Then he slotted in behind Elliot's track and tried to stay as close as possible. He didn't want to get left behind. Neither he nor Schaefer had any idea how many tracks were following.

In fact, three other tracks were following Elliot and Schaefer. Track 206, carrying Corporal Matthew Juska and the injured tracker, Sergeant

Michael Bitz, had slotted in behind 201. In the darkness of the track, Juska had no idea what they were doing or where they were going. From where he was, he could see nothing. What worried him was that they were exposed on the raised part of the road. He yelled at the driver.

"Get off the fucking road."

The marines inside swayed wildly from side to side, drowning in the noise of the diesel engine, the smack of rounds hitting the outside of the track, and the roar of a plane overhead. *Where the fuck are we going?*

Tagging behind track 206 was track 210, filled with twenty-five marines, none of them injured, including Staff Sergeant Anthony Pompos. Pompos didn't quite know what he was doing there. As the shells and mortars had landed around them, they had become separated from the rest of the company, and someone had made a call to get back in the track.

"We are going to link up with the rest of Charlie Company."

The hatches were closed and it was pitch black. Pompos assumed that they were just going to drive a few hundred meters to avoid the incoming and to link up with the rest of Charlie closer to the bridge. What he didn't know was that in the chaos, the AAV driver had decided to join the rest of the medevac convoy and head all the way back down Ambush Alley.

Bringing up the rear of the five-vehicle medevac convoy was Corporal Michael Brown and a group of marines in track 207.

Circling overhead, the A-10 pilots looked down through their binoculars to see what damage they had done. The pilots saw that they had destroyed what they thought were enemy vehicles to the north of the bridge. But they also now saw five vehicles moving toward the bridge, heading back into the city. Gyrate 73 called back down to Mouth.

"Hey, you've got vehicles from the northern target sector progressing into the city."

Mouth was alarmed. He assumed they were enemy vehicles coming into the city to attack them. He cleared the pilots hot to take out the vehicles, insisting on an east-to-west attack heading to avoid the possibility of missiles spilling over from the target area and landing in the city.

"This is Mouth. Those vehicles must not get into the city."

The A-10s had been circling the area and firing on the target area north of the canal bridge for about twenty minutes. Now they had to make sure that the vehicles heading into the city did not get there. Gyrate 74 came in on a strafing run and fired off a Maverick.

In the troop compartment of track 201, Casey Robinson had no idea that they were now heading back down Ambush Alley. If he had known, he wouldn't have jumped in. He felt his track being pounded from all sides. A massive explosion rocked the track and lifted it up in the air. He thought they were going to topple over, but they came back down again with a thump. His insides were shaking and his teeth were rattling with each new boom as mortars and shells landed around them. Inside, no one was saying much. He saw a line of pale, strained faces. At each whistle of a shell, they clenched their insides, waiting to see if this was the one that would explode them into tiny pieces.

Boom.

Another explosion thudded into the tracks. This time it blew open the rear hatch, leaving it swinging madly on its hinges. Those inside inched forward into the track, moving their legs as far from the swinging hatch as possible. As it banged against its frame, Robinson could see the dust and rocks whipped up outside while the track hurtled forward. Wounded marines were pumping out blood, and Robinson felt it dripping all over him. The belly of the track was sticky with the stuff. There was no corpsman with them, so they were relying on buddy aid. Marines grabbed anything they could find, ripping up T-shirts, scarves, and clothes to use as bandages to stem the flow of blood. His squad leader, Corporal Wentzel, who had been injured by shrapnel, was balled up in a corner sobbing. Blood was pouring down Martin's forehead and Seegert was holding a bloody arm. Robinson noticed that they both seemed to still be in the game.

Above the medevac convoy, Gyrate 73 now positioned his plane in the shooter block for another bomb run. He came in on an east-west heading with two Maverick missiles. He saw what he thought was a small-size truck, heading across the bridge. He locked onto the vehicle as it was just south of the bridge and got ready to release one of the Mavericks.

On the ground, Corporal Elliot, in the commander's hatch of the lead vehicle, Charlie 208, had sped across the Saddam Canal Bridge and into the mouth of Ambush Alley. Ahead of him lay the long stretch of road that would lead him to the Euphrates Bridge, the battalion aid station, and safety. He was still bleeding from a shrapnel wound to the neck. There were eleven marines with him. His driver, Lance Corporal Trevino, had earlier put the body of Corporal Chanawongse in the troop compartment. Now it was also loaded with the injured mortarmen, Corporal Jose Garibay, Private First Class Tamario Burkett, and Private Jonathan Gifford, who had been hit when Iraqi rounds smashed into Lieutenant Reid's mortar position. He also had a 2nd Platoon squad leader, Sergeant Brendon Reiss, who had been injured by mortar or artillery fire. Providing security for the track were Lance Corporal Donald J. Cline Jr., Lance Corporal Thomas Blair, Corporal Patrick Nixon, Lance Corporal Michael Williams, and twenty-year-old Private First Class Nolan Hutchings. Elliot's track was also loaded with white phosphorous and illumination ammo for the 60 mm mortar in the troop compartment. With him in the up-gun station there were ninety-six rounds of 40 mm ammo and two hundred rounds of .50-cal ammo.

Elliot looked for threats as the track reached the mouth of Ambush Alley. He didn't hear the A-10 overhead. Out of nowhere there was an ear-shattering noise, a huge explosion, and heat and light seemed to pour into Elliot's turret. He felt the vehicle rock, fill with black smoke, and come to a halt. *What the fuck is happening?*

"Everybody, get out. Get out. Get out of the track."

He forced his way out of the turret and slid down the side of the track onto the dirt road. There was a searing pain in his leg. He yelled to the nine marines in back of the track.

"Get out. Get out."

Trevino had felt the track lift in the air as an explosion came in on top of them. He pulled himself out of the driver's hatch and slid down the other side of the track.

"Get out of the rear door."

Elliot didn't realize that all nine marines in the troop compartment had been blown apart by the blast.

Castleberry, driving track 201, was sticking close to Elliot's track when he saw the white flash shoot into 208's cargo hatch. There was a huge explosion, and he saw Elliot's track jump several feet off the ground. One side of the track just ripped open. Pieces of flesh flew out into the road in front of him. Blood hit his vision block, turning the toughened glass red.

From the turret of 201, Schaefer saw 208 lift in the air so high that he could see the underside of the vehicle. Thick black smoke poured out, and a hand and an arm bounced across the road in front of him. Blood and debris stuck to the gun mounts and the bulletproof glass around his turret. *Nobody can survive that.*

From the air, Gyrate 73 could see that he had scored a direct hit. He and his wingman received a delighted call from *Mouth.*

"Hey, you're putting smiles on the faces of the guys down here."

"Well, you've got a couple of Guard guys up here trying to do our best."

Robinson and the other marines in the troop compartment of 201 were oblivious to the A-10s overhead and the explosion that had blown track 208 apart. They just felt the track swing from side to side, shaken by loud booms. Through the gaps in the crowded track, Robinson could see Castleberry going crazy, swinging the steering mechanism first one way and then the other.

Castleberry first steered hard right to avoid smashing into track 208 and then hard left. He felt the track shudder. The steering wasn't responding. He screamed into the intercom.

"Sergeant. We've lost steering. We're going down."

"What the fuck, Castleberry?"

Schaefer's first thought was that Castleberry had fucked up. He had set him right so many times during training that he thought he'd done something stupid again.

"Hold on."

Castleberry was heading straight for some sort of telephone pole. The only thing he could think to do was run it over. He gunned the 525-horsepower engine, hoping to smash through it.

"Hold on. Hold on."

He braced himself as the track hit the pole, bounced off to the left, and headed toward some houses on the east side of Ambush Alley. Castleberry stamped on the brakes and the track came to a halt in front of a two-story concrete house. At the same time, something ripped open his hatch, shredded his CVC communications helmet, and blew him right down into his seat.

Schaefer, on the right side of the vehicle, felt heat come up through the turret. He thought he'd been wounded and grabbed his back, feeling for signs of hot, sticky blood. He was fine, but the track was completely immobile. He turned around to see everybody in the rear of the track staring at him with wild, confused eyes.

"Everyone out. Everyone out. Get the fuck out."

Then he got on the radio to the other tracks. He knew that some of them might have been hit. But if they stayed in the middle of Ambush Alley, none of them would survive.

"Don't stop. Keep on moving."

From the air, the A-10 pilots saw that they had scored a couple of direct hits on the vehicles below. Some of the vehicles seemed to be maneuvering off the main road to take cover in some of the side streets. It made another gun run risky. They knew that the farther into the city they chased the vehicles, the greater the likelihood that they would hit civilians or even marines.

Gyrate 73 still had one Maverick left. He locked on to another vehicle still out in the open and rolled in for his final approach. Then, just as he was about to release the missile, the radio crackled.

"Cease fire, cease fire, cease fire."

Gyrate 73 and Gyrate 74 were confused.

"Hey, did you hear that? Who called it? What's going on?"

On the ground, Mouth, the Bravo FAC, also heard the cease-fire call on the radio. He grabbed his FiST leader.

"Hey, what's wrong?"

"Battalion thinks there may be some friendlies north of the bridge."

Mouth's first thought was that battalion had been confused about which bridge he was targeting. *They think I'm targeting areas to the north of the southern bridge, not the northern bridge.*

"Check fire. Abort, abort, abort."

"What's going on?"

"Hey, we think we might have had a Blue on Blue, some guys might be up north at the canal, but we're not sure. No one really knows. I'm checking it out."

Gyrate 74 couldn't believe what he was hearing. Seconds earlier, he had been absolutely convinced that they were killing enemy units. Now, he wasn't so sure.

"You got to be kidding. But you cleared me hot."

Mouth again wondered why the pilot was emphasizing the issue of clearance. Under Type 3 CAS, pilots didn't need clearance. He assumed the pilot didn't know the correct CAS terminology, but he didn't want to get into a debate over the radio.

The radio went silent. The two A-10 pilots circled overhead for a few minutes to see if there was anything else they could do. But fuel was low. They called back to Mouth. They had to head back to Al Jaber Air Base in Kuwait. As they disappeared, Mouth was left wondering whether he had just unknowingly caused U.S. planes to fire on friendly forces, what the military call a Blue on Blue.

14

At the northern bridge, the Charlie Company commander, Captain Dan Wittnam, had been trying to get status reports from his platoon commanders when he saw the five tracks disappear over the bridge. *I don't feel good about this. Where are they going?* Very quickly, he guessed that they were evacuating the wounded. It was disconcerting. He was the company commander, and yet he had not ordered them to load up the wounded and played no part in organizing the convoy that was heading back down Ambush Alley. They had taken off without consulting him. If they'd asked him, he would have told them to stay where they were and help support the securing of the bridge. But the Marine Corps taught its marines to use their initiative. He had to believe that they had done what they thought was the right thing to do in the circumstances. Now Lieutenant Seely ran up to him.

"Sir, that was friendly fire that hit us."

Wittnam couldn't believe it. He had seen the A-10 and heard the gun runs, but he hadn't quite put it together that the A-10 had been shooting at them.

First Lieutenant Reid had escaped the A-10 fire and made his way back to the mortar squad where he had last seen the dead and wounded. He couldn't see Corporal Garibay or the other wounded. *That's good. They've gotten out of there.* He jumped into another ditch and saw that one kid was just staring right at him with huge eyes, freaked out by the sight of Reid's bleeding face. Reid tried to reassure him.

"Don't worry about it. We'll be okay."

Now Reid decided to cross the highway and see what the situation was on the west side of the road. As he crested the road, he saw that there was at least a platoon of marines on the other side. He had no idea they were there. He had not been able to see them because of the elevated highway. He was pissed off with himself. *I'm the fire support guy. I'm supposed to know where everyone is at.* He just stood there for a moment. *What the hell is going on?* One of his marines, Corporal James Peterson, a SMAW team leader from Texas, ran over, grabbed him, and threw him in the rear of a track. There was a medic inside who put a splint on his arm and bandages around his head. He tried to find out what was going on, but no one really knew.

"We need to get the fuck out of here."

Reid felt vulnerable in the track. He meant that they needed to get out of the AAV and find better positions on the ground, but the marines around him seized on it as an excuse to try to escape south.

"Lieutenant Reid says we need to get out of here. Let's get out of here. Let's fire up this track and let's go."

The driver of the track quickly calmed them down. He'd seen some of the tracks in the medevac convoy explode as they crossed the bridge.

"We ain't going nowhere. Two tracks have just got blown up trying to cross the bridge."

Quirk, Labarge, and several others from 3rd Platoon were lying in one of the ditches alongside the road, numb with fear. They thought they could hear the A-10 still circling. They had no idea that some of the tracks had already started to head back south.

"The A-10 is fucking lighting us up, we've got to get out of here."

With about ten other marines Quirk ran toward one of the tracks on the east side of the road not far from the canal bridge, opened the rear hatch, and clambered inside. They were struggling for breath from running so fast and were so thirsty that they could hardly feel their tongues. A marine threw over some canteens and they all started chugging water down, grabbing ammo and filling their magazines in between each gulp. Quirk was glad to escape the mayhem outside.

In the gun turret of the same track was the AAV platoon commander, Lieutenant Conor Tracy. He had seen the squad of marines making their way toward the track, duckwalking to avoid the rounds whizzing overhead. When he turned back again, he realized that they had all jumped into the back of his track. He bent down and looked in the troop compartment to see a line of frightened young marines.

"What the hell are you guys doing in here?"

Quirk had never seen the marine before and didn't recognize him as the AAV platoon commander. All he knew was that it was some sort of officer.

"It's as crazy as fuck out there. We're not fucking going out there."

"Bullshit. We got a war to fight, boys."

Quirk thought the guy was mad. *He hasn't got a clue what's going on.*

Just at that moment, there was a string of huge explosions that shook the track. Like a character from a cartoon, the officer dove for cover. Quirk almost had to stifle a laugh.

"Right. We're getting out of here."

Then more incoming shells started to rock the track. There was the sound of shattering glass and tearing metal as the track shuddered and bounced from side to side.

Boom. Boom. Boom.

No one quite knew what the shells were. Some thought they were from the A-10, others thought they were incoming mortar rounds. Tracy thought it was track 211, which was finally exploding from all the ammo inside. Whatever it was, some of the marines around Quirk started breaking down in sobs.

One of them was the same guy who had frozen going up Ambush Alley. He started to rock back and forth, then he grabbed Quirk and hugged him. Sobbing, he started to talk to himself.

"It's going to be okay. This is going to be over. Don't worry, we're going to be fine."

Quirk looked down at the marine hugging him and didn't know what to do. He too was scared. *The situation is fucking crazy, but I don't feel like crying.* He just went numb and thought about two things. *I need water. I need to load that ammo.*

Another marine, a buddy of his and a pretty hard-core guy, started sobbing to himself in a corner of the track. Not loud bawling, just a few sobs. For a second, Quirk started getting emotional, too. His bottom lip trembled. *Dear God, give me a calm heart.* He stopped himself from sinking into the terrifying dark depths. *I can't be thinking like that. Fuck it. No. Drink water and load the ammo.*

The track took off. Quirk felt it swinging from side to side as it was buffeted by incoming fire. He had no idea where they were or where they were going. Quirk just sat there waiting for the explosion that would land right on top of them and take them all out. He loaded up more magazines and inserted one into his M16. He turned to the tracker sitting next to him. He was the tracker from 211, the track Quirk had originally been in. For days, Quirk had felt resentful that trackers didn't get out and fight like the infantry grunts.

"We're condition one. When this ramp drops, you're getting out and fighting with us."

"What do you mean?"

"Do you need to be in this track to operate it?"

"No."

"Well, you're going to fucking get out and fight with us."

"No way, man."

The tracker handed Quirk a magazine and a grenade.

"Fuck you."

A minute later, the ramp dropped.

15

Castleberry couldn't hear a thing as he opened his eyes in the driver's seat of track 201. He was in shock, and his ears were ringing from the explosion that had sent them careering into the telephone pole in the middle of Ambush Alley. He looked up and saw the driver's hatch bobbing up and down above him. He grabbed it with his hand. It was still burning. He heaved it open. *I mustn't forget my rifle and my ammo.* He hauled himself out of the turret and fell to the ground to the left of the track.

Robinson, disorientated and stunned from the explosion, tried to drop the rear ramp. Marines were yelling at each other.

"Get out. Get the fuck out. Oh my God. Get that fucking ramp open."

The hydraulic system took time to work. If he waited for it to be fully released, they risked being hit by another shell. Robinson didn't want to get out of the rear hatch because he could see it was exposed to fire from the road. He clambered through the top hatch and jumped down to the left of the vehicle. As soon as he hit the road, he heard rounds pinging off the side of the track. He instinctively looked for cover and saw a wall, about five feet high, sheltered from most of the incoming fire by the huge hulk of the

AAV. He grabbed his M249 SAW, and, with adrenaline pumping, ran for the wall and leaped over it.

From 201's turret, Schaefer watched the other tracks in the convoy steer around his disabled track and disappear toward the southern bridge. His mind was in turmoil. The whole day was just going from bad to worse. He now needed to get out. He hoped that Castleberry, Robinson, Worthington, and the others were doing the same. *I can't believe this is happening.* He pulled himself out of the gun turret and jumped out to the right of the vehicle into Ambush Alley. He found himself in a dangerously exposed position, caught between the AAV and the west side of the road, where most of the fire was coming from. A crowd of Iraqis were emerging from the alleyways on the other side of Ambush Alley, ready to close in on him. *They're going to overrun me.*

Schaefer turned to see Lieutenant Scott Swantner and another marine at his side. There were three of them now facing what seemed like hordes of advancing Iraqis. *This is it. This is the end.* He had left his rifle back in the track. There was no way out. Then he heard the roar of an AAV. Track 207, commanded by Corporal Brown, had defied Schaefer's order to continue south to the Euphrates Bridge and turned around to come and pick them up. The three marines sprinted a hundred meters down Ambush Alley with the sound of bullets cracking through the air around them. They made it to the open hatch of one of the AAVs and threw themselves into the darkness of the track's belly. Schaefer was used to being in charge, issuing orders and seeing what was going on around him from his turret. Now it was pitch black. He could smell blood, diesel, and urine. He felt the wet mushiness of open flesh. He heard moans and screams and the rattle of rounds hitting the outside of the track. The AAV turned around and headed back south down Ambush Alley. Schaefer had never been so terrified in his life.

About seventy meters or so north of the disabled track 201, Elliot and Trevino were limping away from track 208. Its structure had collapsed, and it was turning into a fireball. They had managed to get out because they were located in the front of the track, not in the troop compartment. They had no idea what had hit their track and who, if anyone, in the rear had survived. They were desperate and disorientated. Elliot couldn't feel his leg and his neck was bleeding. Trevino's eyes were swollen and dripping blood. *It would be suicide to make our way back to the northern bridge.* Elliot saw that one track was pulled up against a telephone pole to the south of where they were. Supporting each other, the two marines dragged themselves toward it, taking cover as best as they could from the shots ringing out in Ambush Alley.

Down by track 201, Robinson was surprised to find that several marines had already gathered behind the same wall that he had jumped over when he had leaped from the disabled vehicle. It opened into a sort of courtyard, and they were dragging the wounded behind a rusty, broken-down bus that was collapsed in the middle of it. He counted Martin, Castleberry, Worthington, Wentzel, Doyle, Milter, Lance Corporal Rodriguez Ortiz, Private First Class Norman Doran, Private First Class Philip Honmichl, Private First Class David Matteson, Lance Corporal Richard Olivas . . . There were no staff sergeants, no lieutenants, no officers at all. They were all young marines, some not long out of high school. He heard the roar of the other tracks driving away and the metallic thud of rounds hammering the disabled track on the other side of the wall. When he peeped over the wall, he saw crowds of Iraqis beginning to close in on the track. *That's it. We're all alone.*

The marines started yelling at each other.

"We got to get better cover."

"Have we got everyone?"

"We need some covering fire."

Robinson looked back over the wall and noticed another track burning about seventy meters away. He saw two figures limp out of the smoke, away from the track, and try to get to their position. *Who the hell is that?* Their faces were black, and their hair was frizzled and singed. At first he thought they were Iraqis. Then he guessed they must be marines. But they were so messed up that he didn't recognize them. Other marines saw them and unloaded a burst of fire to cover for them while they, too, clambered over the wall into the courtyard.

Robinson, his face caked in mud and sweat and strained with anxiety, looked around for some sign of leadership. The most senior marine was Corporal John Wentzel, Robinson's squad leader. To Robinson, it looked as though he had given up the fight. He was still sitting there balled up with his head in his hands. *We've lost our leadership.* Robinson knew Wentzel was injured, but he felt a pang of anger. His old resentment that Wentzel had been promoted to squad leader resurfaced. *I was right about him. He's too soft. I always knew he was a pussy.* They'd been taught that when fear of death takes over there is the tendency to crumble and focus inward. The trick was to fight the fear, to take control of it and turn it into action.

During training, out of all the infantry techniques he'd learned, the one at which Robinson had really excelled was MOUT. Everything he knew about military operations on urban terrain now seemed to flow through his body without him thinking about it. He knew exactly what to do. He saw that Castleberry had the much lighter M203 rifle and grenade launcher. Robinson still had his heavier SAW machine gun.

"Want to trade?"

"Fucking A."

Castleberry was ecstatic to have his hands on a machine gun. He wasn't an infantryman, but he loved the idea of firing such a powerful weapon. He was hyped up by the adrenaline. *Fucking yeah. This is going to be awesome.* He looked around the corner of a wall and came face-to-face with an Iraqi creeping up toward the track, not more than ten meters away. Castleberry pointed the machine gun at the Iraqi fighter and squeezed the trigger. All he heard was the chunk of a round that wouldn't load. *Fuck, he's got an AK. Fuck, he's going to kill me.* He tried again. Nothing. He screamed out.

"Shoot him. Shoot him."

Someone let off a round and the Iraqi collapsed. Castleberry shouted at one of the other marines who had an M203.

"Give me that. I don't know how to use this fucking thing."

They traded weapons, then Castleberry propped himself up behind the wall and started firing off rounds and grenades at anything that moved.

Robinson, no longer weighed down by his SAW, set to work. He stayed low, kept tight with the others, and scanned up, down, left, and right in quick bursts. He was filled with the same buzz he experienced when he was a kid while surfing back home in Santa Cruz. Then he was focused on the changing waves, controlling his energy for that one moment when, with an explosive push, he would thrust himself up on the board and ride toward the beach. Every fiber in his body was now alert to what was going on around him. In training, they called it KOCOA—take in the Key terrain, Observe the fields of fire, take Cover and concealment, watch out for Obstacles, look for Avenues of approach. It was more intense than training in the wide-open desert. That's how he liked it. When he thought about trying for Force Reconnaissance, he often imagined he would excel on a dangerous urban quick-reaction mission. Now here he was, in the thick of it. He was street fighting.

"Hey, I'm over here. Hey, get me out of here."

Robinson peeked his head over the courtyard wall and saw Corporal James Carl still lying against the side of the track, yelling in pain. Rounds were pinging off the track around him. Most of the injured had been helped away from the track. Carl had somehow been left behind.

"Hey. Over here. I'm here. Come back."

Robinson could tell he was trying hard to stay tough, but there was real desperation in his voice.

He grabbed Doran, and the two of them jumped over the wall and ran toward Carl. By the time they got there, Corporal Jake Worthington, the Javelin gunner, was already in the dirt next to Carl, struggling to throw him over his shoulder in a fireman's carry.

Worthington had been running for the courtyard when he'd realized that they'd left a marine behind at the track. In Worthington's eyes, he was an injured marine, suffering and in pain, who needed help. He didn't know that it was Corporal Carl. He'd tried to put him over his shoulder to carry him away from the incoming rounds, but he didn't have the strength. He just didn't have anything left. He couldn't even lift him off the ground. Worthington saw rounds walking toward him, hitting the hull of the track and the dirt around his feet. He turned around to see a massive explosion as the deadlined track 208 went up in a fireball. *I'm going to be that dumb-ass who goes to help someone and gets himself shot. I'm going to die.* He looked up and saw Robinson and Doran coming to help. He was overwhelmed with gratitude. *They've just saved my life.*

Worthington grabbed one of Carl's arms and Doran the other. Then, while Robinson sprayed rounds from his M203 out into the street, the two dragged Carl away from the track. To Worthington, it looked as though Carl's femoral artery was cut because blood was just pouring out of his leg. *No way are we going to get him over that wall. He's gonna die.* Robinson let out another burst of fire and they dragged him to a blue-and-white iron gate set into a wall a short way from where the others were taking cover. Doran kicked the gate, but it didn't budge. The four of them were now several meters away from the shelter of the track, exposed in the middle of Ambush Alley. Doran kicked the iron gate again. This time it gave way, and the four of them tumbled into the courtyard of a house.

From the back room, a middle-aged Iraqi man came running out, shouting and quivering at the sight of the marines. He had his hands up in supplication. Robinson pointed his rifle at him.

"Get out of here. Get the fuck out."

The man gesticulated wildly with his arms, screaming at them in Arabic.

"Get the fuck out."

Robinson couldn't access any of the Arabic words that he'd learned. He made a sweeping motion with his gun to get him to move out, but the man just stood there, shouting at him in a stream of Arabic. Then he let out a lone English word.

"Family."

Robinson understood.

"Family. Okay. Go get your family."

From the back room, a young girl and an older woman joined them. Robinson saw that they were terrified. The young girl pulled her clothes around her, concerned that strange men were looking at her.

The older woman started to walk fast toward Worthington. In a panic, he aimed his rifle at her, ready to shoot. *If she takes one more step toward me I'm gonna kill her.* She took a step forward, reached out, and grabbed a scarf from a shelf behind him. She turned and ran panic stricken out of the back door. Worthington felt humiliated. *I was about to shoot her, and all she wanted was her scarf.*

The man turned back toward them. This time he spoke in broken English.

"Do you want anything?"

Robinson looked up, surprised.

"Yeah. Water. Water. Agua."

Worthington chuckled.

"Hey, dude, he's Iraqi, not Spanish."

The whole situation was terrifying, but Worthington couldn't help but laugh.

"Whatever. I'm Californian."

Robinson motioned again with his rifle.

"Get out of here."

This time the man turned and ran out. Now they had time to look around. They were in a room about six meters square with carpets, a sofa, plain wooden furniture, and windows with grilles. Bags of flour or rice had been improvised as sandbags against the windows.

"We got to clear these rooms."

Using room-entry techniques Robinson had learned from MOUT training, he ran through the house with Doran, checking that there was no one else in any of the other downstairs rooms. Robinson kept low, stayed away from windows, and darted into rooms while Doran covered for him, his rifle at the ready. He scanned up and down, to the left and right, kept fire discipline by not spraying rounds, cleared the room, and then moved on to the next one. He hurried through it, realizing that he ought to have taken more care. But it seemed to work. They had everyone out. The house was basic but homely, with five or six rooms—several steps up from the mud huts that they had seen on their way from Kuwait.

With the downstairs clear, Worthington lay Carl in the front room. He took out his Swiss Army knife and hacked through Carl's chemical suit trousers. The charcoal-lined suit was sodden with blood. He saw three wounds. One was a gaping hole in his thigh that was pumping blood. Two other wounds were on the shin of his leg, which was bloody and swollen. Worthington dropped his knife. Blood from Carl's wounds squirted toward it with such force that the knife was covered with it and washed away. Worthington never found it again. He grabbed his first-aid kit from his butt pack and stabilized Carl by pushing bandages into the hole in his leg. Every muscle in Carl's body was clenched with pain. As Worthington started to apply the pressure bandages, Carl groaned in agony.

Robinson bounded up a staircase and emerged onto a flat roof with a small bricked-up room. There was a laundry line spanning its length and a small parapet, about two feet high, running around the roof's perimeter. He checked his situational awareness. He knew that the rest of the marines were in a courtyard below him on the other side of the parapet. He didn't want to put his head over the wall because he knew it would surprise them and they would shoot him.

He yelled back into the alley.

"Is that you, Robinson?"

He dared to look over the wall and saw Martin aiming an M16 right at his head from below.

"Shit, I almost killed you."

"The house is clear. Get over here."

"How d'you get in?"

It was too dangerous to go back into Ambush Alley and around the front. Castleberry, Honmichl, and Martin collected some loose bricks and built some steps to help them all get over the wall. Robinson stood on top of the wall and covered them while, one by one, they climbed over and fell into the cleared house. It reminded Robinson of training. *Just like an obstacle course at Camp Lejeune.*

At that moment, an Iraqi who looked like the same man they had kicked out earlier came running into the house through the back door, gesticulating and ranting. Most marines had at some stage received their laminated card with the rules of engagement on it. "Treat civilians and their property with respect and dignity." "Give a receipt to the property's owner." Now, though, surrounded by a hostile force, in hostile territory, the rules of engagement looked different. A screaming Iraqi, even one who just wanted his property back, was a dead Iraqi. Several marines let out a burst of gunfire and the man dropped to the ground. They piled up furniture against the back door to stop anyone else from running in.

There were now four serious casualties and about twenty more or less able-bodied marines inside the house. Some of the marines began to panic. Jared Martin, blood still streaming down his eye from the shrapnel wound he received up at the bridge, tried to get his head together. *We've got to calm down. Is everyone okay now? What's going to happen next? We're low on water and ammo.* They knew they still had supplies in the track, including several boxes of ammo inside, but the track was still smoking. The whole thing might go up. Martin remembered that in the rush to get out, they had left behind the broken body of his buddy Fribley. He wished they had brought him with them.

Robinson was dying of thirst from running around. He realized he was unbearably hot. There was so much going on that he hadn't noticed it before. He threw off his chemical suit blouse and gas mask and got rid of his rubber overboots. He felt a hundred pounds lighter. He ran up to the roof with Castleberry, Martin, Ortiz, and some of the others. There they clicked into action. They divided up the areas they were going to cover, building up a base of fire around the SAW gun, the machine gun that was the backbone of a squad's defense. It was an excellent position.

"You got that building and that building. Next guy, you got that building and that building."

By posting marines a few meters apart, they could build overlapping sectors of fire and cover the whole street in front of them. They did a quick general scan of the buildings opposite. Then, as they'd been taught, they each made detailed scans of the street, gradually working their way outward in fifty-meter strips till they were looking at the rooftops opposite.

It was only now that Robinson realized exactly where they were. He heard the explosion of huge mortars raining down in the distance to his right, sending up billowing mushroom clouds. *It sounds like World War III.* He believed the noise was coming from the north side of the Saddam Canal, by the bridge where they had been fighting earlier. *The rest of Charlie Company must still be under attack.* He worked out that to his left was the Euphrates Bridge, which they had crossed several hours earlier. He looked at the disabled track 201 in the street, in front of the house. From the way it was facing, he worked out their orientation. They must have left the northern bridge and been traveling south when they got hit. *That means we are on our own in the middle of Ambush Alley.*

There were crowds of Iraqis about twenty meters from them, hiding in the alleyways opposite, inching closer. More of them started massing in the street. Robinson noticed that, strangely, some of them started waving, as if in welcome. He had no idea whether they were innocent civilians or fighters. He hadn't been taught how to fight like this. All of a sudden a burst of gunfire erupted from within the crowd. The marines on the roof opened up. Some in the crowd scattered. Others fell to the ground.

Castleberry was amazed at what a perfect place they'd found. From the roof they could see almost everything. They could also take shelter behind the low parapet. It was like their own fort. *It's like defending the Alamo.* It wasn't a comfortable sight, though. In the alleyways in front, to the left, and to the right, black-robed figures congregated, as though they were ready for an assault on the building.

"Hajjis at the track."

Marines let out a burst of fire as an Iraqi tried to run across the street and steal a ruck hanging from the side of the track. He ducked for cover. Then another one darted out. This time the marines on the roof hit him with a burst of gunfire. He shuddered to a halt and fell to the ground as the rounds punched him in the torso. Another burst of gunfire stopped his writhing. More Iraqis made the suicide run to the track. Some of them managed to pull down the rucks hanging off the track. Others were just cut down in the middle of the street. Young boys were sent out on the raiding missions. Maybe the Iraqis thought the Americans wouldn't shoot at young kids. Castleberry couldn't understand why fathers, uncles, and older brothers would let the young boys risk their lives. It bothered him. But he shot them anyway. *This is like shooting fish in a barrel.*

It was a continuous stream of orders and reassurance to each other. Nobody was in charge. They went with whoever shouted loudest and whoever came up with a good idea. But it was working. They were still alive.

"I need more ammo."

"Milter, watch out. Hajjis behind you."

"Who needs some 203s?"

"I'm out of rounds, I'm out of rounds."

"I need water over here."

"Hajjis running for the track."

They'd only been there fifteen minutes and already the area around track 201 was scattered with dead Iraqis. Castleberry couldn't explain why they kept rushing out into the street, only to be mowed down by the marines on the roof. *You'd have thought they would have got the idea.*

Farther up the road, strewn around the burning track 208, Robinson saw pieces of dead marines. He could hardly look at the sight. The track was still burning and beginning to cook off. Inside were boxes of ammo. The track was letting off sparks and flames. He regretted that they were losing so much ammo and firepower from the guns mounted on the track. *But at least the hajjis can't get at it to break down our defense.* It didn't stop them from trying, though. Young Iraqi boys dashed to the track and tried to pull down the rucks attached to its side, or grabbed Kevlars and equipment from the dead marines lying on the ground.

Robinson knew that they now had to let battalion know where they were. He watched the radio telephone operator, Lance Corporal Sena, doing his radio operator thing while crouched behind the parapet. He was fiddling with the handheld radio.

"The battery is dead. I can't get no comms. I can't get no comms."

Robinson's heart sank. *If we can't get comms, they won't find us. We're stuck.* He found Wentzel. Wentzel was no longer balled up. He was more energized. He now looked to be more in the game.

"I need to get back to the track and get some batteries for the radio."

Wentzel wouldn't let him go. He was worried that if the Iraqis started firing on the track again it might hit the ammo stored inside and then the whole thing would blow.

He went downstairs to find Worthington. Both Worthington and Wentzel were corporals. Theoretically, they had the same authority. If Wentzel wouldn't let him go, maybe Worthington would. He found Worthington still patching up Carl in the front room.

"I need to get back to the track."

"I know, but let's wait."

"Wait for what?"

"Wait till we've got a situation here. Just hang on."

Robinson didn't like the answer. They needed to get supplies from the track. The Marine Corps had taught him aggressiveness, boldness, initiative. But now he felt driven by something instinctive. Something he hadn't learned. Something he'd always lived with. He wanted to go to the track just to get something done, to get anything done. He felt a constant battle between giving in to fear and being inspired by it. He'd learned through Marine infantry school that fear was infectious. It could spread hopelessness and despair. Or it could be controlled and channeled to inspire those around him to fight. He left Worthington and put his energies into strengthening the defense for the house. Their position was good, but there was some dead space in a small alley to the left of them where, even from the roof, they still couldn't see anyone approaching. *If we can get the house next door, we will be in a much safer position.* He grabbed Olivas and Milter, ran downstairs, climbed over the eight-foot-high wall separating the houses, and ran into the courtyard of the house next door. The family inside took off pretty quick. This time Robinson knew what to expect from the layout of the rooms. He cleared the house by the book, methodically going from room to room. He kept low and tight with Olivas and Milter while they covered him. There was no one else inside the house. He went up the stone stairs onto the roof. There was a full view of both sides of Ambush Alley.

The first few minutes after the marines had taken over the house were chaotic and disorientating. Now Castleberry's initial, overwhelming panic had begun to subside. He had regained some situational awareness, and they had repelled the first wave of Iraqi fighters. He hadn't seen Sergeant Schaefer or Lieutenant Swantner and had no idea whether they had survived. Now he looked up to see Robinson on the roof of the house next door. On ship and in Kuwait, Castleberry had talked with Robinson about his desire to join Force Recon. Now he saw him strutting about on the roof of the house next door as if he owned it. *I don't believe it. He's having a good time. He's in full Recon mode.*

"You are beautiful, man. You are beautiful."

"This house is clear, dude. We're good."

"Get back over this side."

Looking at the space between the two houses, Robinson saw that if you had the balls you could get from one house to the other by jumping the gap between the two roofs rather than going back to ground level and climbing over walls. He felt the same nervous excitement he used to have when he was about to ride an awesome wave, a wave that might be too powerful for him. He took a breath, gave himself a short run-up, and jumped the gap.

In the sitting room downstairs, Worthington was talking to Carl, trying to keep him calm. The area had been turned into the casualty collection point and Lance Corporal Kyle Smith, with his trademark bandanna, was now beside him helping him treat the three other casualties. As Worthington reached over to hand out one of Smith's Newport cigarettes to the wounded, he banged his foot against Carl's leg. Carl screamed in pain.

"I'm sorry, dude, I'm sorry."

As he tried to move out of the way, he hit him again. Carl yelped. Worthington thought about giving him some Valium from his NBC pack. But Valium slows down the heart rate. Instead, he tried to take his mind away from the pain by talking about what they were going to do when they got out of there. Worthington knew that Carl wanted to open a bar with Corporal Glass when he left the Marines. For a while, they talked about the perfect bar, what drinks it would stock, where the barstools would be, what sort of music it would play. Sometimes Carl would join in. Other times he just lay there looking straight up in the air, his arms out to the side, legs perfectly still, muscles flexed with pain. When Worthington thought he could do no more, he grabbed the squad automatic weapon that was lying next to him, ready to join the fight. He was dismayed to find that although the SAW had a belt of ammo, about a hundred rounds, it was covered in mud.

If anyone could get it functioning again it was Worthington. The infantry trained all its marines to be expert riflemen. But Worthington was more than that. He was in Weapons Company and was at ease with any weapon system: the M240G, the M249, the M16, and the M203. He grabbed some cleaning gear that he had in his butt pack, took out an all-purpose brush, scraped the mud from the ammo, opened up the insides of the SAW, scraped it out, put it back together, and ran upstairs to see what was going on. At each corner of the roof there were two marines facing different directions, covering every part of the street below. Marines were picking people off blocks away. *This is an amazing sight.* Worthington was impressed and ran back downstairs to see what else he could do.

Sena's radio was still not working. Robinson knew that battalion was unaware of their location. If they didn't get batteries for the radio, they were stuck. Again he ran around looking for Wentzel and Worthington. This time, they both agreed that Robinson could make a run for the track to try to bring back some batteries and whatever else he could find. Worthington asked him to bring back the CLU, the command launch unit thermal-imaging sight system for his Javelin missile. With the CLU, he could track anything that had a different heat signature from its background. It meant that he would be able to see and target anything that moved, day or night.

Worthington organized suppressing fire from the roof and the downstairs courtyard while Robinson grabbed Milter and Olivas and headed for the gate onto the street.

The distance from the gate to the track was about twenty strides. During that time, they would be exposed to fire coming down Ambush Alley. They all counted.

"One, two, three."

On three, Robinson and Milter let out a burst of gunfire while Olivas ran into the street and jumped into the back of the track and began throwing out whatever he could find. There was still a danger that the whole thing could blow, and none of them wanted to spend any more time than necessary around that track. Olivas was tossing out several AT4s, portable 84 mm antitank rockets with disposable fiberglass launchers. Robinson winced at the sound of all that ammo banging on the ground. *It's not the textbook way to handle these weapons.* He threw out some small-arms ammo and the CLU for the Javelin that Worthington wanted. He didn't bring out any of the Javelin missiles. Other marines started grabbing the stuff and hauling it back into the house. Olivas hopped out of the track and charged back into the house. Milter and Robinson looked at each other.

"Did he get the batteries?"

"I don't think he did."

Robinson cursed him under his breath. *That's the whole reason why we're here.* He asked Milter for cover and hopped into the track himself, turning over the debris inside until he found the batteries for the radio. All the time he heard the eerie *ping, ping* of rounds hitting the track's aluminum skin. He grabbed some more ammo and stepped over Fribley's body, which was still lying in the rear. *I've got to get the hell out of here.*

Castleberry made his way across the downstairs room and headed for the roof. As he went past the casualty collection point where Smith was tending the wounded, one of the injured yelled out his name.

"Castleberry?"

"Elli. Holy fuck. I thought you were dead."

It was only now that Castleberry realized that the two marines who had limped toward them down Ambush Alley from the burning track were two of his fellow trackers, Corporal Elliot and Lance Corporal Trevino. Trevino had his hand on Elliot's neck and Elliot had his hand on Trevino's head, each trying to compress the other's wounds. Trevino's eyes were oozing saliva-like goop and blood.

"I can't see. I can't see shit."

Castleberry saw that they were both in a state of shock. They weren't screaming, even though their wounds were hemorrhaging badly. Elliot was pale with fear. The back of his leg was gone.

"What's going on? What's happening?"

"You're going to be fine. It's going to be okay. We're going to make it out of here."

Castleberry had no idea whether that was the truth, but, if he was in their position, that's what he would have wanted to hear.

Elliot lay there falling in and out of consciousness, listening to the shells land around them, hearing the rounds smacking against the wall. He could no longer feel his leg. His Achilles tendon had been sliced. His face was sore and burning hot. *It's only a matter of time before the house is hit. The hajjis are going to overrun us.* He felt that his energy was ebbing away and that he wouldn't have the strength to fight. *We're probably not going to make it.* As time went on, it didn't really matter to him anymore.

Castleberry, too, was feeling the strain. He'd already thought he was going to die once that day, when the RPGs nearly hit his track going through Ambush Alley. Now there was no doubt in his mind that he was not going to last the day. *I'm going to be going home in a cedar box.* He heard the sound of incoming fire, there were pieces of dead people all around, and he could hear the track up the road still cooking off with enormous explosions. Everything popped into his head all at once. *How will my wife spend the insurance money? What sort of life will she have? What sort of car will she buy with the money? Sergeant Schaefer is dead. I'm just one more on the list. I guess I'll be buried in Arlington Cemetery. How will Mom and Dad take it? I'm going to die.* For a few moments he lost hope. He wondered why no one had come to rescue them. He wondered what he was doing there in a strange house in the middle of Iraq. He felt like the loneliest man in the world. He'd never believed in the political reasons for going to war. *I don't care two squirts of piss about Iraq and the Iraqi people.* But he believed in the marines around him. He fought his way back up from the depths of the blackness and got back into the zone. *I'm not dead. I've got to live, and I'm gonna fight. It's time to kill some hajjis.* He got back up to the parapet and started going at it. He felt he was surviving on fear and adrenaline. He was not fighting for President George W. Bush, or the Stars and Stripes, or Mom's apple pie. He was fighting for the men on either side of him. For the first time in his Marine Corps experience there was no one telling Castleberry what to do. He was just one of a group of young men trying to stay alive and keep each other alive.

Iraqi fighters were now emerging from the backstreets to take the places of those whose bodies littered the street in front of the house. *They are so brave, but so stupid.* Robinson watched another Iraqi emerge from an alley and raise an RPG launcher to his shoulder. Before he could get his shot off, marines from the roof fired down on him. He was punched backward into the dirt, dropping his weapon. It lay there in the middle of the street. Robinson watched as other Iraqis ran out to pick it up. The marines gunned them down before they could reach it. *Holy shit. This is like hajji bait.* Someone hit the RPG with a direct hit and the grenade exploded, turning the weapon into a ball of twisted metal. After that the Iraqis stopped running for it.

From one end of the street, the figure of an old man emerged into Ambush Alley. He walked slowly and deliberately up the street, his arms out in supplication. It was such a strange sight that the whole roof stopped firing. He turned and started walking across the street toward the house. The marines scanned his hands, as they'd been trained, to see if he was carrying a weapon. As he got closer, Robinson saw that he was wearing bulky clothes. *Why's he wearing so many clothes when it's so hot?* The thought crossed everybody's mind that he might be some sort of suicide bomber. The marines on the roof started yelling at him to stop. Someone let out a warning shot. The man kept walking.

Robinson dug around in his head for the little Arabic that he knew.

"*Imshi.* Go away."

"*Al ardh.* On your belly."

"*Idayk fauk.* Put your hands up."

Someone fired another warning shot at his feet. The man just kept walking toward them. *This is too eerie.* Robinson was closest.

"Robinson. For fuck's sake, take a shot."

Robinson hit him in the neck and the old man sank to the ground, looking at him. Robinson shot him again and the old man sank to his hands and knees, still staring. It looked as though he was trying to say something, or make some sort of noise. He was gurgling. Robinson took another shot and the old man fell onto his hands, still looking at him. There was blood everywhere. Robinson could swear the man was staring right at him. He shot him twice more. The old man collapsed onto his belly, his gaze turned the other way.

Castleberry had a view directly into a small alleyway from his position on the roof. For several minutes, he had seen an Iraqi with an RPG ducking out from behind it, ready to shoot off a grenade. Castleberry had shot at him but missed. The Iraqi came out again, this time lower, and managed to let off a shot. Castleberry missed him again. Moments later, two robed women emerged from a door farther down the street and very calmly began to walk toward the alleyway. Castleberry looked at their hands. He couldn't see a weapon, so he didn't shoot. It was confusing, though. *There are bodies all over the place and they look like they're out for an afternoon stroll.* As they reached the alleyway, they stopped. Between their shoulders, Castleberry saw the outline of an RPG. The same man stepped out. Castleberry shot right through the women and three bodies dropped. *This is weirding me out. Who were they? Was one of them the man's wife? Or maybe his sister? Or were they men dressed as women?*

Downstairs, Worthington went out into the front courtyard. Ortiz had taken the position looking down the street to the right, and Smith had taken the position facing back down the alleyway. Worthington saw a place by the gate where he could set up his SAW to cover the street to the left. He found a drum of SAW ammo lying on some sort of water barrel. *Maybe Robinson got it from the track.* He set his SAW up overlooking the wall. He saw, heard, and felt everything with an intensity that he had never known. He felt that he had enhanced vision. If he looked at a window or a spot on a roof he noticed every little movement. Iraqi fighters popped out from behind dusty alleyways and balconies to take shots at them. He'd thought combat would be like a video game but as soon as he'd heard the first hiss and pop next to his ear he knew that this was for real.

Iraqi fighters across the street were pushing young children out into Ambush Alley. They were getting them to point out the Americans' positions. Worthington had a debate with himself. *Do I shoot or don't I? Can I live with this?* From the roofs, marines shot at women and children and watched them die. He knew it would haunt him for years to come. But he also knew that he would never think that they should have acted differently.

For the second time that day, he was sure he was going to die in Ambush Alley. *Nobody knows where we are.* From the front pocket of his

Kevlar jacket, where the antiballistic porcelain plate should have been, he pulled out some letters and a photo of his girlfriend. He'd chosen to leave the bulletproof plate buried in his ruck. *Her photo and letters will protect my heart.* He fingered his bear-tooth necklace. Just before Worthington left for Iraq, his adoptive dad had taken the four canine teeth out of a bear skull he'd had since the 1970s and made four necklaces. His dad kept one, he'd taken another, and he'd given the other two to his brother-in-law and his girlfriend. Worthington was part Native American and his symbol was the bear. He had bear claws attached to his rifle, his Kevlar jacket, and his pack. When he got back home, they were going to meet up and put all the bear teeth together. The symbol of the bear would protect him.

Robinson felt their position was getting better as each minute passed. As they defended the house from the roof, some marines compared their plight to the last stand at the Alamo. Nobody mentioned it, but all the defenders of the Alamo were wiped out. Even though Robinson's nerves were stretched, he couldn't help but laugh when, in the middle of it all, Milter, who was kind of goofy anyway, started going on about his tiger-striped underwear. It had been a running joke in Kuwait. *Marines just don't wear tiger-striped thongs.* But Milter just loved to dance around with them and show them off under his chemical suit. Everyone got a kick out of it. Even now, in the midst of chaos, Milter carried on with the joke.

"I hope I don't die because they'll cut off my cammies and everyone will see that I wear a tiger-striped thong."

Everyone laughed. Robinson really didn't feel like laughing. *But it's kinda funny.*

16

On the northern bridge, Captain Wittnam had a problem on his hands. Over fifty young marines had disappeared in the medevac convoy and were no longer in the fight for the bridge. He now had less than two platoons of infantry to defend the bridge. And among those that remained, scattered about the field were many feeling scared and jumpy. The A-10 running on them had shaken them all. He focused back on his mission. It was to seize the bridge and hold it. *There is no way we are going to abandon the bridge after we've fought so hard to get it.* RPG and mortar rounds were still coming at them from all directions. Once more he ran up and down the lines to offer reassurance.

"Keep doing what you're doing. Consolidate your ammunition. The other companies are fighting their way toward us. They'll be here soon."

He still expected Alpha or Bravo to come hurtling over the bridge at any moment. He wished he had the tanks with him to provide some real firepower. After the disastrous A-10 strafing run, he didn't want to call in close air support. Anyway, he didn't have a FAC to control it. With the direct hit on the mortar squad, his mortar assets were severely limited and running low on ammunition. He only had a couple of mobile tracks with functioning weapons systems. He had very few weapons systems that could operate at long range, beyond a thousand meters. He was relying on the individual marines with their M16 rifles to keep the enemy at bay. He got on the radio again, and now, for the first time in what seemed like hours, he managed to get a message through to the forward command.

"Timberwolf, this is Palehorse 6. We are taking heavy casualties."

He could tell from the urgent voices at the forward CP that Bravo and Alpha were also in one hell of a fight. No one could promise him when they could get support up to the northern bridge. There was nothing for it except to continue the fight.

"We're going to stay here until you can link up with us."

Lieutenant Conor Tracy dodged rounds as he crawled through the swampy area on the west side of the highway, just north of the canal. The level of incoming was unremitting. He'd seen the medvac convoy hurtle past and had tried to flag them down, but either they hadn't seen him, or they were just too anxious to get out of there. *Shit. There goes a lot of firepower.* Then he'd watched in horror as one of the tracks exploded just as it had crossed the bridge. He'd seen people running along the banks of the canal but couldn't tell whether they were marines or the enemy. He hoped it was marines who had safely escaped the burning track.

He had been exhilarated when the first shots had been fired and seduced by the violence of battle. Now it was different. He was weary with exhaustion. *I'm not having fun anymore.* He climbed back into the track and fired the grenade launcher and the .50 cal from the gun position of his track at buildings to his north. Figures were appearing on the roofs in the distance, getting off shots at him. RPGs and mortars exploded only a few meters away. Looking around, he saw the worried, mud-caked faces of marines lying in the dirt, trying to pick out targets. He felt a surge of panic pass through the infantry on the ground. *Our position is on the point of collapsing.*

As the AAV platoon commander, he was keeping count of what vehicles he had to support the company. He'd counted five vehicles going over the bridge, but another one must have gone either earlier or later because he only counted five vehicles with him on the northern bridge. He had watched two of them strafed by the A-10. Another was a mobility kill. It could still fire its guns, but it wasn't going anywhere. He did a mental calculation. That morning he'd started with twelve fully functioning vehicles. He'd lost one to mechanical failure by the railway bridge just before they attacked the city. Six had gone back down Ambush Alley, and three others were disabled or destroyed. That left him with only two fully functioning tracks, 202 and 204. There was no way they could get the rest of the company into two tracks if they had to make a sudden escape. He remembered being briefed that there was a company of Iraqi commandos in the 23rd Infantry Brigade military compound to the north. At any moment, he expected to see them come down on foot from the north and fight them for the bridge. *We're trapped. They've targeted that bridge so we can't go south. They are going to send foot-mobile troops down toward us from the north.* For the first time, Tracy seriously considered the possibility that he was going to be captured as a POW.

He worked his way south to link up with Captain Wittnam. On the west side of the road, he found First Sergeant Henao and Gunnery Sergeant Myers in one of the irrigation ditches. They were sodden and muddy. He lay next to them with rounds going off all around them, showering them with stones and mud. Then a mortar round landed only meters from them. Tracy felt the world around him spin. When he came to, he found himself lying in the mud with Gunny Myers on top of him. Myers scrambled to his feet and ran off. Tracy just lay there thinking he was about to die. He felt jealous that Myers could just get to his feet and run away like that. *That's me. I'm done.* He forced himself to sit up. Then he stood up. Then he took off running toward where he'd left his AAV. He got in the track and tried the battalion forward CP again. He got no reply. But then he picked up the voice of the Alpha S3, the battalion's assistant operations officer, Captain Joel Hernley, who was in a command-and-control track by the Euphrates Bridge with the main command post. He yelled at him down the radio.

"This is Tracy. I'm with Charlie. We need some help."

"There is antiaircraft fire and enemy forces on the northern bridge."

"I know. I'm north of that bridge."

"Yes, Tracy, I understand. You are north of the south bridge."

"No, I am north of the fucking north bridge."

There was a silence before he heard Hernley's voice again.

"Oh shit."

Tracy couldn't believe it. Nobody in command seemed to know what their position was.

He spotted Wittnam in a fighting hole and crawled over to him. He knew that they were in trouble. He wondered whether they might have to abandon the bridge. There was just too much incoming fire.

"What are we going to do, sir?"

"We're going to hold the bridge and stay here until we get backup."

"Roger that, sir."

Tracy was grateful. He had been racked with confusion over what they were going to do now. Wittnam had just clarified their mission. It gave him new heart.

First Lieutenant Reid was still in the medical track, parked up on the west side of the road. He heard the small-arms fire ricocheting off the side of the vehicle. His face was swollen and bloody, and a corpsman was fixing him up with bandages. *What are we going to do now?* Henao jumped in the rear hatch of the track to get an update on the casualties. He looked hard at Reid.

"Buesing is dead. There are others dead. But I don't want to tell you who else."

Reid already knew that Buesing had been killed. He also knew that Henao was referring to his platoon sergeant, Philip Jordan.

Captain Wittnam also came over and Reid saw him flinch when he looked at his face.

"Oh Jesus."

"It's okay, sir, I'm fine. What do we need to do?"

"We need to get everybody over to the east side of the road."

The east side of the road would offer them some shelter from the gunfire coming in at them from the area of the city to the southwest of their position. Reid saw Wittnam pick up a light machine gun and urge those still left on the west side of the road to cross over to the east. Marines teamed up in pairs, sprinted across the road, and sought cover on the other side. As Reid crossed he realized his pistol, still attached by its lanyard, was dragging behind him in the dirt. It was of no use to him. He could hardly see through the mess of flesh and blood and bandages wrapped around his head, and his right hand was too messed up to even hold it. He gave the pistol to a young marine. Reid was exhausted and his head was spinning. He lay down on the east side of the road until he was helped into the troop compartment of another track along with Espinoza, Torres, Private First Class Jason Keough, and a bunch of others. No one was talking much. He saw Staff Sergeant Lonnie Parker climb on Torres's leg and sit on him to stop the bleeding. Espinoza was slouched, alone and in pain, toward the front of the track. Keough though was making jokes. He was a wild one. Weeks before, Keough had been told he was going to be administratively separated—thrown out of the Marine Corps—for drug use. He turned to Reid.

"Do you still think they are going to admin sep me after this is all over?" Everyone in the track laughed.

Reid looked down at himself. He had no helmet, no map and no binos. He couldn't even hold a weapon. *I can't do jackshit. How will I ever come to terms with what is happening today?*

17

A few hundred meters north of the foot of the Euphrates Bridge, Sergeant Frank Walker, Lance Corporal Dante Reece, and Lance Corporal Christopher Rigolato from Alpha's 2nd Platoon were dug in behind walls and ditches at their position at the southern end of Ambush Alley. They were trying to protect the perimeter around the bridge by taking out enemy fighters running through the warren of alleys in front of them. Rigolato could see the numbers of people in the streets still swelling. It made him nervous. He was beginning to have trouble identifying who was a threat. A woman walked out with her hands up. She then ducked away to reveal an Iraqi fighter letting loose with an AK-47.

Iraqis sprinted across the road, running for their lives, but Rigolato wasn't sure if they were hostiles. Several children got caught in the crossfire and crumpled to the ground. The 60 mm mortars were taking out lumps of people's houses, exploding balconies and rooftops. Rigolato was glad the marines had superior marksmanship. The way some of the Iraqis were fighting was suicidal. He watched as one man emerged from cover and dropped down on one knee. But before he could put the RPG launcher to his shoulder, he was cut down in a hail of fire.

Above the noise of gunfire and RPG explosions the group of marines heard the roar of a military vehicle. They looked up to see a lone track, heading south through Ambush Alley, back toward them. Smoke was pouring out of the back. They were confused. *Who the fuck is that? Where did that track come from?* It came limping through their lines, and as it passed they could see it was dragging its rear ramp, leaving a trail of sparks. Just before the track reached the foot of the Euphrates Bridge, it came to a halt in the middle of the street. It was being buffeted from both sides by AK-47 fire and RPGs. Rigolato watched in horror as the white plume of an RPG smashed into its right flank, shaking it mercilessly. The track jumped up off the ground, coming back down again with a loud thud. Seconds later, another RPG flew into its top hatch, detonating the ammo inside and shattering the vehicle's frame.

Rigolato gasped as the track burst into flames. Yet the sight mesmerized him. *There will be mass casualties. No one can survive that.* Next to him, Reece, who thought that his platoon was having a hard time of it, now saw that someone else was in bigger trouble. *This is really crazy. They're cut up real bad. Someone has been in the wolf's mouth.* They both wondered whether any of their buddies were inside.

Walker assumed the track belonged to another of Alpha Company's platoons. He had no idea that it was Charlie Company's track 206, which had set off from the northern bridge minutes earlier to evacuate the wounded. Moments later, another track appeared down Ambush Alley, braking suddenly to avoid smashing into the back of track 206. It was Charlie's track 210, filled with the twenty-five able-bodied marines who had mistakenly joined up with the medevac convoy. Track 210 pulled past the destroyed track and continued toward the safety of Alpha's position at the Euphrates Bridge. When the ramp dropped, the disorientated young marines from Charlie emerged from the rear. Many of them had no idea that they were back at the Euphrates Bridge and that the marines crouched behind the walls were from Alpha Company.

As 206 burned, marines from Alpha's 3rd Platoon who were dug in by the bridge, closest to where the track had been hit, ran up Ambush Alley toward the smoldering structure. Under fire, they began digging through the debris to pull out survivors. It was carnage. There were pools of blood, bits of flesh melted onto hot metal, a severed leg still wearing a boot lying among playing cards, a magazine, cans of Coke, and a small bloodstained teddy bear. Swearing and panicked and shouting at each other, they tried to make sense of the chaos. None of them had ever seen anything like this.

"They are fucking dead, they are dead. Oh my God. Get in there. Get in there now and pull them out."

"Fuck. Help me. Fuck. Fuck. Fucking get over here and help me."

"Oh my God, I can't believe this. Did you see his leg? It was blown off. It was blown off."

From their position north of the destroyed track, Rigolato, Reece, and Walker saw the marines crowding around the rear, trying to pull bodies from the wreckage. One body wouldn't fit into the back of a Hummer, so the stretcher remained upright, the dead man's leg partly blown away. *No one can have survived the blast.* Then they started receiving rounds from a building behind them. They turned their focus away from the blackened track and got on with the task of taking cover and watching out for their position.

Gunnery Sergeant Justin Lehew and some marines from 3rd Platoon continued to fight their way through the debris in the troop compartment of the track. They pulled out two mutilated bodies, but they were so badly mashed up they didn't recognize them as thirty-one-year-old Sergeant Michael Bitz, whose wife had given birth to twins a month before, and twenty-two-year-old Lance Corporal Thomas Slocum. The insides of the track were so blackened and twisted that they were about to give up hope of finding any other survivors when one of the rescue team thought he heard a cough. *There must be another marine inside.* They searched through the rubble again with renewed vigor. Buried inside was Corporal Matthew Juska. He was unconscious but alive.

At the foot of the Euphrates Bridge, Captain Brooks had seen the track explode in Ambush Alley. He also saw some of the tracks speeding into his position from Ambush Alley. He had no idea that the AAVs were from Charlie Company. He assumed that the wrecked track in the middle of the road was one of his. A marine ran up to him with the bad news.

"We've got casualties, sir."

For Brooks, it all changed at that moment. War had become a terrible force. He'd known, of course, that there was always the possibility of taking casualties, but he never really thought it would happen. He wondered who they were but then stopped himself. *I've got to act. I've got to get a helo in there to save lives.* His forward air controller had already got on guard to an emergency channel and called for a helicopter to evacuate the wounded.

Looking around, Brooks saw that the other tracks were vulnerable. News of the casualties was spreading. He feared that his marines would lose heart. He got out of his track and ran down the lines of his marines.

"You're doing a good job."

"Keep doing what you are doing."

He wanted them to see his face. He wanted them to see that he was calm, that he thought everything was going well. The knowledge that his men took very seriously the distinguished fighting tradition of the United States Marine Corps gave him some comfort. *They don't want to be the first ones to screw things up.*

What are my options? His mission was to hang on to the Euphrates Bridge until 2nd Battalion, 8th Marines conducted a relief in place with him. Then he was to link up with Bravo and Charlie at the northern bridge. The relief in place was supposed to be a straightforward formality. He had gotten together with the company commanders from 2/8 a few days earlier. They had all agreed that it should only take them an hour to reach the Euphrates Bridge and relieve him. Brooks guessed that he had already been there for nearly three hours. His plan didn't call for him to seize a city block, fortify it, and dig in for the long haul. None of them had predicted that the Iraqis would be so determined. If he was going to stay there any longer, he would have to change tactics. He now had four tanks with him, but deep inside, he was worried. *What is going to happen?*

Once again he got back on the radio, frustrated that it took him so long to break through all the chatter.

"Timberwolf, this is Tomahawk 6. I need to know where 2/8 is. We are taking casualties. An RPG has just destroyed one of my amtracks. I have definitely got KIAs, and I don't know how many. I need to hand over the bridge to 2/8 and work my way north. My best place is with Charlie Company."

Brooks was burning with frustration. He wanted to move. Even with the tanks, his position was still not completely secure. There was probably a good reason why 2/8 hadn't come to relieve him, but he cursed them nevertheless. *Where the fuck are they?*

18

From their pause in an open area just to the east of Ambush Alley, about halfway between the southern bridge and the northern bridge, Lieutenant Colonel Grabowski and Major Sosa could see both ways up the Alley. They saw two disabled tracks in the distance, off to the north. To the south, the blast of explosions, the billowing smoke, and the helos flying overhead told them that Alpha was still engaged in a firefight by the Euphrates Bridge. Neither of them yet had a clear idea of exactly what was going on. Some moments earlier, Sosa had been surprised to see one of Charlie's amtracks sweep toward him from the northern bridge. It was track 207, commanded by Corporal Brown, one of the five tracks from the Charlie medevac convoy on its way south to evacuate the wounded. Lieutenant Swantner had spotted Sosa in the middle of the road. He yelled out to him.

"Captain Wittnam is dead. Charlie is taking casualties."

Sosa and Grabowki stared at each other in silence. They had heard the reports of casualties at Alpha's position, but this was different. This was someone they knew. Someone they worked with every day. Could it be true?

Dan is dead. Charlie is hurting. Sosa was now worried. *We might not accomplish our mission.* All sorts of options went through his head. He couldn't build up a picture of what was going on. There were sporadic reports that the vehicles in the mud had been pulled free and had then got stuck again. He went back to the basics of the mission. *We've got to get to the north of the city. We've got to help Charlie hold that northern bridge.* Maybe it was hard-hearted, but he wanted to push forward for the bridge. He didn't want to wait until the mired vehicles were pulled out. *The infantry platoon we've left with our tanks can look after themselves. I've got to get combat power forward. I've got to win back effective command and control.* His mind was buzzing with questions. *What instructions can I give to the companies to get them from where they are to where they need to be?*

He ran up to Grabowski.

"Sir, we've got to get north. We've got to send Bravo up to the northern bridge to help Charlie."

Grabowski was frustrated. He too wasn't clear about the exact location of the different companies or what was going on in their positions. But he was reluctant to leave the tanks, Humvees, and amtracks stuck in the mud. *If you have an asset, you don't abandon it.* Charlie was being fired on by the A-10 and was taking casualties. Now he had also picked up Brooks's urgent radio transmission telling him about the casualties at Alpha's position and asking for 2/8 to relieve him. Grabowski was silent for a moment. It was going from bad to worse. *Oh God. What do I tell this guy?* He tried to remain calm, yet his head was spinning with the update on casualties and all its ramifications. He couldn't authorize Alpha to move out until 2/8 had arrived to replace them. And 2/8 was not his responsibility. They were tied into what regiment was doing. All he could do was reassure Mike Brooks that he would communicate with regiment and find 2/8's location.

"Tomahawk, this is Timberwolf 6. I need you to hang on there. Do what you can to evacuate the casualties and keep me abreast of the situation. We'll get 2/8 up there as soon as possible. Let me know when 2/8 links up with you."

On the south side of the Euphrates Bridge, the regimental commander of 2nd Marines, Colonel Ronald Bailey, was moving his command post up from its position several miles south of the city toward the dump by the railroad bridge. He needed to stay within communications range of 1st Battalion, 2nd Marines as the battalion moved into Nasiriyah. Each time he stopped, he set up his Humvees in a protective perimeter around his staff. A platoon of marines was guarding the Humvees. In the center of the defense, he and his staff worked the radios to find out what was going on.

As the regimental commander, it was his job to help shape the fight for the battalions under his command. For months they had worked out a careful plan of how the battalions would move into Nasiriyah but from the radio reports coming in, it was clear that the battle was not working out like that. He was almost overwhelmed by the amount of information coming at him from different directions. It was hectic and heavy. His staff besieged him with confused and changing messages about what was happening to 1st Battalion, 2nd Marines inside the city. *The one thing I do know is that they are in one hell of a fight.*

He got onto his battalion staff.

"We need to know where 2/8 is."

Twice Grabowski had asked him to get 2nd Battalion, 8th Marines up to the Euphrates Bridge to relieve Captain Brooks's Alpha Company. From the tone of Grabowski's voice, he knew it was urgent. He didn't ask Grabowski too many questions, and he didn't monitor the battalion net. That was like spying on someone else's e-mail. He certainly didn't know that they had tanks stuck in the mud. He was hazy on Charlie's position. He had no idea that they had marines holed up in a house in Ambush Alley. He left Grabowski alone until he asked for help. *It's Rick's fight. I can only help him win it.*

"Two-Eight is still south of the railway bridge."

It was one of the regimental staff confirming that 2/8 was making slow progress along the road into the city. They were under attack the whole way, held up by enemy snipers and RPG teams lining the route. Bailey knew that he couldn't just order 2/8 to go straight for the bridge. Part of the regiment's mission was to clear the route into the city so that the combat service support units to the rear of the column wouldn't have to fight their way through. He'd chosen 2/8 to clear the route because they'd had extra MOUT training. But they were in soft-skinned trucks, not AAVs or tanks. There were just too many pieces to move around. Whenever he raised his head from the intensity of discussions with his staff, he was aware that shots were flying overhead. There were crowds of civilians heading away from the city, and he had to monitor them constantly to make sure they weren't suicide bombers or some sort of threat. He wasn't surprised that they now found themselves in such a fight. When the intel had come in about the Iraqis welcoming the Marines into Nasiriyah, he didn't take it seriously. *If someone was going to invade my country, I'd fight like hell to get them out of there.*

Bailey had grown up with stories of the military from his grandfather, who had fought in the U.S. Army under General Patton. Like many African Americans, Bailey had more of an affinity with the Army. The Army had a longer tradition of recruiting African Americans. The U.S. Marine Corps only recruited African Americans from the mid-1940s. That's why he'd been on an Army ROTC program, studying biology and chemistry at a small college in Tennessee. He'd wanted to go to jump school to be a Ranger, but there weren't enough places and he didn't want to wait an extra year. It was only when he met a Marine captain at the student center who goaded him about not being tough enough for the Corps that Bailey started to become interested. *Me, not tough enough? I'll show you.* He decided to go to the summer Platoon Leaders Class at the Marine Corps base in Quantico, Virginia. When he got back to college, he sported a military-style haircut and went around giving the Marine "hoorah" cry. He was captain of the football team, and it wasn't long before the rest of his players started cutting their hair and acting like marines, too. With the promise of $900 back pay, he turned his back on the idea of becoming a teacher or a professional football coach and signed up for the Marines. He took his football training with him, though. He likened his role in the Marine Corps to the best college football coaches, such as Woody Hayes at Ohio State and Ara Parseghian at Notre Dame. They talked about winning and he wanted that same aggressive spirit in his marines. The Marine Corps' history, traditions, and customs excited him. He loved the commercial in which a young recruit climbs a wall and around him appear flashes of the Corps's history and weaponry to support him on his ascent. *We are standing on the shoulders of our history and the traditions of our Corps.* He loved it that his call sign was Viking 6 in recognition of the 2nd Marines' long history of cold-weather training in Norway. *That's what it's about. Tradition and history.*

For years, he had been frustrated. Each time there was a major fight, he was elsewhere. He missed out on Beirut. When Grenada happened, he was at school. Then, during Desert Storm, he was on ceremonial duties at Marine Barracks in Washington, D.C. He felt like an unused player in a football game who was always sitting on the sidelines. He took comfort in the fact that Dwight D. Eisenhower didn't see combat until he became a general officer.

Twenty-eight years after joining the Marine Corps, he was finally at war. *Now I'm playing. Now I'm in combat as part of the toughest and the best.* It was like a big football game. Nothing he'd learned in training prepared him for the reality of it. *Once the adrenaline flows, no one knows how they are going to react.*

He concentrated on getting all the regimental assets working for the battalion. He was also concerned about the flanks. *We need to bolster our force to get through the rest of the day. We need to make sure we have the firepower to hold onto what we've got.* He thought about what he could do to anchor his position as the day went on. The 1st Marine Division was still pressing to go through. There was nothing on the road between 2/8, heading for the Euphrates Bridge, and his regimental HQ. He started working on a plan to get 3rd Battalion, 2nd Marines and the LAR battalion to reinforce his position.

"Have we got air up there?"

The question was aimed at his air officer, call sign Bear. Bailey wanted to make sure Grabowski had all the assets he needed, whether it be attack aircraft or casevac helos.

As he watched the smoke billowing up on the horizon, the helicopters pounding the enemy positions, and the civilians fleeing the city, he didn't debate the right or wrong of what they were doing. He took an oath that he would uphold the Constitution of the United States. He was patriotic. He would do what the country asked him to do. He was asked to go to war and he was there. One hundred percent.

19

Captain Eric Garcia was at Task Force Tarawa's command post, some sixty-five kilometers south of Nasiriyah, when he got the call to scramble. He was in the middle of a brief with air officers from the task force, getting updates on the weather, intel, and the combat situation. Reports were coming in that 1st Battalion, 2nd Marines were suffering casualties in Nasiriyah and needed a casevac immediately. Garcia had been briefed that the enemy threat was medium to high, and he was told to expect a hot LZ. He had already had one casevac mission canceled. *Now at last I can get to the front line and play my part.* A few hours earlier, he had flown in from the USS *Saipan,* floating off Kuwait, to conduct a turnover with the existing casevac crews. They did three days in the field, then three days rest back on ship. It had been a quiet start to the war. Nothing much had come in since his ship had arrived in the Persian Gulf except for a few training accidents and minor civilian injuries. Garcia's war had consisted of sitting for three days in a landing zone at Camp Ryan in Kuwait with nothing to do except keep fit, check and recheck his equipment, and go to briefings.

It was early afternoon when he lifted his twin rotor CH-46 helo off the ground. Nicknamed the "frog," the CH-46 was a squat and bulbous,

Vietnam-era Marine transport helicopter that could carry twelve personnel with equipment. They were robust and hardy helicopters. Many of them still displayed patches covering up bullet holes from Vietnam and Korea.

The sky was clear and visibility was over seven miles as he directed the helo over a parched landscape toward Nasiriyah, using Route 7 as a guide. All he could hear through his headphones was the throb of the twin rotors and calm radio chatter directing him into the city. To his right was another CH-46 as his wingman. They always flew in pairs. Out in front were Huey and Cobra gunships to escort him into the city. The CH-46 only carried defensive weapons. On each side of the helo sat a gunner manning a .50-caliber machine gun. Garcia was happy to have the two gunships to clear the way for them. Up ahead, a cloud of smoke rose into the sky as the artillery fired a round. When it exploded, it sent a thick black plume of smoke spiraling into the air from its target. *This is for real. There's real stuff going on here.*

Garcia never quite understood how he'd got to be a Marine pilot. As a young kid, growing up in El Paso, Texas, he'd certainly had no burning ambition to fly planes or helicopters. Yes, he'd joined the Marine Corps reserves straight out of high school and had trained as an artilleryman, but he wasn't planning to make a career out of it. What he really wanted to do was go to premed school. His parents, both born in Mexico, had become American citizens and were proud of what he was doing with his life. Then, somewhere along the way, he ran into a marine who suggested he try out for Officer Candidate School. Before he knew it, he was taking his flight exam. The Marine Corps paid for twenty-five hours flying time in a small commercial plane, and he was hooked. Flight training at the naval air station in Pensacola was something else. There he got to train in a T-34, a small, fixed-wing plane with a turbine engine. It was like going from a Volkswagen to a Ferrari. There was no turning back. He got his wings in December 1996, and he'd been flying CH-46s ever since. He was fond of the old workhorse. The helo was reaching the end of its life cycle and lately he'd been testing its replacement, the new Osprey with retractable rotors that allowed it to lift like a helo but fly at the speed of a fixed-wing plane. But the CH-46 would do for now. He knew its speed, range, and carrying limitations. *You can't treat it like a race car, but it's steady and reliable.*

"Parole 26, this is Parole 25."

Garcia called up his wingman.

"When we get there, I want you to hold off just to the east."

Ahead he could see the dusty mass of the labyrinthine low-rise buildings of Nasiriyah. Puffs of smoke billowed up between the buildings. *The grunts are involved in some sort of firefight.* Marine pilots, especially the helicopter pilots, had a good relationship with the infantry on the ground. The grunts liked to complain that jet pilots were soft because they didn't get down and dirty on the ground. They went easy on the helo pilots because they supported them directly in combat. Garcia got on the radio for an update on casualties. He knew for sure that they were going in for at least two marines. As he hovered south of the city, all his thoughts focused on his job: staying clear of the gunships that had escorted him in, listening to the radio, and making sure that he was aware of what was going on around him. *I'm going to get in there and do what I need to do.*

In the rear of the CH-46, Navy corpsman Hospital Man 3rd Class Moses Gloria was giving his Black Hawk bag one last check. He'd been sent to Afghanistan right after 9/11 and had treated several combat injuries, so he knew what medical equipment he wanted to carry. He'd modified the bag he'd been given and added a few things. He'd taken Israeli bandages that he found more adaptable than the standard Vietnam- and Korea-vintage dressings. He also brought along QuikClot, a powder that speeded up the coagulation of blood.

"It's just like pixie dust. Sprinkle it on a wound and it will stop the bleeding."

That's what they told him in training, but he hadn't yet used it in combat. He tried to keep calm and said a bunch of Hail Marys to himself. He was amazed at how hyped up he was. When he'd returned from Afghanistan he'd thought of himself as a combat veteran who knew it all, even though he was only twenty-six. The other medics thought he was a jackass and full of it. The truth was, he was still suffering from the experience. When he got back, he found he put on loads of weight from eating crappy food, drinking too much beer, partying too much, chasing too many women. Now he knew it was his way of trying to forget about the bad things he'd seen. Even seeing those hollering and giggling girls having a good time in the mall used to upset him. *Jeez, they don't know what life is about. They shouldn't laugh. There's too much nasty stuff out there.* It was sometime before he realized that their carefree existence was the way of life he was trying to protect.

"Hail Mary, full of grace, the Lord is with thee."

Looking out of the window, he could see the reassuring presence of a

Cobra gunship, their escort. The marines had come up with the idea of casevac to save more lives. Medevac meant taking injured from one safe place to another. Casevac meant getting the wounded out of a war zone. When the call had first come through, there was talk of mass casualties. Now he heard Captain Garcia calling in over the radio to clarify the mission. Moses Gloria didn't know whether the casualties were civilians, Brits, or marines. He just knew they were going into a hot LZ. They were going to land in an area where they would be targeted.

". . . pray for us sinners, now and at the hour of our death."

Moses Gloria had been born on an army base in Honolulu. His parents were from the Philippines, but his dad had joined the U.S. Navy and Gloria had spent most of his childhood traveling from base to base in Saudi, Italy, Greece—pretty much all over the world. He thought of Maryland as home because he'd got a scholarship to the University of Maryland in College Park. He had ambitions of being a lawyer or a politician, but the pressure of being the first in the family to go to school got to him. His grades started slipping, and he dropped out of school. Joining the Navy was the safest thing he knew. It was only when he got to corpsman training that he realized that he might not spend all his time in a clean white naval hospital on shore surrounded by pretty nurses. They'd showed him and other new recruits a video of the Vietnam movie, *Full Metal Jacket*.

"See that guy who's running around while marines are yelling out, 'Doc'? Well, that's you."

The Marine Corps didn't train its own combat medics. It took those trained by the Navy. Most Navy corpsmen like Gloria ended up being with the Marines, and most guys liked it. Gloria didn't look like the sort of guy who would be happy running around a battlefield in the dirt. He was short and chubby. He looked as though he enjoyed the good things in life. Yet he found he got a lot more respect from the marines than from officers in the Navy. The grunts just loved their docs. They were held in special esteem. Gloria would have to put up with the grunts making fun of the rest of the Navy, but they treated him as one of their own.

Garcia was now a couple of kilometers south of the city. He saw the Cobra and the Huey go in with guns blazing to clear the ground and make sure it was safe. Apart from the two corpsmen in the rear, he had his copilot and two aircrew who manned the guns and loaded the equipment. They were all vulnerable. The CH-46 had very little armor. The cockpit might stop a round, but the main body of the helo was just thin metal. A round, or piece of metal traveling at speed, would penetrate right through it. In the cockpit, Garcia sat on a bulletproof seat and wore fragmentary armor, which would stop shrapnel but not a well-aimed shot. If an RPG hit one of the rotors it would desync them; they would hit each other and the helo would drop out of the sky.

He now had direct comms with Captain Jim Jones, the forward air controller on the ground, whose call sign was Koolaid.

"Parole 25, you are clear to land."

Garcia's body tensed. He was the lead as his wingman anchored toward the east. He flew over some palm groves, uneasy because he couldn't see what was underneath. He reached the river, followed the bridge across, and saw vehicles maneuvering on the road and figures fighting it out in the streets below.

"Parole 25. Watch for the smoke."

It was Koolaid, letting him know where to land. Instructions were coming over the radio thick and fast. Garcia focused on avoiding the accompanying Huey. He didn't have time to feel scared. He saw the purple smoke and dropped onto an east-west road. It was pretty open, and he saw an ambulance off to the side of the road. Garcia brought the bird in. As soon as they landed, they started taking fire.

"Parole 25. You have to reposition."

The FAC sounded calm. They were in a bad spot. He wanted to bring him back down, farther north along the north-south road. Garcia didn't know it, but that was the road the marines were calling Ambush Alley.

"Roger that. Show me where you want me."

"Popping smoke."

One of the lessons the Marines had learned in Vietnam was that neither the ground forces nor the pilot would announce which color smoke was being popped. The Vietcong would listen in and pop the color called to try to lure the helo into an ambush.

"I see purple smoke."

Garcia confirmed the color and came in for a second time. The smoke was billowing up between some power lines. It was too tight, so he looked for somewhere with more space. Right across the street he saw an alleyway. *It's tight, but we can get the CH-46 in there.* As he came down, he saw marines forming a perimeter to protect the helo. Garcia circled the CH-46 and slowly dropped the bird into the middle of the alleyway between two six-foot-high walls.

As the helo came to a rest, he heard the AAVs around him directing suppressing fire toward two buildings to his right. His copilot, Captain Tod Schroeder, got jumpy, pulled out a 9 mm sidearm, and held it out of the window. Garcia thought it was kind of funny. *Why's he doing that? We've got two .50-cal machine guns on either side of us.*

He monitored the chatter between the FAC and other aircraft. A huge dog was standing to the side of the road, taking it all in impassively. Garcia turned to Schroeder.

"It can't be that bad if the dog is not freaking out."

Just at that moment, a Huey flew overhead and the dog took off in fright. *So much for my theory.*

Moses Gloria checked his medical gear one last time. In the rear of the helo, he had the litters prepared to bring in the casualties. He went through his ABCs. *Airway, breathing, circulation. Make sure we have our airways out, nasals and orals are reachable, bandages open and ready to go, IVs set and flowing.*

He heard the pilot and crew chiefs talking on the radio.

"Taking fire from eleven o'clock. Now from two o'clock."

"Shall we fire back?"

"Hold fire until it's direct fire."

He prayed one last time and waited for the first casualties to arrive.

"Hail Mary, full of grace . . ."

20

As the CH-46 came in to land, Captain Dyer, in *Dark Side*, was maneuvering his tank around the foot of the Euphrates Bridge. Next to him, his FAC, Major Hawkins, was busy talking on his handheld radio, running air down Ambush Alley and making sure that helos were still flying over the tanks stuck in the mud in the east of the city. Dyer had his own priority, though. A lone sniper had been shooting at him for the past thirty minutes and he had been unable to locate him. *I've got to find him. It's only a matter of time before he gets me.*

Each tank was working an area of about five hundred meters. Each time Dyer maneuvered his tank within his area to get in a better position to help the marines on the ground, the sniper seemed to seek him out.

Another round cracked past his ear. *That was close.* It sounded like a baseball bat striking concrete. *I've got to find that son of a bitch.* The bullet had come from one of the buildings on the east side of the street, but it was difficult to know which one. *He must be properly trained. He is located somewhere deep inside, hidden well away from the window.* He hoped he wasn't firing from too high up, because his gun tube could only be elevated to a certain height. He scanned the windows for any signs of the sniper.

At that moment, his radio crackled with a transmission. The message was unusually loud and clear.

"This is Palehorse 3. We need assistance. We need tank support."

Dyer was concerned. That was the call sign for a Charlie Company platoon commander. On battalion tac 1 you might hear the commander or his deputy, sometimes called the 6 or the 5, but not the 3, the platoon commander. *You get your ass handed to you if you are on the battalion net and not supposed to be there. Something is badly wrong.*

"Palehorse 3, this is Panzer 5. Roll to 158."

Dyer wanted to speak to him on the company net so that they could get away from the cacophony of chatter on the battalion net.

"Panzer 5, this is Palehorse 3."

"Roger. Send it."

It was Lieutenant Seely, Charlie Company's 3rd Platoon commander.

"We are cut off behind enemy lines and we are completely surrounded and we are taking casualties. We have a platoon cut off from the rest of the company and our forward observer is dead. Our FiST leader is wounded. I've tried Timberwolf, but I'm getting no response."

"What's your position?"

The radio went quiet while Seely was checking his grid coordinates. Just then, Dyer saw a muzzle flash from a window on the third story of a distant building on the right side of the road. At the same time, an AK round cracked past his ear. *There you are, you son of a bitch!* It was the sniper. He yelled at his gunner.

"Bell. Kill that son of a bitch. Colocate an MPAT round with that fucking sniper. Fire the main gun!"

Boom.

The round just blew a big hole in the window and the surrounding wall.

The floor of the building where he'd seen the muzzle flash just disintegrated. The sniping stopped.

Dyer looked down to see Hawkins in a crumpled heap at the bottom of the turret. Unaware that Dyer was about to fire the main gun, Hawkins had been hanging out of the turret watching the helos make their gun run. The concussive force of the main gun had knocked him off his feet. *Oh my God, he's dead.* To Dyer's relief, Hawkins stirred and threw him an accusatory stare.

Palehorse 3 came back on the radio with a grid reference. Dyer couldn't believe it when he heard it.

"Say again."

The grid reference would put them beyond the Saddam Canal Bridge. *That means Charlie is well north of where anyone can help them.*

"Roger. Stand by."

He didn't want to leave the poor guy hanging on the radio, but he needed to talk to Major Peeples.

Near Dyer's tank, as the search team looked through the wreckage of Charlie track 206 for survivors, Alpha's marines saw another AAV speeding south through Ambush Alley into their position. The Alpha marines didn't know it, but it was Charlie 207, the track driven by Corporal Brown, which had turned round to pick up Lieutenant Swantner and Sergeant Schaefer when they had jumped out of the deadlined track 201. Inside, Schaefer was shaking with fear and his blood was pumping with adrenaline. Of the five medevac tracks in the convoy that had set off together from the northern bridge, only two, 210 and 207, had made it safely back to the southern bridge.

Brown brought the track to a halt just north of the Euphrates Bridge. Schaefer jumped out, ecstatic to be out of the terrifying darkness. He didn't know where to go or what to do. There were so many things he thought he should be doing that he didn't know where to start. He saw one of Alpha's tracks, bristling with antennae, parked off to the side of the road on the east side of the bridge. He presumed it was the C7 command track. He was hyped up and desperate. *I've got to get some help to Charlie. I've got to let them know what a fucking mess it is up there.* He wrenched open the back hatch of the track, finally relieved to be in a position to help. A captain, closest to the door, stepped back in shock. *The poor guy thinks I'm an Iraqi come to kill him.* Inside there was a bank of radios, boards with Post-it notes, and marines with headsets plotting positions on maps.

The words tumbled out. Schaefer explained who he was, about the fight that Charlie was having on the northern bridge, about the destroyed tracks in Ambush Alley, that the marines inside might have been killed while trying to get out. He said that Captain Wittnam and Lieutenant Tracy might also be dead.

The captain shook his head. He said there was too much going on at the Euphrates Bridge and that they didn't have any one they could spare.

"There's nothing we can do to help you right now."

Schaefer was frustrated and disgusted. He ran over to one of the tanks, *Desert Knight,* and banged on the hatch. An officer popped his head out. It was Major Peeples.

"What do you need?"

Schaefer told him that Charlie Company was stranded on the northern bridge, that they were taking casualties and that they needed help.

"I'll see what I can do."

Schaefer jumped off the tank and headed back to his track. He was in a world of his own, pissed off, manic with frustration and anger. It was a world that was crumbling around him. The Marine Corps had been his life since he was eighteen. It had given him a home and friends. He'd joined because he'd gotten tired of his parents, back home in Charleston, South Carolina, manipulating him and using their money to control him. He'd gone to a military academy, but it cost $16,000 a year, and they kept on saying that unless he got better grades, they would stop paying his fees. By the end of his freshman year, he was sick of them and decided to jack it in and join the Marines. *They walk taller and prouder than the other branches of the military. Who wouldn't want to join them?* As a tracker, he'd been sent to Bosnia and Egypt, but Iraq was the first time he'd seen combat. When his dad found out he was going, he was disparaging.

"Son, you'll be nothing but a bullet catcher."

His father's comment had pissed him off at the time. But now he wondered whether the Marine Corps really was the secure home he'd thought it was. As he crossed the open street, he took fire from some Iraqis in a building off to the side. Instead of taking cover, he just stood there in the middle of the dusty street, punching out rounds from his M16. He was possessed, temporarily insane with hate and fury. Part of him knew that standing in the open like that was against everything he had ever been taught. But part of him didn't care anymore.

Some marine snipers looked at him with astonishment as he made his way back to his track.

"Where are you going, Sergeant?"

"I'm going back up there."

"We'll go with you."

Brown was waiting for him. Schaefer didn't know whether Castleberry and the others from track 201 were alive or dead. He felt bad that he'd left them there. They were his marines to look after, and he'd abandoned them. Overwhelming feelings of guilt mixed with anger and bitterness at the way the marine captain had reacted when he'd asked for his help began to take over. He didn't stop to think what a dangerous and stupid move it was to go back along Ambush Alley for a third time in a single AAV. Brown turned to Schaefer.

"I think we're going to die."

"Probably so."

"Let's do it."

Major Peeples now knew that he was not the only one who was experiencing difficulty in communicating with the battalion staff. Captain Brooks was also finding it difficult to break through the chatter and give out important information. But at least his knowledge of the battlefield was becoming clearer. Captain Dyer had just informed him about the distress call he had received from Charlie on the northern bridge. It confirmed what the Charlie AAV platoon commander, Sergeant Schaefer, had just told him. *Charlie Company is in trouble, and the battalion commander doesn't know what the hell is going on.* Peeples had never been in combat before, but it had been drummed into him during training that sometimes the battalion command structure is not going to be able to control the fight. To reassert control of the battle, marines were trained to break down into squads or into the smallest unit of four-man fire teams. A large, chaotic battle can still be won by breaking it down into smaller fights. Ducking to avoid the incoming small-arms fire, Peeples ran over to Brooks.

"Charlie Company is having a rough time. They are taking a lot of casualties. They need some tanks up there."

Peeples saw Brooks's face drop. He knew Brooks didn't want to lose those tanks. Since they'd arrived, they had begun to turn the tide.

"Are you going to take all four tanks?"

Peeples saw the distress on Brooks's face. *His face looks as though I've just kicked him in the nuts.*

"I'm going to leave two here with you, and I'm going to take the other two north."

He jumped back on *Desert Knight* and told the driver that they were going to drive straight through Ambush Alley.

"Here's what you are going to do. You are going to pull back the cadillacs as far as possible and you are going to shoot down this road as fast as we can go. Do you understand?"

"Roger that, sir."

Peeples called his XO, Scott Dyer, to follow him in *Dark Side.*

"Captain Dyer, get your tank on the road and follow me."

Dyer maneuvered his tank behind *Desert Knight.* He saw that the other two tanks from 3rd Platoon, Red 1 and Red 2, were not following them.

"Panzer 6, this is Panzer 5. I don't see Red 1 moving. Is Red 1 coming?"

"Negative, I'm leaving Red here. I need to leave some tank support for Alpha Company. It's just you and me."

Dyer had seen the number of Iraqis that were running up and down Ambush Alley resupplying their ammo and getting into position. He'd seen the machine-gun and RPG positions along the road. He really didn't want to be driving all the way up it. Another RPG whooshed past his head as they took off up Ambush Alley. *Oh shit. The major must have brass balls. Huge brass balls.*

21

Captain Mike Brooks's heart sunk as he watched Peeples disappear with two tanks into the mouth of Ambush Alley. He now had only two tanks to safeguard his position at the Euphrates Bridge. The aggression and initiative displayed by Peeples had impressed Brooks. He didn't wait for orders from the battalion commander. *Would his actions stand up in a doctrinal textbook? Maybe. Maybe not. Anyway, he is now carrying a lot of the success of the battalion on his shoulders.*

Brooks now had a much clearer picture of the battlefield. It was now confirmed that the AAV that had been hit in his position was not one of his tracks. The track and its dead and wounded were from Charlie Company. He also now knew, from survivors from the convoy, that Charlie Company had taken the northern bridge but were in one hell of a fight to hold on to it. But he had heard nothing from Bravo or the forward command post for some time. *I guess they are still heading north around the east side of the city. It must be taking longer than planned.* He didn't know that several tanks and tracks were stuck in the mud. He had never asked the battalion commander. He had just wanted simple answers to his simple questions. He had too many things going on where he was located to find out what was happening at the forward CP. Nevertheless, he felt uncomfortable not knowing where the other units were. *It's not good warfighting skills.* You need to know where everyone is to reduce fratricide. Because he did not know exactly where the other battalion units were, his FiST was forced to coordinate fire support by knowing where friendly forces weren't.

They were still receiving RPG and small-arms fire from the buildings at the mouth of Ambush Alley. Rounds were still cracking over his head, and mortar shells and RPGs were exploding only yards away.

He ran back to his C7 to work out what he was going to do. He did know that the three companies were now in separate parts of the city and unable to support each other. *The longer it goes on like that, the bigger a problem it will become.* Brooks had assets with him—the 81 mm mortar platoon, a CAAT section, tanks, a forward air controller, and now a platoon of Charlie's own marines—that would make a huge difference in Charlie's fight. *The longer we sit here, the more dire the situation is going to be.*

He couldn't move until 2nd Battalion, 8th Marines conducted the relief in place. There was no sign of them on the bridge. He tried to think one step ahead, formulating in his mind suggestions that he could throw at the battalion commander. He knew that Dan Wittnam, Charlie Company's commander, was in trouble. Dan was a close friend. Personal loyalty was involved, too. *Dan needs help. Bravo is stuck to the east. I am the only person who can help him.* He was realizing that he needed to leave the Euphrates Bridge and head north along Ambush Alley to help out Charlie at the Saddam Canal Bridge. Now he wanted to speak to the battalion commander or the operations officer so that he could make it happen.

"Timberwolf, this is Tomahawk 6. Do you read me?"

There was nothing.

He tried to reach the main command post.

"Main, this is Tomahawk 6."

He thought back to war games and training. *If ever there were a tactical problem thrown at you in peacetime, this would rival any of them.* But he wasn't training. This was for real. *This is the sort of situation you only ever read about.* He had to make a decision, and there was no one to help him.

Should he move now and help Charlie, even though 2/8 had not arrived to secure the Euphrates Bridge? Commander's Intent told him that at the end of the day, his mission was to help secure the northern bridge. The longer he waited, the more likely it was that Charlie would have to surrender the bridge. *I am not going to stand by idly and allow Charlie Company to get chopped up or take further casualties when I could be in a position to assist them.*

Brooks moved around with the field radio to get a clearer signal. Although the buildings were only one or two stories, they seemed to be interfering with reception. He tried a different radio, but it didn't help. Finally, he got through to the assistant operations officer, Captain Hernley, at the main CP some fifteen kilometers away. He almost shouted at the voice at the end of the line.

"I have no comms with the battalion commander. I need to know where 2/8 is so I can turn the bridge over to them."

"Two-Eight is already in position."

Brooks looked back to the Euphrates Bridge. Then he looked at the casevac helicopter still waiting in an alleyway off Ambush Alley for the wounded from track 206 to be loaded up.

"I don't see 'em. Can you check that? I'm evacuating casualties. As soon as this helo lifts, I'm going to call you again and I'm going to tell you what I'm going to do."

Brooks ran over to his men, warning them to prepare to move out.

"Pass the word. When the helo lifts, we are going to make best possible speed to Charlie's position."

Fifty meters away, the 81 mm mortar platoon was still firing. He yelled at them.

"When this helo lifts, we're leaving."

He saw them looking at him blankly. They had no idea who the hell he was.

"I'm the fucking company commander. And when this helo lifts, we are leaving."

They sprang into action.

He ran back to the track and got on the radio to Hernley.

"What's the status of 2/8?"

"To the best of my knowledge, 2/8 is in position on the bridge. They say they are on the bridge."

Brooks once again stood up and looked across the span of the bridge.

"Listen. I'm on the fucking bridge and I don't fucking see them."

Brooks made a quick calculation. The railway bridge had confused him earlier in the day. *Either they are on the railway bridge, not the Euphrates Bridge, in which case it will take them too long to get here, or they are holding and not coming.* He asked himself whether he was prepared to undergo the scrutiny of leaving before he'd done a positive handover to 2/8. He decided he was. He reached for the radio.

"When this helo lifts, I'm going to go up north and relieve the pressure on Charlie."

22

The Charlie marines had now been in the house on Ambush Alley for about an hour, and for the first time they felt as though they had a semblance of control. They expected a Marine convoy to come and rescue them at any moment. With all its technical and military know-how, the Marine Corps must be able to get to them. For the past few minutes, it had been calm. But there was something about the way the black-robed figures appeared and then disappeared from alleyways and windows that made them feel that it was about to kick off again. Castleberry was perched behind the parapet with a good view down Ambush Alley when he saw a motorbike with two soldiers on it coming up the street toward them. They were the first uniformed soldiers he'd seen all day. The guy on the back was firing an AK at the house as he sped along the street. All the marines on the roof got into firing positions.

They'd killed so many people that Castleberry didn't feel much anymore. *It has turned into a game to see who can kill the most Iraqis.* When the motorbike came into firing range, all the marines on the roof were on it. There were bursts of gunfire from M16s, M249s, M203s. It was a 203 grenade that hit the motorbike first, punching a hole through the driver as the bike spilled from under him. The marines on the roof let out a cheer. The passenger tried to pick up the bike and kick-start it. He was a sitting duck. There was another burst of gunfire. *We've wasted him in a hail of fire.* The roof erupted again in cheering.

Worthington, down in the courtyard, saw the marines yelling and hollering with delight, doing a victory dance as if they'd scored a touchdown.

"Yo, that's what I'm talking about. Whoa."

Robinson was so hyped up that any movement was now a threat. He spotted a white pickup truck careering down the road. *This is dangerous. If the car manages to knock down a wall, they will overrun us.* He took aim with his machine gun and fired. The truck veered wildly off the road and exploded.

Castleberry recognized the change in atmosphere. Killing had become routine and easy. An old man with a stick walked right along Ambush Alley in front of the house. Nobody was taking any chances. A marine fired at him. The old man crumpled to his knees, his face looking in the direction of the house. Milter was freaked out.

"He's looking at me. He's fucking looking at me."

Castleberry could see that the old man wasn't looking at anyone. There was no movement. He was obviously dead. It didn't stop Milter.

"That old man is looking at me. He's staring right at me."

Somebody shot the old man again to force his gaze in another direction.

Castleberry didn't know how long they would be able to hold out. He saw Sena still working with the radio. There was a weak signal, but there was so much chatter going on that he couldn't break through. He heard Sena trying to call back to Captain Wittnam on the northern bridge.

"Palehorse 6, we're south of the bridge one hundred meters, in a house to the east of the MSR."

Again there was nothing.

"Why can't we get any fucking comms?"

Castleberry wanted a go at it. He thought of himself as pretty useful with anything technical. At home in Seattle, while his brother had messed about with computers, Castleberry had done more manual things—fixing cars, stereos, anything that was broken. He turned the radio off for ten minutes to see if the batteries would recharge. This time he tried his AAV platoon commander, Lieutenant Tracy, call sign Whaler. If he was still on the northern bridge with Charlie, maybe the signal would reach him.

"Whaler. This is Castleberry, over. Tracy. This is Castleberry, over."

On the northern bridge, Tracy had just climbed back into his track when he heard a faint noise on the radio. Through the static, he could just make out the name of Castleberry. He grabbed the radio.

"Castleberry, this is Tracy. Where are you? Over."

Castleberry was elated at the response. It was the first time they had made contact with anybody since they'd taken over the house. He tried to tell Tracy about the dash down Ambush Alley and being stranded in the house. All Tracy could hear was empty static.

"You're breaking up. I can't understand."

Castleberry was getting frustrated. He started to yell into the radio. He knew it was stupid, but he thought that if he shouted louder, something might get through.

"Castleberry. This is Tracy. I'm losing you. Click once if you can hear me."

Castleberry clicked the radio key once.

"Good. Click once for yes, twice for no. Are you south of the north bridge?

He clicked the radio key once for yes.

"Are you at Alpha's position?"

Castleberry clicked twice for no.

"Are you in your vehicle?"

Castleberry clicked twice again.

Tracy was worried. *That's not good news.*

"Are you in the city?"

Castleberry clicked once for yes. Tracy paused, trying to come to terms with the fact that there was at least one marine stranded in the city without support.

On the roof, it had been quiet now for about fifteen minutes. Robinson found his mind wandering. He thought about his wife. They had met because they were both swimmers. He hadn't written to her much in Kuwait, just a couple of brief notes scribbled on the back of some cardboard, or an MRE packet on which he'd written her address and *Free Postage*. The last one he'd written didn't say much more than "Hey, how's it going?" He hadn't described much about life in Kuwait or what he did all day. *She's a clever girl. She can work it out.* But now he didn't know how he was going to explain to her about the house in Ambush Alley and the killing and the chaos. She had moved to Camp Lejeune with him but hated it on the East Coast and moved back to California, where she worked as a travel agent. He had missed having her around. After she left, he had to share a small room on base that contained a sink and three bunks with two other guys. The good thing was she flew back to see him every couple of weeks. She hated him going to Iraq and said he might die out there. But he made a promise to her that he wouldn't get killed because he wanted to have kids with her. He'd even refused to write a death letter like some of the other marines did. He thought it was bad luck. *I hope I'll be able to keep my promise about having kids.*

He wondered who would look through his pack if he died. There was an understanding among the marines that they would sanitize each other's packs. They would get rid of the porn magazines and other private stuff that it wasn't good for family or girlfriends to see. He'd heard of a marine who was killed in combat and whose wife had received, among his personal effects, letters a girlfriend had written to him. That wasn't good.

He had no idea how long they'd been in the house. Time was of no relevance. It could have been five minutes; it could have been five hours. They were all feeling the strain and beginning to sag. Robinson watched someone write a death letter and give it to a fellow marine. He saw Martin, with blood streaming down his face, still posting security on the roof and was amazed that he didn't act injured. It was the same with Seegert. He'd been on the roof like everyone else. Now Robinson saw that his triceps had been shredded. He thought about the injured marines downstairs. *All I want to do is get them home.* He hoped that if he were wounded, someone would look after him, too. Only hours earlier, he had remembered feeling all macho and that the marines would crush anything that stood in their way. Now he was terrified. *We just might not make it out of this one. I'm scared. I want to go home.* But home was such a long way away.

"Hey, there's something big going on over there."

Robinson woke from his reverie. He looked south and saw Cobras circling among the buildings away to the east of Ambush Alley. *Something is going down a couple of klicks away.* He thought for a moment that the helos were going to turn and swoop toward them. Then they would be in trouble.

Worthington grabbed some metal foil from the house and tried to signal to the Cobras in the sky. It didn't seem to work. He broke some glass and tried to reflect the sun toward the eyes of the pilots. Other marines grabbed laundry and the orange air panel from inside the track and waved them at the helos in the distance. But the helos ignored the marines and just kept pounding the buildings in front. Smoke billowed out from between the buildings followed by a long crackle of gunfire and an enormous boom. *Maybe Bravo is finally on its way to get us out of here?* But if he was honest with himself, he was no longer sure where any of the companies were or whether anyone was going to come and get them out.

Robinson, Olivas, Martin, and Castleberry sat under the shelter of the parapet on the roof. Worthington manned his SAW position in the courtyard. Smith worked on Carl, Trevino, and Elliot in the front room. They felt alone, abandoned, let down. In the midst of the anxiety and tension there was now a new, even more uncomfortable sensation taking root. They didn't recognize it yet, but it was the early traces of what was growing into a burning, bitter anger.

23

Major Peeples and Captain Dyer, in their tanks *Desert Knight* and *Dark Side,* accelerated to forty-five miles per hour as they screamed up Ambush Alley toward the Saddam Canal Bridge. Small-arms fire pinged off the side of the tanks, but they were going so fast that Peeples hardly noticed it. Halfway along, he saw what looked like a marine step out into the road and try and flag him down. It was Major Sosa, with pistol drawn. Peeples drew up beside him. *What the hell is he doing?*

Sosa yelled up at him.

"Charlie Company needs you up north."

"I know that. That's where I'm going."

"Well, get going then."

Peeples jumped up again on his tank. It was a strange conversation. But at least he now knew the location of the battalion forward command post. He sped north toward the canal bridge, hardly noticing the amount of fire raining down on him. Just before reaching it something caught his eye. He saw a burning AAV, and in the dirt around it, the torso of a marine. He'd never seen a dead marine before. It was a sight that burned into his memory. He faced forward again and continued toward the bridge.

Just behind him in *Dark Side,* Dyer's driver, Lance Corporal Shirley, was swerving the tank in and out of the telephone poles to avoid the RPG rounds that were coming at them from both sides of the road. In the turret, Dyer was targeting a retreating RPG gunner with his coax. As he swung the turret back to a forward position, he caught a glimpse of a red cloth and the distinctive shape of some marine helmets on the roof of a house on the east side of Ambush Alley. It was not much more than a flash, but he guessed that they were marines. He wondered what they were doing there. He logged the house's position in his mind. There was no way he was going to stop. He was going at forty-five miles per hour and was under fire.

Following Peeples's tank, he rolled up to and across the flat span of the canal bridge and got his first view of the battlefield on the north side. *Holy shit.* Dyer again thought of a movie. The air was thick with dirt, smoke, and flying metal. Mud was being thrown up in the air as mortars and artillery shells impacted on the ground. He saw there was hardly any space between the impact holes. Small-arms fire whizzed around him. *This is like the opening scene of* Saving Private Ryan.

Lying in a swamp near the span of the canal bridge, marines from Charlie Company's 2nd Platoon were trying to identify targets. They had been receiving fire from under the bridge all day. They could see figures running about in the reeds trying to take potshots at them. Lance Corporal Eric Killeen was worried. If there were a concerted push from the north, they would be sandwiched.

Tracy was trying to organize his two remaining fully functioning vehicles into a defensive perimeter. He hadn't fired the gun on his track for some time. He'd assumed that the Iraqis thought they'd all quit when the AAVs went south. He didn't want to let them know that those two tracks were still functioning. *I've just got to sit here quietly and not attract any attention.*

Captain Dan Wittnam was by the bridge, taking cover under the raised road that headed north. For several hours he'd been expecting tank support to arrive. It was about 1600, and soon it would get dark. *Where are those fucking tanks?*

From across the bridge, the marines of Charlie Company heard a rumble and felt the ground shake. Killeen thought Iraqi tanks were on their way. He thought the company was almost certainly lost.

Wittnam and Tracy also heard the roar. They raised their heads above the road and saw two M1A1 Abrams rumbling over the bridge. Tracy's stomach leaped. *This is the greatest thing I've ever seen.*

From the turret of his M1A1 tank, Peeples saw that Charlie Company was getting hit hard. Mortar shells were coming in from the southern bank of the canal; rounds were coming in from the west and east. He headed for the AAV with the diamond symbol denoting the commander's track. As soon as he stopped, Dan Wittnam jumped onto the tank. He looked beat up and anxious.

"What do you need?"

Wittnam pointed to some buildings back toward the city from where they were taking most of the artillery fire. Peeples ordered his loader to load a high-explosive round. *Any second, the Iraqis are going to bracket fire on me. I've got to find them before they get me.* His gunner sent out a laser shot to get a range on a building and then fired the main gun. There was a deafening boom. The building crumbled. Wittnam stayed on the tank, pointing out targets.

"We're taking fire from that building there. The one with the machine gun on the roof."

"Roger that. I see it. Hey, gunner, I want you to put two rounds right on that building with the red door."

"Roger that."

The gunner looked through the crosshairs on his sight and fired a couple of times. The tank rocked back. *Boom. Boom.* The building exploded.

Wittnam was relieved. *We're gonna have the north side of this bridge for the rest of the war.*

"Panzer 5, this is Palehorse 3. We are separated from the rest of the company and we are getting heavy fire from the north."

It was Lieutenant Seely, the same marine on the radio who had alerted Captain Dyer to Charlie's plight. Peeples directed Dyer and his tank to head north and find them. From the turret, Dyer looked for Lieutenant Seely and the platoon of marines who had become separated from the rest of Charlie. About five hundred meters away, he discovered them, a ragged platoon of marines, dug in like ticks, targeting a large building complex to the north with nothing but machine guns and M16 rifles. They had no mortars with them, and their FiST members had been cut up in the fight. Artillery and mortar shells were landing all around them. Dyer remembered from briefings that the large white building was an Iraqi army complex. He got onto his gunner, Corporal Bell.

"Put some rounds into those buildings. Fire into the high points. And hose the whole complex down with the coax."

The turret traversed until the barrel of the gun pointed at the complex.

He fired the main gun, and the marines around him cheered as a fountain of dust exploded from behind the building's white walls.

Tracy, hunkered down by the canal, now remembered the radio message he had received from Castleberry. He knew that at least one marine was somewhere in the city. *And what about the figures I saw running along the bank of the canal when one of the convoy tracks was hit crossing back into the city? They could be marines, too.* He couldn't look for them with his two remaining tracks. They were too vulnerable. The only vehicle that had the armor and firepower to venture back down Ambush Alley was a tank. He got hold of Major Peeples.

"We have marines in the city."

Peeples recalled the conversation he'd had with Sergeant Schaefer of Charlie Company. He, too, had told him that there were marines in the city. There were no comms with the battalion commander. He decided that he was the only one who was in a position to provide any help. He spoke to Captain Wittnam.

"I'm going to leave my XO here, but I'm going back into the city to find those missing marines."

Once more, *Desert Knight* took off into Ambush Alley.

24

The marines in the two houses along Ambush Alley had been holed up for two hours. They were hot, thirsty, and exhausted. The initial euphoria that had kept them alive during those early frantic moments was ebbing away. They had still not managed to get any meaningful radio message out to the forward command. There was the distinct possibility that no one knew they were there. Lance Corporal Jared Martin, sweat, dirt, and dried blood staining his face, looked up at the sky from his position on the roof. *We have about two hours before the sun goes down. Then we're gonna be real screwed.*

A few minutes earlier, they had heard the rumble of tanks coming from the south toward them. They had all scrambled to wave the tanks down.

Someone had grabbed the orange air panel. Worthington, Doran, and Martin had waved their rifles and Kevlar helmets. But the tanks had thundered by without stopping. Soon there was nothing but a cloud of dust and a distant rumble. The atmosphere on the roof had descended into despair. They all had the same thought. *We are going to die here.*

Jared Martin forced himself to stay in the game. Within his sector of fire there was a small alleyway on the other side of the street. Several times an Iraqi had emerged from behind the wall and raised an RPG to his shoulder. Each time he came out, Martin got off a round to send him diving back behind the wall before he could fire. Martin waited for him. This time he was too late. He saw the Iraqi dive into the street and fire off the RPG before he could get his M16 round off. Martin watched as the RPG arced toward him, trailing its thick white smoke. *It's going to hit us.* Just before it made contact, it veered off into a power line above his head, exploding in a shower of sparks. *Next time that hajji comes out, I'm going to drop him.* A minute later, the Iraqi appeared behind the same corner. Martin was ready. He let off a burst from the M16 and the man crumpled.

Castleberry and Robinson were realizing that they were not going to get out of there. Robinson had already started to plan the defense of the houses in case they had to spend the night there. During training, they had always been encouraged to think *What If?* It was something that came naturally to Robinson. He had spent his whole life working out how to get out of difficult situations, from having an escape route if the police caught him fighting on the Santa Cruz beaches, to a story he could tell if he was accused of using steroids. Now his mind was buzzing with tasks they needed to do if they were going to make the houses secure before nightfall. Then the marines on the roof heard another distant rumble of an armored vehicle from the southern end of Ambush Alley.

"Hey, get up here, everyone. We've got vehicles."

From the sound, Castleberry recognized that this time it wasn't a tank. It was an AAV. All of them grabbed something to wave. Castleberry saw that someone was waving some pink ladies underwear.

As a tracker, Castleberry recognized every track in his platoon. He was amazed therefore to see that the lone vehicle coming up the road was Brown's track. He didn't know that Schaefer was inside, on his way back to Charlie's position at the northern bridge. He watched the vehicle come toward them at speed. At the same moment, an Iraqi came out of an alley and took a knee, ready to fire an RPG at the track.

"Stop. Don't do it. Don't do it. Stop."

Castleberry yelled at the Iraqi uselessly. He was a long way away, but Castleberry, in a fury, unloaded a full magazine of thirty rounds at him. *That's our ticket out of here. I'm not going to let him screw us. I'm going to shoot this guy.*

The AAV accelerated and disappeared back into the dust toward the northern bridge. It didn't even appear to have seen them. Castleberry could see that the sight of it broke the spirit of some of the marines.

"It's okay, guys. He'll be back. We'll be out of here."

Castleberry tried to encourage them. He said that the trackers had seen them. In fact, he was just as dismayed. *We're fucked. We're screwed.* But he kept his thoughts to himself. *If I were them, I wouldn't want to hear that.*

He thought about the time he'd spent with his wife, just before he'd left for Kuwait. It now upset him that they hadn't spent more time together. They'd been high school sweethearts, and they married a year ago. She was visiting her parents when he got the news that he was going to Iraq. It was just after New Year's, and by the time she was back they had only five days together. And most of the time he was working his butt off getting ready to depart. That sucked. When they got the order to go, they drove the amtracks to Camp Lejeune's Onslow Beach and swam the tracks out to the ships. The lines on the ship to call home for a few minutes were so long that he had decided against calling her. He wondered now whether that was a mistake.

On the roof, Private First Class Robinson's black thoughts were returning. *What the fuck am I doing here?* He thought of all his buddies that he'd grown up with in Santa Cruz and wondered what they would be doing now. Some would be surfing, others would be earning good money in the construction business. He thought of them partying on the beach. *None of them are holed up in a shitty house in a far-off country being shot at by hajjis.*

It was unbelievable. They were part of the most formidable military force in the world, yet none of its might, expertise, or technology had been able to get them out. They were surviving on their own guts and wits. Robinson wasn't looking to blame anyone, but it was hard not to feel that those higher up had let them down badly.

The clatter of a Huey woke him up. He was horrified to see it bearing down on them, guns aimed directly at their positions. Everyone on the roof put their fists on their head to signal they were friendlies and started yelling.

"Friendly. Friendly."

The helicopter came in for a closer look and gave them the thumbs-up sign. He flew over them, went across the street, and launched some missiles at buildings across the way.

Castleberry, Robinson, and Worthington talked to each other. They talked about a lot of things. Castleberry smoked a cigarette, even though he hated the things. They talked about their girls and wives, about getting them all together once they got out of this mess. It seemed like hours since the tanks had thundered past without seeing them; in fact, it was only about thirty minutes. And then they heard the roar of a tank again.

Peeples had crossed the northern bridge and was scanning the buildings along Ambush Alley, looking for signs of marines in the city. He guessed they must be near where he had seen the torso of the dead marine on his way northward earlier. He spotted movement on the east side of the street and saw the disabled AAV. He ordered his driver to pull up alongside a building. He jumped off, ducking to avoid the fire, and ran to a house. He'd got the wrong one. He needed to be next door. He crawled through a fence to get there. Waiting for him on the other side was a group of marines. They were ecstatic and hyped up. He was the first officer they had seen since they'd been holed up in the house. Now people knew where they were.

"What the hell is going on? How can I help?"

"There are guys who've been bleeding for two hours. If we don't get them out of here right away, they're gonna die."

There was no room in the tank and not much room on top. But Peeples saw a way that he could get some of them out of there. By turning the turret sideways, he could put the injured marines on the flat, exposed part of the tank and drive them back to the northern bridge.

Castleberry was pleased. *What an awesome idea.* If they could get the wounded to safety, the marines left in the house would feel much happier about staying there longer. Smith, Wentzel, and Olivas helped him load up the injured men onto the tank while the marines on the roof covered them with fast and furious fire. Some of the wounded could be helped along;

others had to be carried because their legs were shot out. Castleberry held Elliot's hand as he loaded him onto the tank.

"It's going to be okay, Elli. We're going to get you out of here. You're going to be okay."

"Thank God. Thank you. Thank you."

Castleberry gave Elliot's hand a squeeze.

"When you get back, you can have a shave and a rest. Save your energy. You'll be fine."

Peeples then came up with a plan to get everyone back.

"Right, fellas. This is what we are going to do. I'm going to drive my tank slowly back to the north bridge and you can walk by the side of the tank so you are protected on one flank. You'll just have to deal with the other flank yourselves."

Castleberry and Robinson looked at each other. They had never heard such an absurd idea in their lives. *Walk back up Ambush Alley with people coming out from the side of the road shooting at us!*

Worthington was horrified. *I've been across the bridge twice already, and I'm not going back across with anything less than a battalion.*

"That's not going to work, sir. We have too many people. If we start getting hit, we're going to be fucked."

He was also worried about leaving behind the CLU, the sighting system for his Javelin.

"Sir, I cannot leave without my sight. It costs two hundred and fifty thousand dollars."

Peeples couldn't believe it. They were in the middle of a war zone, and he was worrying about a piece of equipment.

"We can forget about the damn sight."

Peeples thought they had the place pretty secure. Maybe they could hold out a little longer. He climbed back onto his tank and gunned up the tank, ready to take off with the wounded.

"We'll get the rest of you out of there soon enough."

For Castleberry, Worthington, and Robinson, it was a huge relief to have got the wounded away. The worst part was sitting there watching their fellow marines slowly bleeding to death while there was nothing any of them could do for them. As the tank left, Castleberry looked at his hands. There was blood up to his elbows. It wasn't enemy blood. It was blood from his own marines. It was a sight that he knew would live with him forever.

Marines on the roof were ready to fight again. They were reinvigorated.

They had enough ammo and no wounded to slow them down. Once again, Ortiz felt the adrenaline coursing through his veins. *We gotta do what we gotta do to survive.*

25

Back at Task Force Tarawa's command post, Brigadier General Rich Natonski was trying to picture the battlefield. He was working out of two light armored vehicles, positioned back to back, with a tent covering the gap. He'd let Lieutenant General James T. Conway, commander of the 1st Marine Expeditionary Force, know that his lead elements had run into the Maintenance Company's convoy. The general had been as surprised as they all were. Now, six hours later, he was struggling to keep up with developments. Reports coming back to him were sporadic and confused. He hadn't been expecting a big fight in Nasiriyah. He'd known that the Iraqi 11th Infantry Division was based up there, but they'd received reports that its soldiers were carrying civilian clothes. As soon as the first shots were fired, he thought they would get rid of their uniforms and run away. That's how he'd planned the battle. But it wasn't happening like that. He could hear the artillery going off. All hell was breaking loose. *It's like the gunfight at the OK Corral.*

One of his staff came through with the latest information.

"Sir, they are reporting mass casualties."

What is going on? Natonski felt the fog of war descend on him. He'd read a lot about it, but he'd never experienced it so clearly. In spite of all the planning, the battlefield had become confusing, chaotic, uncertain, and unstable. Nobody seemed to have a clear idea of where the different companies were located. There were reports that Bravo and the forward CP were lost somewhere in the city. There was hardly any news from Charlie at all. He found it hard to believe that the remnants of the Iraqi army and a few fedayeen fighters had the firepower or determination to hold up one of his armored battalions. *Where the hell are they?*

Protected by marines from Bravo Company, Lieutenant Colonel Grabowski was plotting his next move on an improvised map he'd drawn in the dirt at his position in the open area to the east of Ambush Alley. Just when he thought that he was reestablishing some sort of control, he began to receive reports from his air officer that a Huey pilot had spotted some marines on the roof of a house in Ambush Alley. *What is going on? How did they get there?* He was surprised at how little he knew of what was going on around him. In training during the CAX at Twentynine Palms, they were given a scenario and had to react to it. That was difficult. But now he realized how difficult it was to react to a scenario that was constantly changing and which you didn't fully understand. He called his staff together, drew lines in the sand on his improvised map, and began to work out a plan to get the marines out of there. The Huey pilot had given them a rough location for the house: a few hundred meters north of their pause, on the east side of the road. As soon as they got confirmation that the tanks and tracks stuck in the bog were out, they would move up Ambush Alley with their tracks on the west side of the road. He would place his soft-skinned vehicles on the east side of the road to give them some cover from most of the fire, which was coming from an area to the northwest described on their maps as the Martyrs' District. When they got to the house, marines in the soft-skinned Humvees would jump out and grab the marines from inside.

As Grabowski was talking, Major Sosa could see Iraqi civilians walking around the outer edge of the open area where they had stopped. Others were waving flags from rooftops. *What does that mean?* Gradually, more and more people, including women, children, and old men, began to gather and slowly pressed toward them. Some were smiling and waving. Sosa and the marines with him became concerned. *Are they pleased to see us, or is this an orchestrated ploy?* His big fear was that civilians were being used as human shields by the fedayeen and that at any moment someone in the crowd would open up on them.

"Keep those people back."

Shots were fired in the air and interpreters yelled at the crowd to stay away and go back to their houses. Some refused to move and just stood, looking on as if it was normal to have hundreds of marines, tracks, and Humvees bristling with weapons camped out in their backyard.

The women wore traditional burkas. It made him uncomfortable to see the women wrapped in their headscarves. He didn't know much about the culture, but he sensed the oppression. It might have been an excuse, but it made him feel better about what they were doing. To the side of the square, an Iraqi civilian was being looked after by a corpsman. He'd been shot in the abdomen and was lying on a stone slab near the parked vehicles. The corpsman hooked up the IV bag and began to work on him. They bandaged him up and turned him over to some civilians. Sosa watched with unease as the man got up, blood still coming out of his stomach, lit a cigarette, and walked off as though nothing had happened. *He's probably going to die, and he's carrying on as if it were normal life.*

Corporal Neville Welch of Bravo Company was one of those making sure the throng of Iraqis didn't get too close. No one in the crowd seemed to have weapons, but Welch was ready for them. He kept his mantra going in his head. *I am going to get out of this alive. If you want to take me on, I'm going to drop you.* From the rooftops, a fedayeen let off the occasional round. But Welch had good cover, tucked in behind a thick wall in the shelter of a building. His marines had superior marksmanship. If his team saw anyone crawling around on roofs or balconies with hostile intent, they were taken out. He had no idea how long they had been fighting or what was going on elsewhere. His knowledge of the battle was confined to a twenty-square-meter area around him and the few marines by his side. *How will this end?*

26

At the mud bog on the east side of the city, marines were still desperately trying to haul the tanks, Humvees, and tracks out of the mire. It had become worse by the hour. Staff Sergeant Aaron Harrell, the twenty-eight-year-old marine reservist who worked as a CVS pharmacy shift manager, had heard that the tanks from 3rd Platoon, which had been delayed because of the refueling, were going to be arriving any minute to help them out. He saw them charge around a building, heading toward the area covered in pools of green mud and slime that they were calling the shitbog. He tried to wave them down, but he was too late. Captain Cubas and Gunnery Sergeant Alan Kamper of 3rd Platoon had also been deceived by the terrain, and now their tanks also became hopelessly mired in the muck. It didn't matter from which way you came—the ground was nothing more than a thin crust, covering watery mud.

Kamper was horrified to see flames coming out of the rear of his tank. The protection filters in the NBC system, designed to protect them from nuclear, biological, or chemical attack, appeared to have caught fire. There was screaming and yelling as the crew evacuated. The driver, Lance Corporal Joshuah Mouser, hauled himself out of the driver's hatch at the belly of the tank just as an Iraqi, armed with an AK-47, appeared at a door right in front of him. Mouser only had a pistol with which to fire back. The tank's gunner, Sergeant August Nienaber, tossed Mouser his pistol. With a pistol in both hands, he looked like some Western gunslinger. Mouser fired both pistols at once, scaring the Iraqi so much that he dropped his AK and took off running. He picked up the dropped weapon gratefully. He had shot all fifteen of his 9 mm rounds.

"There's enemy infantry coming around the wall."

Harrell, along with several other tankers and Bravo Company's executive officer, First Lieutenant Judson Daniels, ran to help in the fight. The tanks traversed their turrets and managed to fire a couple of rounds to push back any enemy fighters. Cobra helicopters and Huey gunships thundered in low over the area, making gun runs on the enemy to keep them away from the recovery operations.

Gunnery Sergeant Randy Howard looked around at the chaos. At forty-seven years old, and after fourteen years in the reserves, Howard thought he'd seen it all. In civilian life, he had a comfortable job remodeling houses in Kentucky. He took another look around at the yelling, frightened marines, the Iraqi fighters shooting off rounds at him, the tanks sinking in mud halfway up their treads, and wondered what possessed him to join the United States Marine Corps. *I must have been insane.*

What worried him was the state of the young marines from Bravo Company who were posting security. Some were just out of high school. *They need someone to hold their hands.* He hoped they would be able to hold back the crowds of Iraqis from overwhelming the stuck vehicles. They had set up a strong perimeter around the tanks, but he could see that they were wide-eyed with fright and apprehension. In their eyes, he was an old man. In peacetime, it meant they teased him about being old and stuck in his ways. At war, it meant that they looked to him for guidance. He got off his tank and went to each of them to reassure them. He'd seen a lot in life, and although his insides were churning, he was not going to lose his head now. *If you run around acting like a fool, nobody is going to listen to you.*

From the briefings in the weeks before, he'd been given the impression that the Iraqis would be giving them a warm welcome. *I imagined the Iraqi women would be greeting us with flowers in our gun tubes and holding up babies to be kissed.* Instead, he was ducking his head from the rounds streaking around him and making sure the kids posting security stayed awake.

"Hey, keep your eyes open for all those ragheads running around."

Howard tried to get through to the battalion staff on the radio, but there were always too many people talking on the net. They were now low on ammo. Some of his marines had taken the AK-47s from dead Iraqis and were using them to keep the waves of enemy fighters at bay. He looked around once again at the scene. *We badly need the M88 tank retrievers here.* Trying to pull the tanks out with tow cables just wasn't working. The tow cables were too short, and the tracks and mobile tanks couldn't get close enough to pull them out without sinking into the mud themselves.

"Timberwolf. We need the tank retriever up here."

There was no reply.

Howard was pleased that he had Harrell with him. Harrell had been working on the recovery effort and now came up with an idea to make the inch-and-a-quarter steel tow cables longer. He connected two cables using a piece of scrap metal and a clevis, a U-shaped piece of metal, that marines found lying around in the mud. He twisted them together to make them stronger and attached a third cable to give them length. He attached one end to his tank and the other to the tow bolt on Staff Sergeant Insko's tank. As he was working on the recovery effort, a lance corporal, shaking with fear, came up to him.

"Are we going to get out of this hole?"

"We're going to be fine. Get back and work on getting your tank out."

Putting his tank in reverse, Harrell slowly sucked Insko's tank, *Death Mobile,* out of the mud. Then they managed to get Staff Sergeant Dillon's tank free. Things were looking up.

27

At Alpha's position by the Euphrates Bridge, in an alleyway off Ambush Alley, Captain Garcia was waiting patiently for confirmation to lift his CH-46. The casevac was taking longer than he would have wished, but he remained calm and focused. It wasn't the ground fire that was the most immediate threat. He wanted to make sure he knew where the Hueys and Cobras were overhead so that he didn't hit them when he took off.

Marines dragged in the first patient on the back of a wooden board.

They dumped him on the ramp and ran for cover under a hail of fire. Moses Gloria, Hospital Man 2nd Class Mark Kirkland, and the loading chief pulled the wounded marine in. A second patient stumbled forward on foot and fell to the ground a few meters from the aircraft. Gloria ran out, helped him in, and sat him on one of the troop seats at the back. He and Kirkland immediately set to work. Over the roar of the rotors, they yelled at the one marine who was conscious.

"Where are you hit? Are you okay? Do you have any other injuries?"

The marine grabbed his leg, but he didn't want help.

"Just take care of my buddy, I'm fine. Look after my buddy."

The other marine was on a litter on the deck of the helo. Gloria threw in a nasal airway down his nostril and got some IV fluids into him. He was unconscious and had injuries to the lower limbs, but he was stable. If they managed to get him out of there to a shock and trauma medical platoon on the ground, he should make it. The marine was Corporal Matthew Juska, who'd been found alive in the wreckage of track 206.

Gloria went back to the first marine. There was something about his injuries that worried him. The leg was bandaged, but he was losing blood. He did a body sweep under his arms. When he pulled his hands back, they were covered with blood.

"Take your Kevlar jacket off."

Sure as anything, he saw two circular wounds that went straight through the left biceps. The marine looked at him like a deer caught in the headlights. Over the noise of the rotors, Gloria yelled at him.

"Where did you get those from?"

Rounds were now whizzing around outside and bouncing off the helo.

"Did you get this injury before you were in the AAV or on the way to the helo?"

They both realized at the same time that he'd been hit just as he was trying to get on the helo.

In the pilot's seat, Captain Eric Garcia made an effort to keep calm. He could hear the AAVs outside his cockpit firing at the buildings around him. He didn't focus on it too much. He stuck with his job, listening to the FAC talking to the Huey pilots and waiting for the corpsmen and crew in back to tell him it was okay to lift.

"Let us know when you are done there."

Moses Gloria and his fellow corpsman had stabilized both casualties. The call came back from the crew chief.

"We're all set. We're ready to lift."

The level of bullets increased and Garcia pulled up the joystick.

"Let's buster out of here."

Captain Mike Brooks, coordinating the fight from the ground, got goose bumps watching the helicopter take off. Then he got a sick feeling in his stomach. *It's only a matter of seconds till they destroy that helo.*

The helo lifted. By now the word had got around to all Alpha's marines that it was the signal for them to get in their tracks. They were going to head north to link up with Charlie at the northern bridge. Alpha Company marines ran for their tracks, relieved to be getting out of there. Staff Sergeant Pompos, one of the marines from Charlie Company who had made it back down Ambush Alley unscathed, came up to Brooks. He had twenty-five marines with him and not enough vehicles.

"Sir, we don't have a ride for a lot of these marines."

"What do you mean, you don't have a ride? As long as we've got vehicles you've got a ride. It doesn't matter how tightly we pack 'em."

There were thirty marines crammed in each track by the time Brooks got his convoy in position. He put two tanks at the head of the convoy to draw the fire, followed by sixteen AAVs and the entire 81 mm mortar platoon of nine Humvees and four CAAT vehicles. Gunnery Sergeant Lehew, Alpha's AAV platoon sergeant, brought up the rear to make sure no one was left behind. It was just after 1600. Brooks didn't know it, but he and his marines had been fighting at the Euphrates Bridge for nearly three hours. Time had meant nothing to him. He urged his convoy on at top speed. He knew he needed to get to Charlie to help them out at the Saddam Canal Bridge. He hoped that 2/8 was in position to relieve him at the Euphrates Bridge. As they entered the mouth of Ambush Alley, Brooks looked back. He could still see no sign of 2/8.

28

The marines in the house in Ambush Alley lay on the roof tucked in the shelter of the parapet, scanning the road for signs of the enemy. They kept glancing anxiously up the road to their right for signs of a rescue squad. Their faces were caked in sweat and dirt and etched with anxiety.

For the third time that day, they heard the rumble of vehicles coming up Ambush Alley, this time from the Euphrates Bridge on the left side of the road. Looking up from the roof, Robinson, Ortiz, and Martin saw a long convoy of marines speeding toward them. There were tanks, tracks, and Humvees. A whole company was on the move. Robinson's spirits soared. At last they were going to get out of there. *They have come to get us out.* Masonry and dirt exploded into the air as the approaching convoy shot up buildings on both sides of the road along the entire route. Robinson and the others waved their guns and Kevlar helmets to signal that they were friendlies.

As the convoy reached the house, Ortiz, manning a corner of the roof, heard the crack of a round as it ricocheted off a wall. He then felt a smack to his head and dropped to the ground. Robinson saw him drop. *He's not moving. He's dead.* He quickly moved to cover his position. They had survived two hours besieged by hostile forces only to be shot at by their own marines. Martin ducked out of the way of the incoming rounds smacking against the walls around him and cursed themselves for their stupidity. *What a dumb thing to do, waving our rifles around like that.* Ortiz opened his eyes and slowly started to regain vision. He wasn't dead. He had blacked out. The round had gone into the back of the Kevlar helmet, penetrated it, but came out of the top without touching his head. He couldn't hear a thing, though. He just saw people mouthing at him in slow motion. He sat slumped in a corner, completely out of it.

Castleberry and Worthington watched the rest of the convoy just zoom by. *They've fucking missed us.* But as the last vehicle in the convoy drew level with them, a gunnery sergeant in a Humvee, shooting a pump-action shotgun out of the window, spotted them and drew up to the house. He was Gunnery Sergeant Jason Doran, a twenty-year marine veteran.

"What do you need?"

For some reason, Worthington didn't say the obvious. He didn't say, "We need to get out of here right now." He was so tightly focused that he was thinking only of immediate needs. He wasn't thinking of the big picture. Right now, all he knew was that everyone was dead thirsty.

"Water. We need water. And radio batteries."

The gunnery sergeant ran around to the back of the Humvee and threw a five-gallon can of water and a pack of batteries at the marines in the house.

"I'll be back."

Milter ran outside to pick up the water jug. It was empty. In frustration, he hurled it into the air.

All Castleberry and Worthington could see was an empty water jug flying past their line of vision.

"They are fucking empty. And they are the wrong batteries for the fucking radio."

They looked at each other. *Goddamnit. We're fucked again.* Castleberry almost laughed in frustration. *It fucking figures.*

Robinson was getting jumpy. It would soon get dark, and although marines now knew where they were, they were still no closer to getting out of there. *We might just not make it out of here tonight.* Grabbing Ortiz and Olivas, he told Worthington and Wentzel that he was going back to the track to pick up anything else that might be useful.

It was the same drill as before. Ortiz and Olivas covered for him as he waited for the countdown. It was like watching a bull jump out of a gate. When they started firing, he ran out and jumped into the track for a third time. He grabbed some more AT4s and tried to pull out a Javelin antitank missile for Worthington. There were four of them in the track. Getting it was no easy task. They were several meters long, each one weighing thirty-six pounds. Robinson yanked one from behind the benches and pulled it free. He then grabbed anything else he could lay his hands on and threw it all out of the back of the track. Then he tried to do what he had wanted to do all day. He tried to get Fribley out of there. But each time he grabbed him, Fribley's body just came apart in his hands, spilling his intestines all over the floor and over his hands and arms. He was jammed in pretty good between the ramp and the bench. For a second, Robinson got the chills at the macabre scene. Then he went numb and just moved on, leaping out of the track and back into the house. At that moment, he shook off the sight of Fribley's broken body. He wondered whether, in months to come, it would be as easy.

The sun was sinking fast. It was now getting to the point where Castleberry didn't think they would survive the rest of the day. Robinson, Wentzel, Worthington, and Martin began to discuss the unthinkable. They thought of *Black Hawk Down. We might have to shoot our way out of here and patrol back along Ambush Alley on foot.*

III

THE
NORTHERN
BRIDGE

1600–0500 Hours

1

Captain Mike Brooks and the convoy of Alpha Company vehicles shot their way through Ambush Alley toward the northern bridge. Brooks didn't have time to focus on what was going on. They just fired a wall of lead at buildings and bunkers lining the street. Just before the bridge span, Brooks saw the two damaged and twisted AAVs. One of them was no more than a charred hulk still churning out black smoke. He felt it as a slap in the face. *Good Lord. What happened there?*

As they crossed the bridge, Brooks came face-to-face with the horror of war. It was a sight he thought he'd never see. There were marines lying on the ground, bleeding out by the side of the road, their faces contorted with pain and anguish. The lifeless bodies of KIAs, covered in ponchos, were laid out behind a mound of earth. Around them, Charlie's marines were dug in, wide-eyed and fearful, faces caked in blood, sweat, and dirt. A hundred meters beyond the bridge were a couple of AAVs. One, destroyed in the middle of the road, still had smoke spewing out; another was lying in a ditch, as impotent as a beached whale.

Brooks looked for Dan Wittnam. He asked a couple of Charlie marines where their commander was. They just stared at him, too badly shaken to make any sense. Then he saw him by one of the tracks, trying to work the radio. Blood and dirt had dried in blotches on his face and the front of his chemical suit. His legs were covered in thick mud. *Good Lord. What have you been through?* Brooks looked him in the eye, trying to gauge how he was doing.

"Dan, am I glad to see you. How are you doing?"

Wittnam looked back with a steady gaze. Brooks could see that he was being strong and trying to hold it together. But there was real anguish behind those eyes.

"How are you doing, Mike?"

Brooks didn't need to ask him what was going on. That was clear. Neither of them had any idea where Bravo Company and the forward CP were. They looked back into the city, but there was no sign of them. *They must be somewhere in there doing God knows what.*

"Dan, I'm going to get to work on drumming up the defense and getting a solid perimeter. We'll chat more in a few minutes."

Brooks set up a battalion minus defense with the tanks and the CAAT team. It was a way of defending the position without full battalion strength. He wanted to chat more with Dan but could tell that he was preoccupied with the job of accounting for his marines. *It's wearing on him that he doesn't know where everyone is.*

Alpha's arrival at the northern bridge had changed the balance of power. They were now a force to be reckoned with. Alpha's FAC called in air strikes on the buildings around the canal where much of the fire was still coming from. The 81 mm mortar platoon laid down baseplates, attached cannons, and blasted buildings to the north and south. Tanks traversed their turrets while their gunners looked through the crosshairs and locked onto the buildings and bunkers from where they were still receiving fire.

Mike Brooks had seen the difference the tanks had made by the Euphrates Bridge. He now saw it all over again. As soon as the tanks started firing, the incoming stopped. He didn't have time to analyze it fully, but he had the fleeting thought that they had poorly task organized the employment of the tanks. *It would have been better to give tanks to each of the companies.*

Staff Sergeant Anthony Pompos, one of the Charlie Company marines who had run the gauntlet of Ambush Alley with the medevac convoy and had now made it back to the northern bridge, tried to link up with the rest of the marines from his platoon. Even though he had managed to consolidate all those who had mistakenly traveled back to the southern bridge in track 210 with him, there were still some marines missing. As he was trying to account for them all, he ran into Gunnery Sergeant Jason Doran.

"Hey, half my platoon is missing and I don't know where they are at."

It was like a lightbulb went off inside Doran's head.

"There are marines inside the city. I just drove past them. They are from Charlie Company. Help me clear this Humvee up."

Doran and Pompos cleared some equipment out of the Humvee and grabbed a couple of machine gunners. Doran got back into his Humvee and headed back down Ambush Alley.

Robinson, Castleberry, Worthington, and the other marines inside the house on Ambush Alley had been waiting for what seemed like hours since the gunnery sergeant from the Alpha convoy had pulled up to the house and thrown the water jug at them. Robinson thought they were never coming back. *They've left us here. They've forgotten about us.* Now he finally saw the same gunnery sergeant, Jason Doran, hurtling down the road toward them with five Humvees. Castleberry thought he was like something out of a movie. He saw the shotgun at his side and shotgun rounds slotted in his flak jacket. He lit a cigarette just like the Marlboro Man and started pumping off rounds in the direction of some Iraqis. His chin strap was hanging down. *This guy's rough and ready, just like John Wayne.*

Doran ran to the house and shouted at Worthington.

"Hey, man, why didn't you say you needed out of here the first time?"

Worthington couldn't answer. It just didn't occur to him.

"Well, let's get the fuck out of here now."

The marines in the courtyard downstairs piled into the Humvees, followed by those on the roof. Doran ran into the house to make sure that everyone had gotten out. When he got back into the street, he saw a group of marines just hanging around the vehicles.

"What's wrong?"

"We don't know which vehicle we should get into."

"Get the fuck out of here. Get in any of the vehicles. Just get in."

Some piled into the back of Humvees; others had to hang off the sides and lie on the hood. As the Humvees took off, they fired off all the ammo left in their rifles at every window, every alley, every building on both sides of the road. Guns were blazing as the marines fired so many rounds that they burned themselves on the hot barrels. Robinson was relieved to have finally gotten out of the house. He felt much more comfortable in the familiar surroundings of a Marine Corps Humvee. Castleberry didn't. He felt vulnerable. Normally, he was hidden inside the metal compartment of his track. The sides of the Humvees were no more than canvas flaps. *I've just got to get as much lead out there as possible. We're getting out of here. Let's not fuck it up now.* There was a feeling of group elation. During the three-minute drive back to the northern bridge, a wall of lead flew out from both sides of the convoy.

2

Gunnery Sergeant Howard and his tanks had now been stuck in the mud on the east side of the city for over three hours. He was still waiting for the Hercules M88 tank retrievers to show up. There was just no way they were managing to pull out the stuck tanks and tracks with the tow cables they had with them.

He heard the M88s before he saw them. The battalion staff had not wanted support vehicles getting mixed up in the fighting in Nasiriyah. But Gunnery Sergeant Greg Wright, Staff Sergeant Charlie Cooke, and the tank company's mechanics had detached from the battalion log trains to drive the two M88 tank retrievers, unescorted, over the Euphrates Bridge, into the city, and toward the mud bog.

This time, a couple of tankers, led by Sergeant John Ethington, re-conned the route on foot so that the M88s wouldn't get stuck in the mud. Once again it didn't help. Howard's heart sank when he now saw one of the 88s slide into a mud hole. Marines yelled in disbelief. The other 88 ma-neuvered around it and managed to pull it out. The mechanics on that 88 now positioned the vehicle close enough to pull Howard's tank out. Just as the 88 raised its crane arm and pulled Howard's tank out, the 88 began to sink into the mud. Howard now had to use his tank to pull out the 88. *How are we going to get out of this mess?* As they tried to get the C7 amtrack out, the 88 got stuck again. The other 88 couldn't get close enough to pull it out without getting stuck itself.

No matter what combination of vehicles they used to tow each other out of the mud, one of them would always seem to get stuck. It was getting dark. Howard knew that they had to get out of there before nightfall, yet two vehicles, the C7 forward command-and-control track and now one of the M88 tank retrievers, were still stuck. The only way to get enough pur-chase on the ground would be to demolish one of the corner houses. They decided it wasn't a good idea.

A couple of miles north of the mud bog, Major Sosa had seen, through the gap onto Ambush Alley, the long convoy of Alpha's vehicles, led by the tanks, hurtle past them from south to north. As they moved through the town, fire rained down on them from the western side. Sosa was relieved. He finally knew that with so much firepower heading north, they were going to accomplish their mission. *We're going to make this happen.* Now they needed to get the stuck vehicles out so that they could join the fight, too.

Lieutenant Colonel Grabowski also saw the Alpha convoy go through. At last, things were starting to happen. He'd picked up from radio comms that there were now several dead and an unknown number of wounded. He'd had reports that some of the wounded were with Alpha and others with Charlie. He didn't know how many. Some of the reports suggested there were mass casualties. *This was not how it was supposed to be.* Grabowski was frustrated and angry. *The gloves are now off.*

He got his artillery liaison officer, First Lieutenant Kevin Jackson, to call back to the artillery batteries of 1st Battalion, 10th Marines, call sign Nightmare, to shell the Martyrs' District, on the northwest side of the city, where most of the fire had come from. Until now, the city had been a restricted area. To cut down on what the U.S. military euphemistically called "collateral damage," Grabowski and his marines had been told not to fire into residential areas unless they positively identified targets. The bitter fighting over the last five hours had changed all that. Now he ordered artillery shells to strike the city. He watched as the shells came over and landed in the Martyrs' District, sending up fountains of debris and smoke. They hit right on the money.

From his position on the edge of Ambush Alley guarding the forward CP, Corporal McCall, one of the CAAT marines, looked through the 13-power sight system of his TOW. In the distance, he saw a marine AAV disabled against a building and Iraqis dragging objects from the rear of the vehicle. *Were they the bodies of marines or were they packs?* He didn't know that it was track 201, which had been carrying Robinson, Castleberry, and the other marines who had been holed up in the house on Ambush Alley. He had no idea how the AAV had got there. He asked permission from the battalion gunner, Chief Warrant Officer David Dunfee, to engage the track.

"Are you sure there are no friendlies?"

"I can't see, sir."

Dunfee couldn't be sure that there weren't marines still in the track. He wouldn't let McCall shoot. McCall had to sit there and watch the Iraqis dragging stuff away.

Grabowski wasn't going to wait any longer. He'd got the news that almost all the vehicles were out of the mud, except for the C7 and the Hercules M88 tank retriever. They would have to leave them. He got hold of the battalion staff he'd left with the stuck vehicles and told them to move out. Some of the mechanics refused to leave the M88. It was only when Major Peeples gave them a specific order that they agreed to abandon it. Marines stripped as much as they could off the two vehicles and pulled out onto Ambush Alley. Ahead of them, Grabowski and the rest of the forward CP and Bravo Company were already waiting. At last, the remaining vehicles of 1st battalion, 2nd Marines, headed up Ambush Alley in one long convoy. When it reached track 201, marines from the CAAT vehicles jumped into the troop compartment and found the mangled body of Lance Corporal David Fribley. They pulled it free and loaded it into one of the Humvees. Other marines ran into the house to look for the stranded marines. There was no one there. They didn't realize they had all been rescued earlier by Peeples and Doran. It was 1715. As they set off toward the northern bridge, Grabowski saw, on the other side of the road, the charred hulk of track 208 still burning. *No one could have survived that.*

3

Lance Corporal Thomas Quirk had heard the Alpha convoy arriving at the northern bridge, but he was so focused on looking for Iraqis to kill that he didn't pay much attention. He was lying in the dirt behind a mound of earth on the east side of the road, eyes locked on one small sector of marshy terrain where he had seen figures running about. He heard someone over his shoulder yell out.

"Hey, we're through here. Get over here and get in your platoons. Let's get a count."

It was weird. It happened out of the blue. The shooting stopped as though someone had called a time-out. *What am I doing? Where is everyone? Where is my platoon?* It was like suddenly waking up and finding himself in a different world. Quirk did not have a clue what had happened. He'd stayed with the same ten or twelve guys throughout the fight and had no idea where anyone else was or what they'd been doing.

He jumped on a track and headed three hundred meters north of the bridge to the spot where his platoon was getting into formation. Out of thirty marines, there were only eleven left. *Where the fuck is everybody?*

Quirk was agitated. As had happened so often in the past, his brain just went into overdrive.

"Where's Fribley? Where's Carl? Fribley's in my team. Where the fuck is he?"

Private First Class Brian Woznicki tried to calm him down.

"Hey, Corporal, don't worry about it."

"Fuck you. Where's Martin? Where's Olivas?"

"Don't fucking worry about it. Calm down."

"Who's fucking dead? These are my friends. Where the fuck are they?"

Quirk had lost his cool. *Nobody knows where anybody is or what has fucking happened. What kind of fucked-up shit is this?*

He went up to marines in his platoon and asked them where his buddies were. Some marines just hung their heads. He walked up and down the lines, yelling out names.

"Martin, where are you? Martin. Jared Martin. Lance Corporal Jared Martin. Where are you?"

An officer walked past with his head bowed, looking at the ground.

"I hope you find your buddy."

That was the last thing Quirk wanted to hear. The whole day, things had just gone from bad to worse. *For the thirtieth time today, things have just gotten worse. Now we've reached rock bottom.* His buddies Olivas and Martin were not there. If they weren't there, they might be dead. It was too horrible to contemplate.

He ran over to the side of the road where the bodies were lined up, covered with ponchos. As they got there, a chopper came in and blew the ponchos off the bodies. With Woznicki and a bunch of other guys, he ran over and started to cover the bodies up again. Through the gore and blood, he recognized a tattoo on one of the lifeless bodies. The face and body were so mashed up that if it hadn't been for the tattoo, he wouldn't have known who he was looking at. But he'd seen that tattoo many times before on the arm of Corporal Randal Rosacker. He'd never seen a dead person up close before, and now he was staring at a guy he'd hung out with, drunk beer with, talked shit with. They were not best buddies by any stretch of the imagination, but they'd been to bars together and he'd thought the guy was cool. *Holy shit, what the fuck am I looking at?* None of it was registering. So much had happened in such a short amount of time that he was overloaded.

He ran to the casualty collection point and saw Corporal Carl, his team leader, on a stretcher, pale and morphined up. There was a tourniquet around his leg. He was surrounded by medics who were freaking out, screaming at each other. As they carried him away, Carl gave him a thumbs-up.

"Be safe."

It was the creepiest thing Quirk had ever seen. *I can't fucking believe it. Two days ago I was hanging out with these guys, walking around in shorts and goofing around, and now I'm looking around at them and they are in the dirt, bleeding to death.*

That's when he saw Fribley's body, covered by the Stars and Stripes. A huge bloodstain was seeping through the flag in the area of the chest. His mouth went dry. Quirk had always had an American flag in his room as a kid. He'd saluted it countless times, and now he saw it draped over his friend's body, oozing with blood. He knew that he would never be able to look at the American flag the same way again. From now on, every time he closed his eyes, that would be the image he saw.

A TV cameraman was taking pictures. Quirk ran over to him and stood in front of the camera.

"I hope you make a lot of fucking money off this."

The cameraman said something back to him and Quirk just flipped. He ran at him, screaming. Woznicki grabbed him and tried to calm him down.

"It's okay. Leave it. He's just doing his job."

None of it was making any sense to him. *I've fucking shot my fucking rifle all day and I've watched fucking people fall to the fucking ground and see shit getting blown up in such a fucking small period of time. I don't know what the fuck is going on and I'm looking at a bunch of my dead friends lined up in the street and half my platoon is not fucking here and nobody fucking knows what's going on.*

That's when he heard one marine mention that some of his buddies were stranded in a house in the city.

The CAAT vehicles, which had gone back into the city to rescue the marines stranded in Ambush Alley, pulled into the reinforced position. The marines inside were battered and bruised, their vehicles riddled with bullet holes and dents and cracked windshields.

Private First Class Casey Robinson, Lance Corporal Jared Martin, Corporal Jake Worthington, and Lance Corporal Richard Olivas clambered wearily off the Humvees in a daze, unable to digest what they had been through. They were shaking and ragged; the barrels of their weapons were still hot. Sweat and dirt caked their faces. Blood coated their flak vests. For hours they had kept intensely focused on staying alive. Now they felt flat and disorientated. They had no idea where to go or what to do next. Their platoons were scattered all over the battlefield.

Robinson wandered as if in a dream across a battlefield strewn with burning tracks, debris from exploded missiles, empty water bottles, torn pieces of battle dressings. The acrid smell of spent ammo hung in the air. The metallic taste of burning metal stuck to his tongue. By the side of the road, bodies were laid out in a line. Robinson wondered who they were. He saw marines carrying body parts covered in ponchos to the casualty collection point. Cobras were still circling, and the odd round cracked overhead. But it was a different place from where he had been a few hours earlier. He had time to breathe. He saw artillery strikes pound Nasiriyah over to the west, on the south side of the canal. The ground shook. Some marines around him whooped with excitement.

"Let's nuke the whole place."

When he found his platoon, he counted no more than a squad and a half. Half his platoon seemed to be missing.

"Hey, Robinson. We got word that you died. Thank God you are here."

He sat with the others and tried to figure out who was still alive. Someone said Rosacker was dead. Someone else said Juska was dead. Another company of marines had been assigned the gruesome task of loading up the dead and wounded. The higher-ups didn't want Charlie Company marines loading up the Charlie KIAs.

He sat on the ground and did an ACE report, checking his ammo, casualties, and equipment. Then someone shoved an MRE in his hand and he just sat there eating it, tasting nothing.

Worthington looked for the other members of the Javelin team. When someone told him that Rosacker was dead, he went numb. They'd been through the School of Infantry together. It was disturbing. It was too much to compute. Guys he'd been joking with the day before were wide-eyed with apprehension. *No one knows who is alive and who is dead.* All sorts of rumors were flying around about what they'd been through, who had been shot, who was missing.

Martin's first thought when he clambered out of the Humvee was *Where are my buddies?* Someone said one of them was dead. Another said they'd just seen him. Martin didn't know what to think. He knew that those who had stayed on the northern bridge had been hit real hard. *How many of my friends are dead?* What he did know was that he wanted to get away. *We need to leave here and get out.* He forced himself to keep going. But his energy was dropping. The marines who had been in the house with him were beginning to suffer. They had been sustained by fear and adrenaline. Now they felt drained and empty. Martin's bleeding forehead, which he had forgotten about for so long, now throbbed with a sharp pain. Tiredness hit him out of nowhere.

That's when Quirk and Martin found each other. Quirk was shocked at Martin's pale and drawn face. Quirk had had enough.

"I don't want to do this again."

The two of them talked a little about the battle. Martin didn't want to talk about the house on Ambush Alley. He wasn't ready to go into details. Quirk almost felt as though he'd missed out on something. He wanted to have been in the house with the rest of them. At the same time, he was glad he hadn't been there. He remembered how he had been that morning. *We were talking big shit about wanting to go to war and killing people. And now this.* It had started as the most exciting day of Quirk's life and ended as the most horrible day anybody could imagine. *Nobody should ever have to go through such a fucking ridiculous day.*

He looked around and saw the destroyed tracks, the burned-out Humvees, the bodies lying on the ground. *This is sick. This is fucking sick.* He breathed in the air deeply, very deeply and thought, *I'm alive. I fucking made it without a scratch.* But there was no standard operating procedure for what to do next. *I don't know whether to piss or shit, sit, or stand.* No training he'd done had prepared him for this. Instead, they started fooling around. Woznicki showed him the big shrapnel wound he had caught in his butt. Quirk remembered the bit from the movie *Forrest Gump* when Tom Hanks, running through the jungle of Vietnam, gets shot in the ass. Quirk imitated Forrest Gump's voice.

"Something bit me."

The two of them balled up with laughter and repeated their newfound catchphrase.

"Something bit me . . . Something bit me . . . Something bit ME."

They rolled around in giggles. Fooling around was the only way they had to release their anxiety. Then someone put an MRE in his hand.

"You guys, go ahead and break out chow."

Quirk broke open an MRE, put food in his mouth, and chewed. He didn't taste anything. It was just something to do. *That was the longest forty-five minutes of my life.*

A marine next to him looked at his watch.

"Do you know we've been doing this shit for over six hours?"

That blew Quirk away. His buddies told him things that he'd done, things that had happened. Quirk couldn't remember any of them. Bits of the day had just been erased from his memory.

Captain Dyer, the executive officer of Alpha Company, 8th Tank Battalion, was still several hundred meters north of Quirk's position, with his tank facing northward toward the white military complex. For the first time that day, combined arms had begun to work like a dream. For the past thirty minutes, as Dyer took out targets with his main gun, his FAC, Major Hawkins, had been calling in F-16 and A-10 fire to destroy targets to the north. An F-16 streaked across the sky and dropped a guided missile on a radar installation. An A-10 worked the tree line to the north where vehicles were going back and forth, picking up and dropping off combatants. The pilots identified dug-in mortar positions, enabling the tankers to call in artillery fire. Artillery fire also began to take out the mortar and artillery batteries firing at them from inside the complex. Wave after wave of aircraft came in and took out targets on a 270-degree arc to the north of the canal.

He now looked back and saw that Alpha Company had arrived to reinforce Charlie. He was relieved to see two more tanks coming toward him to back him up. It worried him, though, that all the battalion's vehicles were packed in too tightly around the foot of the Saddam Canal Bridge. *If a shell lands, they are going to be wiped out.* He called back to the main CP.

"You need to contact the companies at the bridge and tell them to spread out."

Maybe there was too much going on at the main command post, but Dyer didn't like the answer he received.

"If you can get them to do it then try it out."

It was just another chunk of frustration. *Battalion, that's your job to get the guys to spread out.* Dyer had felt all day long that battalion staff had been interfering in the fight when they didn't need to. And now that there was something that was clearly their responsibility, they didn't want to know. He was still feeling sore that the fire support coordinator had aborted their attack on the tank earlier that morning. *It was frustrating when we couldn't get hold of battalion, but at least they couldn't screw it up for us.* He knew it was unprofessional to think like that, but that's how he felt.

In spite of everything, as he looked back and saw the marines regrouping at the bridge, he felt that the way the U.S. Marines did business had worked. Even though the battalion staff had not been able to coordinate the battle, the three separate companies, from platoon and squad level down to individual marines, had fought their separate fights and got the job done.

He worked out that throughout the day he must have fired at least ten main gun rounds and thousands of machine-gun rounds. But it was getting quiet now. He got hold of his driver, Lance Corporal Shirley, who had been holed up in the driver's seat in the belly of the tank for hours.

"It's safe enough to pop your hatch and get some air."

Just as he did, a mortar round landed so close that he was clobbered in the face with mud. Shirley quickly ducked back down and closed the hatch.

With the lull in the incoming fire and the extra security Alpha's presence had brought them, Lieutenant Conor Tracy, commander of Charlie's AAV platoon, could begin to account for his trackers and his vehicles. He'd started the day with forty-eight men and twelve working vehicles. Now he counted no more than ten men and only two working tracks. He'd been with most of his platoon for a year and a half. He knew almost everything about them. Now he was facing up to the prospect that his platoon was decimated.

He was on the eastern side of the road, working out what he was going to do next, when the first of his missing trackers pulled back into his area in a working AAV. It was Corporal Brown and Sergeant Schaefer, who had followed Major Peeples's tank back up Ambush Alley. Tracy was delighted to see them.

Schaefer, too, was overjoyed to see Tracy. At one stage during the battle, he was convinced that Tracy, his platoon commander, was dead. He'd had to take over the responsibility of leadership, and he didn't like it. He was feeling confused and guilty. A few hours earlier, he had led a convoy of five vehicles south and had now come back with only one functioning track.

"I'm so fucking sorry."

Schaefer and Tracy sat down in the dirt and shared a cigarette, taking cover under an overhang where part of the eastern side of the road had been blown away. Tracy didn't smoke, but someone had given him the cigarette early that morning. He'd kept it in his pocket, and it was so bent out of shape that it looked like the McDonald's logo. Someone had to light it for him. His hands were shaking from shock.

"I'm so fucking sorry that I lost those vehicles."

Schaefer was on the point of breaking down. He analyzed everything he'd done, picked apart every decision he made. He could feel the tears welling up. Guilt started to overwhelm him. He felt bad about taking so many vehicles south, and he felt bad about leaving Castleberry and the others in Ambush Alley. Schaefer, at twenty-five, was one of the senior guys. He'd been with the Camp Lejeune AAVs for four years. He remembered the day Castleberry and the others had arrived at the 2nd AAV Battalion headquarters at Courthouse Bay. He'd enjoyed training them and teaching them everything he knew. Castleberry was highly strung and overexcitable, but Schaefer always felt real proud when he gave him something hard to do and he pulled it off. It was the same with Elliot. He was a good Christian pretty boy who never did anything wrong. But he felt protective toward him and the others. Now he felt as though he'd let them down. He'd abandoned them in Ambush Alley. He was glad Lieutenant Tracy was sitting next to him, because otherwise he would have lost it.

"You did what you thought was right. At least you were able to let them know of the situation at the northern bridge."

Tracy tried to reassure him. He wouldn't have ordered the medevac convoy to go back, but it did mean that someone managed to reach Alpha and warn them of the fight that Charlie was in.

"Don't dwell on it. There's work to be done."

That helped change Schaefer's mind-set. He got up to scour the creeks and irrigation ditches for the bodies of the missing marines. Then he would have to start work on the tracks. For every hour that the track is running, it needs eight hours maintenance. *The idle mind is a dangerous thing. We've got to get back to work.*

One by one, Tracy's trackers started turning up. Everyone that showed up was a gift. Soon he didn't even think of it as losing people. The numbers of those confirmed alive mounted. But it was troubling him that Castleberry hadn't appeared. He recalled the message that Castleberry had clicked through to him on the radio that he was somewhere in the city. *Where is he now?*

As Castleberry arrived back at the northern bridge with the rest of the marines from the Alamo, the first thing he saw was Staff Sergeant John Lefebvre in one of the tracks, with Lance Corporal Jerome Washburn driving. Castleberry was confused. *It should be Chanawongse driving.* It gave him a bad feeling. He didn't yet know that two of his fellow trackers, Corporal Kemaphoom Chanawongse and Sergeant Michael Bitz, had been killed. He reached the rest of the trackers. He was so glad to see them. He burst into tears. It was like returning to his family.

"Hey, we're so glad to see you. We thought you were dead."

Sergeant Matthew Beaver gave him a big, big hug.

"Hey man, it's real good to see you."

"Doc" Fonseca, one of the corpsmen, grabbed him.

"Where are you hurt? What do you need?"

Castleberry's knees and elbows were bloody and raw, but otherwise he was fine. He drank some water and tried to smoke a cigarette, but he was shaking so much that he had to put it down.

"Chanawongse is dead. Bitz is missing."

He went numb. He felt like a zombie. He couldn't think too much. He now understood the term *war torn. They're all fucked-up looking.* He tried to piece it all together. He found Schaefer assessing the damage to one of the tracks. Castleberry listened wide-eyed as Schaefer told him how he had jumped into Brown's track to head back to the Euphrates Bridge and how, when he had asked for help to get them out of Ambush Alley, a battalion captain at the command post had told him there was nothing he could do.

"I told them, but those motherfuckers wouldn't send anyone to help you."

Castleberry stewed. *How is that possible? How did they not know where we were? And when they knew, why didn't they help us?* He looked up at Schaefer.

"I need to be alone for a while."

For the next hour, Castleberry sat there, his head in his arms looking at the ground.

Lieutenant Reid, in the back of the casualty track, was getting nervous. He couldn't see what was going on, and even though there was not much noise outside, he was fearful that the track was going to get hit. *I'm not going to stay here.* He jumped out of the track to find a bunch of people from Alpha Company standing around. He couldn't understand why they looked so nonchalant. *Don't you understand there is a battle going on?* Then it dawned on him that most of the fighting had stopped. He asked around for his buddy from Alpha, Lieutenant Steve Cook. A corpsman came over and had him sit down at the casualty collection point. Then Cook came over.

"I'm glad to see that you are okay."

Their wives were good friends, and just by seeing him, Reid felt closer to home. Another close friend, Lieutenant James Lane, an Alpha platoon commander, came over. Reid's eye was still bloody and swollen, and he was still losing blood from somewhere.

"Where are you hit?"

"I am good to go. Another doc bandaged me up."

"Well, we are going to take your SAPI plate out to make you more comfortable."

They opened up Reid's flak jacket and took out his Small Protective Insert, a bulletproof ceramic plate.

"Holy shit."

"What is it, Doc?"

"There is a hole in your shoulder. I do not see an exit wound. But it doesn't look too bad. You'll be fine."

"Sure thing, Doc."

The medic patched him up and marines came by to see him. He watched their body language closely to see how they reacted to him. *Am I going to have an eye by the end of this?* His head seethed with guilt. He knew several of his men had been killed, including the artillery FO and platoon sergeant. Lieutenant Seely came by and just laughed at him and gave him a friendly tap on the leg. That made him feel better. He remembered with black humor that he and Cook had bet on which bridge would be the toughest to take. Cook had thought the northern bridge would be hardest. Reid had thought it would be the southern bridge. When they were on ship, Charlie had originally been tasked with taking the southern bridge and Alpha the northern bridge. Both of them had been pissed when their missions were switched because they both wanted to be where the action was. *I guess Cook was right.*

Jose Torres was still lying by the casualty collection point. He had no idea what was going on. To him, it was just a bunch of marines coming and going. He felt as though he had been on a roller coaster for several hours, just spinning around as he was driven from track to track. Now he was lying in the dirt waiting for the helos to come in. Every so often, a marine would come past and comfort him, or a corpsman would check up on him. He had a tag attached, which read, "*Urgent—surgery—buttock.*"

Nearby, another marine had the job of keeping the flies, birds, and dogs away from the body parts laid out on ponchos in the mud and the hood of a Humvee.

Overhead, there was the throb of an incoming helicopter.

4

Captain Eric Garcia, piloting his CH-46 helo, had dropped off the two casualties from the first casevac at the "Big Buddy" CSSB or Combat Service Support Battalion, 22 level-one care facility and then flown on to the Jalibah airstrip to refuel. It was there that he had got a call to go back into Nasiriyah. This time they were very clear about the status.

"Parole 25, there is a Mass Cas situation. Mass Cas."

Mass Casualties. Reports were coming in that there might be as many as fifty. He focused on flying the helo back toward Nasiriyah. It wasn't his job to think about the patients or wonder what sort of state they were in. His job was to get his CH-46 back to the battlefield as quickly and safely as possible.

In the rear of the CH-46, Moses Gloria went through his equipment again. But he was distracted. He couldn't help looking through the windows, searching for incoming RPGs. He'd done his job with the two patients on his first casevac mission. But this time he knew it would be different.

Mass Cas. Even the sound made him fearful. He was scared that his brain might freeze when he started to work on someone. He was terrified that the number of casualties would overwhelm him.

"Hail Mary, full of grace, the Lord is with thee . . . please help me make it through the day."

He prayed that nothing would hit the aircraft. He prayed that he would be able to do his job. He prayed that he would remain calm. He prayed that he would not get in such a state that he would start pretending to do stuff that in reality was not going to help. His worst moment had been during refueling, when he knew that he had to get back there and save some lives. But the refueling took time. There was nothing he could do except sit and wait.

Garcia looked down at the outskirts of Nasiriyah. Puffs of black smoke erupted around him. It reminded him of watching an old World War II movie. *There must be an Iraqi antiaircraft artillery battery aiming at me, trying to bring down the helo.* They started taking fire from a palm grove by the river. Now below him he could see the street where they had carried out the first casevac mission a couple of hours earlier. This time the air controller gave him another grid a couple of miles farther north. He flew over the north-south MSR. He was flying over Ambush Alley. Now he could see the blackened hulk of a burned-out AAV just by a bridge over a narrow stretch of waterway. It was still smoking. He couldn't believe that's what could happen to an AAV. He'd never seen anything like that before. He hovered overhead, found a wide road to land on, and brought the helo down.

Gloria looked out of the window and saw that they were hovering above the landing zone. He looked over a wide, desolate area of mud fields covered in debris and smashed vehicles. The site was a reality check. During the previous weeks, he had been lolling around in Kuwait, trying to make use of the facilities. He knew that once they got to Iraq it would be rough, so he spent much of his time on the Air Force side—the Rock, he called it—enjoying the hot chow and showers, the air-conditioned chow halls, the stores selling reading material, the cabins for making calls home. He'd seen the full might of the coalition getting ready for war. There was the U.S. Army, the U.S. Air Force, the Brits, the West Coast and East Coast Marines. He'd thought then that it was going to be a walk in the park, that with such power and organization they would stroll into Baghdad. He'd daydreamed about how he was going to spend the extra money he earned after the war was over.

Now all those thoughts were gone. Moses Gloria could see the full terror of what was waiting for him. There were smoking vehicles; bodies, some covered in camouflage ponchos, some draped in the Stars and Stripes; groups of wounded marines, dazed and confused, held together by bloody bandages and strips of T-shirts. Some were in the arms of their buddies who were trying to comfort them. *This is hell on earth.*

Hail Mary, full of grace.

The helo landed with a bump. He ran down the ramp and began triaging, assessing his patients for severity of injury. There were marines holding bloody limbs that were no longer attached to their bodies. There were gaping lumps of gore where a leg used to be, bones protruding through skin, necks and faces covered with shrapnel wounds oozing thick red blood.

Hail Mary, full of grace, the Lord is with thee. Flashes of people that had ever meant anything to him came into his head.

"Where were you hit?"

He took a deep breath and tried to pull himself together.

"Can you hear what I am saying?"

Something had clicked—muscle memory, training—something that just made him get to work on his patients in spite of all the chaos and terror around him, in spite of all the weird things that were going through his head.

"It's okay. We're going to get you out of here."

He made sure that he went from marine to marine, checking all of them. He felt that a guardian angel was looking over him, helping him do what he had to do to get these guys out of there. There was one marine with a severe chest wound that he wanted to spend time over. But he forced himself to help everybody, to not waste all his supplies on one patient. He started babbling to himself. He was losing it again. He stopped and took a deep breath. One marine's stomach was blowing up. He was bleeding internally. There was nothing he could do for him. He needed major surgery and fast. He tried to make him comfortable.

"Hang on there, buddy, we're going to get you home."

Gloria chose his patients. He took the critical ones with internal injuries, severed limbs, head injuries. He started to send the less critical injuries to a second helo that had just landed. He was horrified to see that a master sergeant was already loading the dead into that helo. Nobody had the heart to tell him to take out the bodies. One of the marines loaded up was covered in the Stars and Stripes. None of the corpsmen or crew chiefs that day would forget the name of that marine. The marine who carried him to the helo had scrawled it on a piece of cardboard—*Fribley.*

"We loved that guy. Get him home."

Gloria looked for seven patients to make up a full load. There was one who was in a bad way—it was some sort of cervical injury, but he was stable. He had a laceration to the head and a couple of superficial wounds to the stomach and his leg, but they weren't bleeders. He had a collar around his neck. But the worse thing was that he couldn't or wouldn't open his eyes. They were squinted down really hard. It reminded Gloria of the MVA victims who'd suffered head trauma or cervical spinal injury from a vehicle accident.

"Can you squeeze my hand?"

The marine, his eyes shut tight, gave Gloria's hand a slight squeeze. He tried getting him to move his leg. There was no movement. He rubbed his sternum to see if he could get some reaction. Nothing. He realized that there was nothing he could do for the marine. It was either shell shock, in which case he'd recover with time, or he was really messed up and had some sort of brain injury. There were limits to what he could do. He moved onto the next one.

He began to package them, putting tags on them with information on their injuries and what medication they'd had. He had to guesstimate what treatment they'd received on the battlefield.

Some of the corpsmen on the ground had done excellent first-aid work with what little they had. Some of them had molle bags with IV fluid and bandages, but much of the equipment had already run out. Marines had used T-shirts to stem the bleeding, belts and shoelaces as tourniquets, duct tape and rifles as splints. They'd done what they had to. Get air into the airways; if he bleeds, plug the hole.

He moved onto his next patient, Sergeant Torres. On his tag, a corpsman had written, "*Urgent—surgery—buttock.*" He pulled back the bloody dressing and found that half the marine's buttock had been blown off. *We're taking a beating down here. This is something we can't handle. This isn't Kansas anymore.* He suddenly had a premonition that this is what it was going to be like every day for the next six months. *We're going to be flying 24/7, balls to the wall, picking up guys in body bags and piecing them together.*

"Okay, get him on the helo."

Mass cas. It was so utterly confusing no matter how hard you planned for it. *This is what is going to happen all over Iraq.* He wondered how he got here. Why wasn't he in some nice white naval hospital somewhere? *I'm not a warrior. I'm trained to heal, not to fight. I'm on the chubby side; I'm not made to run around on a battlefield like this.* All the same, he did what he was trained to do, scared, fearful, doubting his own abilities. He patched up some marines and sent them back to their units to fight again. Others he sent to the helo.

He had his full load of seven patients. If he took more, he would be maxed out and unable to cope. He let Captain Garcia know the casualty status.

"Okay, sir, we have five litter patients and two walking. We have three surgicals and two immediates. Let me know when we have an ETA."

He could usually tell within minutes whether he was going to lose a patient. This time, though, he didn't think he had any "expectants."

"Okay, let's go."

Marines were still ferrying the dead and injured to another helo that had landed next to them. The rotors whirred, the ramp went up, and the helo lifted. Some marines were in too much pain to say anything. Others were joking.

"At least this shrapnel wound will make it easier for me to pick up a girl."

One marine was missing part of an arm, but he was still more worried about the marine next to him.

"I'm all right, Doc. Look after my buddy."

One of those loaded on the helo was Lieutenant Reid. He was worried that the helo was going to get hit. *What a way to go after making it through such a horrible day.* With relief, he felt the helo lift. But he couldn't get the morbid thoughts out of his head. *What if we get a mechanical failure and end up going down?*

While the corpsman made sure that the IV fluid was properly attached, Reid thought back to the number of wounded in his platoon. He looked over and saw Torres and Espinoza on the other side of the helo. He had seen at least three dead. If that's what happened to his platoon, then there might be fifty dead from Charlie Company as a whole. The germ of guilt continued to take root. *I ordered Garibay to get those guys on the track and ordered it to go back. I killed them.* It was too much to think about. But in the weeks to come, alone in the hospital, he would continuously analyze the battle from every angle, and he would become bitter. He felt that they had been micromanaged in training, that the decision making was too centralized. It would take several months before he realized the only thing that still mattered: that nobody—neither the general, the colonel, nor any of the battalion staff—had set out to get anybody hurt. They had all, including him, made decisions based on the information they had at the time. There were some things that no one could control: how hard the wind blew, whether the Iraqi jerked the trigger, whether the enemy mortar was bubbled up or not. Everyone had done their best, but some things were just not known. *Would I like to have more information next time? You're damn right I would.* His one hope was that one day, the truth about that day would come out, regardless of egos, so that everyone could learn from what went wrong. *If the Marine Corps learns and becomes stronger, then my men did not die in vain.*

Alongside Reid, Torres was feverish and cold. As the helo banked, he saw the devastation below, a swirling mass of vehicles, men, smoke, and mud. Breaking through the sound of the rotors, he heard a *tink, tink, tink* of small-arms rounds hitting the helo's hull. *What is going to happen to me?*

Gloria went from patient to patient, checking up on them all, keeping them talking, taking their blood pressures and heart rates. A couple of marines had cut femoral arteries that had been controlled on the ground. He left those wounds alone. He wanted to make sure that the wounds didn't uncauterize. He didn't want to lose any of them now that they were so close to getting help. He looked at the horror around him and decided that when it was over, he would make every day count. *If you're moving, you're breathing. If you're breathing, you're alive. If you're alive, it's a good day. It's a good day.*

"Airburst at two o'clock."

Garcia, in the lead aircraft, pushed his helo through the airbursts and flew back over the city toward Jalibah.

5

The sun was going down as Major Sosa walked around the battlefield on the north side of the canal where Charlie had been fighting. Scattered all around him was the debris of war—twisted metal from RPG hits, pieces of burned flesh, smashed-up vehicles, spent rounds of ammo, empty water bottles, shreds of Marine clothing. The air was thick with the taste and smell of explosives. From the radio reports he'd picked up in the city, he'd had no idea that it was this bad. He was relieved to see that, contrary to

Swantner's earlier information, Dan Wittnam was not dead. But Dan looked haunted, his face streaked with dried blood and dirt. As he went around to the groups of Charlie marines, he found it hard to look at them. Some were sobbing; others were hugging each other in their grief; a few were sitting in the dirt, alone, staring into space. He could tell that they had fought hard. They were cut and beat up. Yet now he had to ask them to do more. He had received intel that fedayeen fighters were going to try to get back into the city on buses from the north. They would now have to deal with that threat and get ready to support the 1st Marine Expeditionary Force's move through the city and on toward Baghdad. He issued a frag, or fragmentary order, to set up a defense for the night at the T intersection a few hundred meters farther north of the bridge. *I gotta ask them to do more— set up for the night, establish a defense, get ready for the passage of lines.* He knew that the marines were only half listening to him. It was almost as though they felt that he had no right to tell them what to do because Sosa hadn't been through what they had. They had other concerns on their minds. What they most wanted was their buddies back. *They won't be able to rest or put the horror of the day behind them until they know where all their buddies are.*

A few meters away, Lieutenant Colonel Grabowski gathered his company commanders together. Around him were Captain Mike Brooks of Alpha, Captain Tim Newland of Bravo, Captain Dan Wittnam of Charlie, Major Bill Peeples of Team Tank, and Captain William Blanchard of the AAVs. They appeared to be exhausted. Dan Wittnam was in a state of shock. Grabowski had received radio reports throughout the day and built up a picture of what had gone on, but he wasn't sure whether he really understood. He paused before speaking.

"Gents. It's been a hell of a day."

One by one, he asked the company commanders how many marines were still unaccounted for. He started with the tank company, then Mike Brooks from Alpha.

"Tanks has got everyone accounted for."

"There are no missing and no KIAs in Alpha Company."

Grabowski was confused. He remembered the radio conversation about casualties when Brooks was still on the southern bridge.

"I thought you had some KIAs?"

"They weren't mine, sir."

For Grabowski, that was excellent news. Alpha was up. It was the same with Bravo. No wounded, no missing in action, and no KIAs. This is not as bad as he'd thought. He then came to Dan Wittnam.

"What about Charlie, Dan? Give me your status."

It was written all over Wittnam's face. He looked long and hard at Grabowski without blinking.

"I've got nine dead, twelve wounded, and nine missing. I think."

"Damn."

Grabowski didn't know what to say. He was stunned. All he could ask them to do was check their numbers again and to get dug in for the night.

"Gents, you've done a hell of a job today. But the fight ain't over yet. We've still got a lot of bad guys out there. We don't know what is going to happen tonight, or tomorrow. I need you to keep your head in the game."

As they turned to leave, Grabowski called Wittnam back. He knew that Charlie's marines had suffered and needed some time to get their heads together. He'd seen that the young marines were feeling bitter and confused.

"I'm putting you in reserve tonight. Do you need anything?"

"No, sir. I just want to find out where my guys are."

As Wittnam walked away, Grabowski thought he had done the wrong thing. Maybe it would have been better to keep them in the front line just to keep them busy.

Grabowski looked up to see Newland of Bravo Company and his FAC, call sign Mouth, coming toward him. They had talked to Wittnam about the A-10 friendly fire incident on the northern bridge, and they now had a good idea of what had happened. As they approached, Grabowski saw that they were carrying the weight of the world on their shoulders. They hardly looked up as they told him how they had not realized that Charlie Company had overtaken them as the lead element. The FAC explained how he had presumed that any vehicles north of the bridge were enemy. He had cleared the A-10 pilot to fire on them without realizing they were marine vehicles. The FAC was distraught. Grabowski tried to give what reassurance he could.

"We are going to report this, and there will be an investigation. You did what you thought was correct, but war is a confusing, bloody mess."

He thought back to the warnings he tried to give young marines who looked forward to war with glee and excitement. *As you grow older, you realize that war is an ugly, brutal business, and it leaves scars forever.*

"Gents, this is what we do for a living. It's ugly. The bottom line is that you both did a tremendous job today and I need you in the fight because we don't know what will be out there tomorrow."

"Roger that."

They both looked up at him, turned, and walked away.

There was so much to get on with that he didn't know where to start. He wanted to talk to the marines from Charlie Company, to tell them what a great job they had done and what a success the mission had been, but now was not the time. And besides, he didn't know quite what to tell them. They were hurting too much. They were surrounded by a shield of emotion. He couldn't tell whether it was resentment, bitterness, anger, or hurt, but it was a shield that kept him out.

He called Colonel Bailey at the regimental HQ with an update on the number of dead, wounded, and missing. He had to use the satellite radio. The VHF radio wouldn't reach back that far.

"Tell General Natonski that we've got his damn bridges. Timberwolf 6 out."

At Task Force Tarawa's command post, well south of Nasiriyah, General Rich Natonski greeted the news that 1/2 had secured the bridges with relief. He'd been under pressure all day from the follow-on forces of the 1st Marine Division to secure the bridges so they could get en route to Baghdad.

"Sir, there are several DUSTWUNs."

"What the hell is DUSTWUN?"

He'd never heard that expression before: duty status whereabouts unknown. Some marines were missing somewhere in the city. He knew it would affect the marines on the ground still fighting. He made a point of making sure to walk the lines in the coming days. He remembered how, as a young marine, he'd been terrified and overawed by the generals. He wanted the young marines to see that he was there with them. But for now, he had to start making plans for the next day. They needed to start clearing the city, and they needed to find the missing marines from Charlie Company and the missing soldiers from the Army's 507th Maintenance Company.

Up by the T intersection, a couple of kilometers north of the canal bridge, Mike Brooks checked and rechecked the security perimeter that marines from Alpha had set up to stop enemy vehicles from the north getting to the canal bridge and back into the city. His marines were digging fighting holes, talking to each other in a soft hum. Others just stared off into the middle distance, reliving the events of the day.

The sun had gone down and it was getting very dark. Brooks was too exhausted to eat. He'd been perturbed by the short conversation he'd had with Grabowski. He felt that the battalion commander still didn't really understand what had happened at the northern bridge that day. Now he just collapsed in the dirt, relieved to be reunited with the rest of the battalion. This was all the family he had with him at the moment. He thought of his wife and three sons back home. He wanted to smell his wife's hair and feel the hugs from his three little boys. *I don't want them ever to have to go through this.* He wondered whether the events of that day would change him, whether he would be scarred by war, whether he would be able to love his wife and sons in the same way as he had done before. He'd now seen dead bodies. It didn't matter whether they were American or Iraqi. There was no Hollywood message telling him that those dead Iraqis were evil. They were dead people, and it wasn't a good sight to see. He already looked forward to the day in years to come when he could meet up with former brothers-in-arms and share stories about the events of March 23, when the visceral pain and sorrow he now felt might be transformed into romantic memories of battle.

Dug into a trench, facing the Iraqi military compound just by the T intersection, Neville Welch was peering into the darkness. He was disturbed by what had happened to Charlie Company. He couldn't sleep. He didn't want to sleep. He was terrified that an Iraqi would crawl up under cover of darkness and slit his throat. *That's all they want. To kill just one of us.* He stayed awake by opening an MRE packet of coffee powder, pouring it down his throat, and washing it down with cold water. He hadn't washed in a week. He hadn't taken a shit in days. The only clean clothing he had on his body was a pair of socks that he'd washed by shaking around in a plastic MRE sleeve filled with water and soap. He climbed out of his hole, walked ten meters away, knelt down, and took a piss. It was the first he'd taken all day.

When he got back, Lance Corporal Nicholas Jones was in his fighting hole. He was glad for another set of eyes. For days, Welch's marines had talked about nothing other than the girls they were going to hook up with once they got home, about getting wasted, having a blast, and getting laid. That night, Jones wanted to talk about God.

"When I get out of this, I'm gonna turn my life around."

Jones told him about the cookies his aunt's church had sent him and how, back home, they were thinking of him and praying for him. They talked for hours, agreeing that God had delivered them from Ambush Alley and that they were relying on God to get them safely back home. For some reason, God had chosen to save them, not the marines from Charlie Company. Welch knew two Charlie marines who were still missing. Lance Corporal Slocum used to be in Welch's platoon. Private First Class Burkett used to come over sometimes and borrow CDs. *It could have been us. We could have been the ones that died.* He gave honor to God and vowed to purge and cleanse himself in the wide, open desert. Then he thought about *Matrix Reloaded.* He'd seen the first *Matrix* movie and had loved the cinematography. But *Matrix Reloaded* had come out just after they left for Iraq. *Oh man, I just gotta see* Matrix Reloaded. *I want to see it so bad.*

In a Charlie Company hole down the line, Lance Corporal Thomas Quirk felt a bitterness rising in his throat. It was a feeling that somehow he'd been let down by the higher-ups. Not Captain Wittnam, his company commander. *He was awesome. I'll go to war with him any fucking day of the week.* Those who were in charge, those who should have known what it was going to be like in Nasiriyah, had let them down. The Iraqis didn't surrender. They fought like the world was going to end, and those in charge didn't know it. And when it had come to the fighting, who had died? It wasn't the commanding officers; it was the grunts, the infantrymen, who had suffered. They were the ones who lived on a need-to-know basis. *Guys like me didn't need to know a fucking thing. Guys like me died.* Quirk was angry. It was the first time he'd been in combat. He knew it was the first time his commanders had been in combat, too, but he felt that they'd failed him. They'd given the order to remove the orange air panels, designed to ward off friendly fire, from the roofs of the tracks. He was glad he hadn't come across the battalion commander. *I wouldn't have been too fucking pleased to see him. They are a bunch of cocksuckers, and I'd like to knock them all down.*

He questioned why so many of his buddies had died. He had known everything about them, and now they were no longer there. *And they knew everything about me.* He was struggling with it all. *It becomes pretty real, real fast. It's something else. It's weird right here.* There was too much information going through his head. *What will happen in the rest of the war? What will happen tomorrow?* And tomorrow might be worse than today.

He thought about writing to his girlfriend. *But what am I going to say?* That he'd killed women and children? There were certain things he just couldn't unload. People wouldn't understand. *Some of the shit that has happened today is so intense that the average dude won't be able to grasp it without thinking of Nazi Germany. Unless you were in it, you won't be able to understand it.* He decided he would just write to her and tell her how great she was.

He had lost his pack from the outside of the burning track 211. It had everything in it: his sleeping gear, ponchos, poncho liner, change of clothes, socks, food, letters from home, pictures of his girlfriend, extra batteries. The marines carried no spare gear with them. But that's how he liked it. *We carry no spare gear because we are harder than the rest of the faggots.* Now he was having to dig his fighting hole with a bayonet because he'd also lost his e-tool, the small spade used to scrape away ground for cover. Next to him, a corporal, the same guy who had been shitting himself all day, was telling him to dig the hole deeper. And all Quirk could reply was "Aye, aye, Corporal."

He felt himself getting crazy again. He tried to pray. *Dear God, give me strength . . .* The words would not come out. He felt breathless and panicky. He wasn't able physically to continue with his prayer. He just couldn't concentrate. He tried again. *Dear God . . .* Each time he started, he wondered what sort of God would make a world where his buddies could be shot up by Iraqis or other Americans, where he would be put in a situation where he was allowed to kill people. He tried to pray, but the words wouldn't come out.

Corporal Jake Worthington tried to sleep but couldn't. He'd seen his buddies killed and wounded, and he'd killed and wounded the enemy. And now he felt abandoned. He felt that every day, for the rest of the war, it would be a struggle. He would need more than a "good job" and a pat on the back from his superiors. He was struggling with raging emotions. He almost felt like going on a rampage and killing those in charge. His first thought was that the regimental and battalion commanders had failed them badly. *You put on the brass. It's your responsibility.* He fingered the bear claw around his neck and took out the letters and photos his girlfriend had sent him. He was already thinking about what he would write to her and how he would have to tell her that he'd changed. *I hope she can be understanding.* He just stared at the sky. He thought of himself as spiritual, but now he felt a long way from God. *You son of a bitch, how could you let this happen?* It was like the devil and the angel appearing on each shoulder, one with the horns, the other with a halo. *See what God did. This is what He did to you.* The other voice chimed in. *No, you've survived. He saved you.*

Lance Corporal Castleberry, Lieutenant Tracy, Sergeant Schaefer, and the rest of the Charlie trackers were crammed into their tracks, trying to get some sleep. They had lost so many tracks that they had to make several trips up to the T intersection to get all of Charlie Company up there. They were feeling sick with loss. Tracy had tried to encourage them. He now had only two trackers unaccounted for. Instead of mourning them, he chose to think that he had now given back thirty-two of his marines he didn't think were alive. He tried to persuade his marines to think like that, too. What was hard was that with so many AAVs destroyed, many of the trackers had lost all their gear. Their personal effects, photos, letters, and books were gone. All those intimate connections with home were severed. They even had to share a toothbrush between twelve people. Tracy very quickly fell asleep on the metal bench in exactly the same spot he'd sat down on. He was exhausted. There was nothing left. Next to him was Schaefer. He couldn't stop thinking about what had happened that day. His head whirred away like a computer. It hadn't gone according to plan. Mistakes had been made. But that was what life was like in the Marine Corps. *If we'd been told to take the bridge with pistols, we would have done it.*

Next to them, Castleberry couldn't sleep. He was boiling with resentment. A few moments earlier, as they were setting up a defense for the night, Lieutenant Colonel Grabowski had approached him and some other marines.

"You did a great job."

Castleberry stared at him, anger and resentment pouring out of his eyes. It was a death stare. He refused to shake his hand. He wanted to buttstroke him. Right then he felt that Grabowski had let them down. He and his staff had refused to send help when they were caught in Ambush Alley. Major Peeples did it on his own. Sergeant Schaefer had done what he had to do. But Grabowski had pussyfooted around. *That's what separates the mice from the men. We had to sit there and suffer for hours, bleeding to death in terrible pain, thinking we were going to die in this stinking house in the middle of fucking Iraq, all because you and your staff refused to send anybody to come and get us.* Castleberry did not know all the facts. But that day, what he'd heard from other marines was enough.

Grabowski hadn't known where his units were, he hadn't insisted on the presence of the tanks, he hadn't known what his forward air controller was doing, he hadn't kept accountability of his marines. Castleberry didn't feel like being generous. Grabowski was in charge and he'd let them down.

The more Castleberry thought about that day, the more wound up he became. *I'm going through some sort of religious meltdown.* His mom had wanted him to go to church. But that night he was losing all sense of religion. He thought about the women and children he shot. He remembered one kid in particular. They'd shot an Iraqi dead from the house in the middle of Ambush Alley. This little kid, maybe the dead man's son, who couldn't have been more than ten years old, ran out and picked up the abandoned AK-47. He lay on the ground and started firing it. Castleberry and some of the others shot the young boy, punching bullet holes right through him. The kid did a sort of combat roll, stood up, and then fell down dead. Castleberry knew that he would shoot hundreds more kids like that to save the life of just one marine. *That's how fucked up this job is. How could God let this happen?* He tortured himself with the vision of Fribley's broken body. *And then you look in the troop compartment of your track and there is a guy there with his entrails pouring out of him, his body blown to pieces and completely desecrated. And yet the day before he was laughing at you because someone had taken a photo of you while you were shitting.* That's what had turned him against God. And now he didn't know how he was supposed to find any sort of faith. *Trouble is, if I believe in God, I'm really screwed because I killed a lot of people out there.*

In the distance, there was the crackle of gunfire and the odd explosion of an artillery shell. Marines tossed and turned and screamed in their sleep. The siren of an ambulance approaching from the north woke up Tracy and Brooks. A group of marines looked at the approaching vehicle, but no one shot. Brooks wondered whether he should check it out. But he let it pass. Chief Warrant Officer Dunfee and Lieutenant Colonel Grabowski also saw the ambulance approach.

"What the fuck is that doing? How did it get through?"

Grabowski took out his pistol. *How am I going to stop an ambulance with a handgun?*

In his tank, *Dark Side,* Captain Dyer saw the ambulance, its light flashing, coming toward them. The tanks from his company had set up a roadblock to stop vehicles from getting to the Saddam Canal Bridge and into the city from the north. They were also there to stop enemy vehicles attacking the battalion from the south. He ordered his marines to pull the ambulance over. He was furious with the line companies for letting the ambulance get this far.

The tankers forced the ambulance to stop. The occupants said they were taking wounded to the hospital. There was one wounded soldier with serious burns to his face, but when they searched the ambulance the marines also found a colonel of the Iraqi 23rd Infantry Brigade who was masquerading as a paramedic. He admitted that he was trying to get back into the city to organize its defense. His uniform and ID were hidden in plastic bags. He was carrying a large amount of U.S. currency.

When Tracy and Brooks heard who they had let through, they kicked themselves. Tracy was really pissed.

I would have loved to find a guy with an Iraqi uniform and a couple of stripes on his shoulders.

Major Sosa sat up in his Humvee planning for the day ahead. He was worried for his marines. They were bitter and resentful that their buddies were still missing. *Not knowing where they are is tearing them apart.* He knew that until they could answer that question, they would not rest easy. They were going to be angry and trigger-happy. *We've got to lick our wounds and regroup.*

Much later, as he wandered over the battlefield to check on some dead Iraqis, some marines from the light armored reconnaissance battalion came up and started posing with cameras in front of the dead men. Standing over the bodies, they grinned and gave the thumbs-up sign as the cameras clicked. Sosa just exploded at them.

"These are fucking human beings. How can you do that?"

In the moonlight, Private First Class Casey Robinson and Lance Corporal Rodriguez Ortiz dug their fighting hole by the T intersection in the shadow of the Iraqi military complex from which they had received a lot of the enemy fire earlier in the day. Ortiz was still feeling anxious and jumpy from the hours spent in the house on Ambush Alley. He had talked about combat, prepared for it, even looked forward to it. But he had never imagined the horror of it. He thought about what he'd been through. *You could put the bravest guy in that situation and he'd break down. We went through it, and it has changed us all forever.*

Robinson just dug. When he had finished one fighting hole, he started on another. He heard marines around him moaning in their sleep. He used his NVGs, his night-vision goggles, to scan for movement. There was lots of dead space behind the wall in the military complex, and he couldn't tell if anyone was moving or not. *They might still be in there. They can kill us whenever they want.*

Out of the darkness, a group of figures did appear. They weren't Iraqi, though. They were British. They came over to where Robinson and his buddies were and asked for some cigarettes. In their strange accent, they started saying that the marines shouldn't go up north, that it was heavy up there. Robinson was impressed by them. *They are older, with beards and mustaches and shit.* They were loaded with ammo, and their all-terrain vehicle was bristling with rockets and M240s. And then they just disappeared into the desert with no support and no word of where they were going or what they were up to. Robinson guessed they were British SAS. And in spite of what he had just gone through, he yearned for the romance of life in the Special Forces.

He dug deeper into his hole. He thought about the marines who weren't there. Those who had died.

He's not going to be there in the morning when I eat breakfast. He's not going to be there to talk to at night, to keep me awake on watch or anything like that. He dreaded going back to Camp Lejeune to see their families. He didn't know what he was going to say. He felt a chill. He had lost his jacket in the house and his sleeping bag and poncho had burned up in his pack on track 201. He was anxious and nervous. It was only the third day of the war. He hadn't thought that war would be like this. *This is the calm before the storm. It's going to get worse. It's going to be like this every day.*

He was still digging as the sun rose.

POSTSCRIPT

On March 23, 2003, eighteen marines from Charlie Company were killed in action between the southern Euphrates Bridge and the northern Saddam Canal Bridge. Over thirty-five were injured. It was the single heaviest loss suffered by the U.S. military during the entire combat phase of Operation Iraqi Freedom.

A day later, the 2nd Light Armored Reconnaissance Battalion successfully passed along Ambush Alley, spearheading the 1st Marine Expeditionary Force's attack toward Baghdad.

The bodies of several of the missing marines were not recovered until days later when, after receiving tips from locals, marine search teams found them buried in the backyards of houses in the city.

On April 1, marines from Task Force Tarawa participated in the rescue of one of the soliders from the Army's 507th Maintenance Convoy, Private Jessica Lynch.

It wasn't until April 2 that Brigadier General Rich Natonski was able to say that Nasiriyah was secure and under American control.

A U.S. Central Command investigation into the A-10 incident concluded that friendly fire might have been responsible for the deaths of up to ten marines, including all nine marines in the troop compartment of track 208. The investigation also found that the A-10 was responsible for injuries to Sergeant Torres and may have been responsible for injuries to another three marines. It was not possible to determine exactly how many vehicles the A-10 pilots hit or when they hit them because the tapes from the gun cameras on the planes went missing. The pilot of Gyrate 73 said he had handed them to the Intelligence debriefer for the mission. But there was no record of the tape being processed. The pilot of Gyrate 74 inadvertently reused the tape and covered over the contents of the March 23 mission.

The A-10 pilots were cleared of any wrongdoing. No unit commanders were held responsible. Mouth, the Bravo Company FAC, was held responsible for the incident.

Eighteen months after the operations in Nasiriyah, many marines from Charlie Company, 1st Battalion, 2nd Marines had been reassigned to 2nd Battalion, 8th Marines and sent to Afghanistan for seven months.

Brigadier General Rich Natonski took command of the 1st Marine Division, based in Camp Pendleton, California.

Lieutenant Colonel Rick Grabowski went to the U.S. Army War College in Carslisle, Pennsylvania, and was promoted to colonel.

Major David Sosa took command of Recruiting Station Sacramento in California.

Major Bill Peeples left the Marine Corps Reserve and remained in the Inactive Ready Reserve. He returned to his job as a city planner and had a second child with his wife.

Captain Scott Dyer remained the executive officer of Alpha Company, 8th Tank Battalion and has been selected to become the commanding officer of Company C, 8th Tank Battalion.

Captain Mike Brooks of Alpha Company was reassigned as the staff secretary to the commanding general, 2nd Marine Division.

Captain Tim Newland of Bravo Company left the Marine Corps.

Captain Dan Wittnam of Charlie Company was promoted to major and returned to Iraq as the commander of a small craft company.

First Lieutenant Ben Reid received shrapnel wounds to his face and right hand and a gunshot wound to his right shoulder. He has recovered from his injuries and was reassigned to train new recruits at Parris Island, South Carolina.

First Lieutenant Conor Tracy was reassigned to the Basic School at Quantico, Virginia, to train newly commissioned officers.

Sergeant William Schaefer and Lance Corporal Edward Castleberry remained at Camp Lejeune.

Sergeant Jose Torres has a damaged right leg and left buttock. He is fighting to prove himself fit enough to stay in the Marine Corps. He was promoted to staff sergeant.

Corporal Neville Welch was reassigned to the Headquarters and Service Company, 1st Battalion, 2nd Marines. He saw *Matrix Reloaded* and hated it so much that he asked for his money back. He regretted he'd spent so much time in Iraq thinking about it.

Corporal Matthew Juska sustained a closed head injury and is recovering.

Corporal Randy Glass had eleven surgeries to remove shrapnel, dead muscle, and metal pins from his leg. He left the Marine Corps and returned home to Pennsylvania.

Corporal Jared Martin had eight chunks of shrapnel removed from his hands and legs on the battlefield. Other pieces of shrapnel were later removed from his elbow, upper arm, and below his right eye.

Corporal Manny Espinoza had several surgeries to repair damage done to his intestines from a shrapnel wound. The day before he left the Marine Corps, Lieutenant Reid presented him with a Bronze Star for his heroic actions on March 23.

Lance Corporal Bradley Seegert received burns and blast wounds to his right arm and is recovering.

Private Jason Keough was severely wounded in his right leg and is recovering. He was not administratively separated from the Marine Corps.

Four months after getting back from Iraq, Private First Class Casey Robinson was told that he would be accepted into Force Recon. A few days later, on October 15, 2003, military police searched his car. They found steroids. A few months after that, he and Lance Corporal Thomas Quirk were sent to the brig for thirty days for beating up a junior marine. In May 2004, Robinson was demoted to private. In June 2004, his wife gave birth to a baby boy, Ethan. In March 2005, Robinson was awarded the Bronze Star for his actions at Nasiriyah on March 23, 2003.

INDEX

ABOUT THE AUTHOR

TIM PRITCHARD is a London-based journalist and filmmaker who has made several award-winning documentaries for the BBC, Channel 4, PBS, and the Discovery Channel. This is his first book.

ABOUT THE TYPE

This book was set in Caledonia, a typeface designed in 1939 by William Addison Dwiggins for the Merganthaler Linotype Company. Its name is the ancient Roman term for Scotland, because the face was intended to have a Scotch-Roman flavor. Caledonia is considered to be a well-proportioned, businesslike face with little contrast between its thick and thin lines.